Phil Stant was born in E[...] school, he joined the Arm[...] with postings in the Falkla[...] team working alongside the SAS. Eventually he returned to his primary love of football where he played for teams including Huddersfield, Fulham, Cardiff, Brighton and Lincoln City, whom he also managed for a year in 2000. He now works for the Football League as a Youth Development Monitor.

Ooh Ah Stantona

THE AUTOBIOGRAPHY OF THE SAS HERO
WHO BECAME A FOOTBALL LEGEND

Phil Stant

JOHN BLAKE

Published by John Blake Publishing Ltd,
3 Bramber Court, 2 Bramber Road,
London W14 9PB, England

www.blake.co.uk

First published in paperback in 2008

ISBN 978 1 84454 516 2

British Library Cataloguing-in-Publication Data:

A catalogue record for this book is available from the British Library.

Design by www.envydesign.co.uk and Hayley Stant

Printed in the UK by CPI Bookmarque, Croydon, CRO 4TD

1 3 5 7 9 10 8 6 4 2

Papers used by John Blake Publishing are natural, recyclable products
made from wood grown in sustainable forests. The manufacturing processes
conform to the environmental regulations of the country of origin.

Every attempt has been made to contact the relevant copyright-holders,
but some were unobtainable. We would be grateful if the appropriate
people could contact us.

Dedicated to all of the people who have served
in conflicts and wars to give us the society of today,
not some talentless celebrity wannabe from a
TV reality show!

Foreword

They used to say that I only picked Stanty for my teams because he smoked. His team-mates would always loudly point this out as I bummed another fag off him. The truth is, as a dozen managers will tell you, Phil was a top-class goalscorer in the lower divisions who could guarantee any boss twenty goals a season. Gold dust.

But it wasn't the Benson and Hedges or the goals that made Stanty stand out. It was the measure of the man. His background is unique in football. How long would some of today's Premiership millionaires last in the SAS? On away trips with Bury I used to tell Stanty to sit next to me on the bus and tell me stories of his days in the forces. The miles passed easily as he explained to me how he could demolish a building with a box of matches or wreak havoc around the world with a tin of baking powder. Stanty is a diamond with a northern accent as thick and rich as a black pudding. He often led the forward line for me alone, and, fittingly, he's proud of writing every word in this book himself.

Enjoy your chance to read some of the stories that inspired me and his team-mates to help us win promotion.

Stan Ternent

Acknowledgements

With thanks to Mum, who has in the past mistaken my deodorant for my shaving foam, and to Dad. Thanks to my sister Shirley, who I apologise to for selling her guitar, but there was no need to respond by making me a dog meat sandwich. Thanks to all the chairmen, managers, coaches, players, groundsmen, physios, journalists, agents and coach drivers who have had to put up with my tantrums as well as my ego. Thanks to the Football League and to the young professionals who have allowed me to develop their careers in my role as a youth development monitor for the Football League.

With thanks to my inspiration, Barry McGuigan's father, Pat, who sang *Danny Boy* before his son's world title fight in 1985.

Thanks to the Olympic athlete who after years of hard

work stands on the winner's podium to collect their gold medal while the flag is raised to the national anthem. Thanks to the underdog in any walk of life but especially in sport.

Thanks to Clive Hebard and John Blake Publishing, and all at ITV who made the return trip to the Falklands possible, particularly Frazer Shephard, Phil Braund and Paul Leuenberger. Finally, thanks to Arlette Betts, who made us feel welcome and really helped out.

Contents

Introduction

Think you know soccer hardmen? Vinnie Jones... Chopper Harris...Roy Keane...Tommy Smith...Norman Hunter. Hard? Not likely!

What's a flying tackle when you've dodged flying bullets? What's the inconvenience of a sending off compared to the hell of a war-zone watching your mates die before your eyes? Phil Stant is a breath of fresh air in today's world of pampered soccer ponces who earn £80,000 a week and spend just 90 minutes of it on the pitch and the rest at the hairdresser.

Phil had a life before he became a professional footballer. And what a life! His account of his role in the Falklands War is breathtaking in its intensity, raw with its emotion and – when he briefly talks footy with an Argie prisoner of war – hilarious.

Phil's reaction as he watched the burned-out wreckage

of *Sir Galahad* become a war grave belies the myth that all footballers are insensitive morons.

But hard? This is the man who played for the SAS first eleven! This is the man who worked for bomb disposal! This is the man who finally put down his gun and entertained thousands of fans on Saturday afternoons as a professional footballer all over the country.

And this is the account of his life of extremes: Death, duty and the occasional drubbing. Phil Stant may not have the right foot of David Beckham. But there's not a footballer alive who's had the life of Phil Stant.

Tony Livesey, *Sports Newspapers*

Chapter One

Rumour had it that a counter-attack by the Argentinean Special Services was on its way.

I looked up and saw Lft Stevens heading towards my location. He was running as quickly as he could. I was stood in my trench; a foot deep in water and my feet were bloody freezing.

So were my hands as they gripped my submachine gun. The 'Rupert' was breathless as he reached the trench.

'What the fuck does he want now?' I wondered.

'Private Stant,' he shouted. 'Here's two grenades, wait until the enemy is right on top of you, then let them have it.' With that he thrust two grenades into my freezing hands.

He was a young 'Rupert', or 'Rodney' as we used to call them. He was just out of basic officer training at Sandhurst and looked about fifteen years old; in reality, though, he was the same age as me. As I took the grenades out of his hands, I looked into his face and saw an expression that said: 'I'm shitting myself.' But he wasn't the only one.

I shouted back: 'I'm missing the fucking World Cup for this shit.'

The 1982 World Cup finals were in full swing in Spain and yet there I was in a trench full of freezing water with two grenades for company.

The officer stopped and just stared back at me with a blank expression on his face before running off to the next foxhole with his deliveries.

I didn't mean it, of course, or maybe I did, I don't know now, but anyway, I'd been football mad for as long as I could remember. I was now beginning to wonder what the fuck I was doing on the Falkland Islands. It was true that, until then, I'd seen every World Cup since Mexico 1970.

Born in Bolton on 13 October 1962 in the top bedroom of 14 Grasmere Street, I had no recollection of 1966 and all that. My first taste of real football came in 1969 when my dad took me to Burnden Park for the first time. This was the home of the 'Trotters' – Bolton Wanderers.

They were in the old Third Division: Eddie Hopkinson was approaching the end of his career and George Best was in his prime. However, even though Wanderers were my team, I made my dad buy me a Manchester United shirt. In those days, United's shirts were made of red cotton with a white neckband.

Mum then sewed the No. 11 on the back – Georgie's number at the time. Mum and Dad split up in 1969. My dad was a long-distance lorry driver and I knew that there would be no more trips with him in the lorry after that.

Money was also tight, so trips to Brunden Park were also thin on the ground.

We would always go down to the ground at midday for a 3pm kick-off. By 12.15, we were outside the pub with me sat in the car. Here I would happily sit with a bottle of pop and a bag of crisps, decked out in a black and white scarf and clutching my rattle.

The pop and crisps were offered to keep me quiet while dad had a session with his mates.

Every now and then one of them would come out with a fresh bottle and another bag of crisps. Usually, when it got to 2.50pm, I began to worry that he wasn't coming back at all. This was something that happened all too often and it would often transpire that I would miss the game altogether.

When he did come out, however, it was great. We would stand on the near-empty embankment, underneath the old scoreboard. Of course, Dad and his mates hardly watched the game. He was too busy stood at the bar continuing his session, while I used to kick paper cups up and down the deserted terraces while the game was going on. At half-time, at one game, he lifted me over the barrier with my paper cup. This cup was as good as a shiny new Casey ball as far as I was concerned. I scaled the ditch – which was a feature of the old Burnden Park and which, to me, was like climbing Mount Everest – to make it to the hallowed turf. I had done all this to the amusement and encouragement of Dad and his mates.

I remember looking into the sparse crowd and seeing other boys my age looking back at me with pure envy.

I placed the paper cup about two yards from the goal-line, turned round and walked a few yards back. Then, I ran back and kicked the cup as hard as I could straight into the middle of the goal. It finished up just over the line and a big cheer could be heard from my dad and his mates as I celebrated my first ever goal on a Football League ground.

I was so happy that it could have been Wembley in front of 100,000 people as far as I was concerned. Suddenly, I became aware that the groundsman was chasing me.

'What the fuck's up with thee,' said my dad.

To which the red-faced groundsman replied: 'He's damaging the pitch.'

'Is he fuck,' said Dad, standing his ground.

His words did not placate his verbal sparring partner.

'Next time, I'll get the police,' was the groundsman's final offering as he dutifully stamped down the divots on the pitch.

My dad had had enough. 'Oh fuck off,' he said, turning towards the direction of the bar.

'Yeah, fuck off you miserable bastard,' shouted one of my dad's mates. They were all having a good chuckle by this time.

But I had made an impression. One of my dad's mates said: 'By 'eck Phil, you were just like Johnny Byrom.'

'Was he fuck,' countered Dad. 'Our Phil scored from two yards.'

Howls of laughter followed as my dad and his mates made their way back up the terraces.

Number 14 Grasmere Street was an old terraced house in a row of about thirty. They were all built at the turn of the century and were already classed as derelict.

They were all two-up, two-down houses with a backyard that led into a back street. Dad had been the main breadwinner in the family for Mum, my sister Shirley and I. Before becoming a truck driver, he worked down the mines. It was there that he lost three fingers in an accident. When he was at home, he always used to leave very early in the mornings. He would always wear his flat cap and have a Capstan full strength between his lips as he woke the neighbours by revving up his truck. It was hard for Mum after they separated, but she did her best.

Our house, on reflection, was a dump. Winter was the worst because the toilet at the bottom of the yard was always freezing up and there was no light in there. There were two bedrooms upstairs and a piss bucket on the small landing; it was always getting knocked over and it usually bounced down the stairs and into the kitchen. There was only one main rule with the piss bucket: Mum insisted that nobody could do a number two in it.

But sod that. There was no way that I was going down the yard in the freezing cold to the pitch-black bog that was always full of spiders. No, if I was caught short during the night, I used the bucket for a number two and faced both Mum and the consequences in the morning. Either that or I would blame Shirley.

The house was always damp as there was no central heating or anything like that back then. There was just a small coal fire in the living room. This had two doors, one that led into the kitchen and the one onto the street. We would come down the stairs in the morning behind Mum and wait for her to run into the living room and switch the light on. Then we would hear her stamping all around the room. After a couple of minutes she would say it was fine for us to come in. We would creep in while mum was brushing away all the dead cockroaches into a dustpan.

All the time she was doing this, she kept on muttering that they had come from the dirty cow next door. This was a reference to Mrs Walsh, an old lady who lived next door with her forty-two-year-old son.

The highlight of the week was bath night in front of the fire in the old tin bath which was kept hung up outside in the yard. It took ages to fill with kettles of water. Shirley always went first as we listened to the top twenty and then 'Sing Something Simple' on the old wireless we had. Then Mum would be off to the corner shop and we would share a bag of sweets while watching a black and white TV in the corner of the living room. This was on hire from Telebank and you had to put shillings in a box at the back to make it work.

It was always going off in the middle of programmes and then Mum would say it was bedtime, simply because she had no more shillings to feed it with.

My first school was Chalfont Street, a goal-kick away from our front door. The headmaster ran it with a rod of iron.

Mr Richardson, or 'Pop' Ritchie as he was known by his

delinquents, was six feet tall with a balding head and a big, bushy moustache. He was always very smart and always wore a suit and tie. I think he felt sorry for me because he would occasionally call me into his office. I would stand outside, shitting myself and trying to think what I'd done wrong.

'Come in Stant,' he would bellow.

Once inside, however, he would turn into a father-like figure and ask me how my home life was. All the while I would be standing there with my arse hanging out of my trousers. I could usually tell by the tone of his voice that I wasn't in trouble, but I was always watching him to see if he picked up the cane that was situated by the side of his desk.

He would pull out a bag that contained boys' clothing, as he had a son who was of a similar age to me. These bags could contain a jumper or trousers, sometimes even shoes.

'Try these on boy,' he would say and then he would ask if they were the right fit.

When I told him that they were, he would say: 'Good, collect them after school and don't tell anybody.'

And that's how it was. I don't think mum was embarrassed, but she would only allow me to wear them for best or on Sundays when we used to travel to Little Lever to visit my aunties and uncles.

The best time for me was always after school when we would go to the end of the street where, on the corner house, there was always a goalpost chalked on the wall. This was our Wembley.

There was a lamppost three or four yards away which combined as a floodlight and a central defender: we christened it 'Jackie Charlton' because it was so tall. Every now and then somebody would take it on themselves to re-chalk the goalpost so that it always looked white. God knows how Mr and Mrs Skilling, an elderly couple who lived in the house, survived the constant banging on the wall as the ball was fired into the top or bottom corner of the goal.

In the following years, 'Jackie' made numerous clearances from shots aimed for the top corner. The recurring problems were stoppages by the referee, mainly for cars or old ladies walking slowly on the goal-line. Sometimes it would be the Alsatian from number 23 Ullswater Street. Many a game had to be abandoned because this fearsome dog had burst the ball.

The main stoppage, however, would come from: 'Philip, your tea is ready' – it was a shout that brought a premature end to many a keenly contested encounter. After tea, I would be back for the evening kick-off under the floodlights.

Many families were out of work, but when somebody got a colour TV, the whole street had to have a look. Our next-door neighbours on the other side were Elsie and Bill.

Elsie was an alcoholic, and most nights she would be found down the pub. Our Shirley and I would take great delight in waiting at the bedroom window to witness her nightly struggle home. She would curse anyone and everyone on the way home. Her wig was always disjointed and every few seconds, if she hadn't fallen over, someone would be called a bastard or told to 'fuck off'. Once, she fell into the milk crates outside the local corner shop and was attacked by the owner's Alsatian. This was our late-night entertainment, but during the day she was as nice as pie.

Another bit of nocturnal fun was to be had at the Warburton bakery, which wasn't far away. If you went down there late at night you could see people in the shadows waiting for the chance to open up a window and nick a loaf of freshly baked bread off the conveyor belt, which was within easy reach once the window was open. They would then scurry home with loaves of bread under their coats.

My first recollection of the World Cup finals came in 1970, when England were competing as reigning champions. It was a hot, sunny day, but I was glued to the black and white TV watching England play West Germany. We were 2–0 up with goals from Alan Mullery and Martin Peters. England looked to be coasting through to the next round, but then up popped Seeler, Beckenbaur and Muller with a classic strike to send us out.

Mum was fed up of me returning from school with my shoes scuffed and it was always the right foot that was damaged.

I would come up with the same excuse that 'I'd fallen over', but anyone with any commonsense would have realised that it was because I played football with my right foot. I was soon practising with my left and, to my joy, it wasn't long before I would scuff both shoes: just to annoy Mum even more. The end result was a new pair of pit boots. 'Ruin them if you dare,' was her challenge.

Playing in the schoolyard with these was like playing with diver's boots on, but one thing was for sure, no kid ever came in for a tackle, otherwise they would have had badly bruised shins. They also had their other uses...

One Wednesday afternoon when I'd moved on to Sharples High School, a fixture had been arranged against our local rivals, Smithills High School on Astley Bridge Park, which separated both schools. I was determined to be part of the team. Word had got round and we were expecting a large crowd. Football, no ... a mass gang fight between two rival schools, yes.

About 100 of us arrived first and we inspected the pitch. Not long after, our rivals made their entrance and we started to walk towards each other, led by our gladiator and cock of the school, Mark Leyland. Then it started. The fight lasted for about thirty seconds before five police cars came charging onto the scene with sirens blazing. Everybody scattered using every available exit, including yours truly.

I reached Blackburn Road, where I took a seat outside Frank Peacock's sports shop. It all went quiet, so I decided to catch the bus home and had just got up when three Smithills lads came round the corner.

'Act cool,' I thought when they came up and said:

'Hey, were you on Astley Bridge Park twenty minutes ago?'

'No,' I said.

'Yes you were. You were the one who threw the first brick, you twat.'

That was all I heard before the first punch landed right on my nose and I collapsed under a torrent of punches and kicks before they ran off.

I caught the next bus home with blood running out of my nose. I reached the house as Mum was making tea; beans on toast, or was it egg, chips and beans?

'How did the game go?' she asked.

'Very physical,' I replied as I went to my room.

'Did you save any?' she said.

'No, but I managed to block one or two,' I said as I shut the bedroom door. The result? I suppose you could say that it was a draw.

The next day in assembly, headmaster Kenyon stood up and barked that he wanted anyone who was on Astley Bridge Park the previous afternoon to stand up.

Slowly people began to get to their feet.

'Leyland, you was there. Stant, you was there. Jones, you was there. Stand up.' Within a minute, 70 per cent of the school was on its feet, players and spectators alike.

It ended up with five of us – the nucleus of the side, I suppose – getting the slipper.

'Fuck me, not Lightfoot,' we muttered, as we shuffled about outside the deputy head's office. Mr Lightfoot, the deputy head, was also a rugby player and a fanatic; when you got the slipper from him, you certainly knew about it.

'Oh fuck, here it comes,' I mumbled to myself as Lightfoot did his usual hop, skip and a jump before that rubber plimsoll connected with your arse five times. Needless to say, we couldn't sit down for the rest of the day, but at least I didn't have go to my maths lesson.

I was playing for the school team and also a local team on a Saturday called All Souls in the Bolton Boys' Federation. I would play for the school in the morning and All Souls in the afternoon, where hidings of 10–0, 15–0 and once even 32–0 were regular occurrences. But I had also found something else: punk rock. It was a new sound and it intrigued me so much that I sprayed my pit boots silver, much to my mum's horror.

When we moved to a new house on a new estate, there was a football pitch at the side of our house: I was in heaven. We were also situated near to a block of flats called Skagen Court. We had a lot fun in those flats. I even managed to spray my name in red standing on the ledge of the balcony; you could see it for miles. The biggest fun, though, was to play in the lifts.

You could enter the shaft through a trapdoor at the top of the lift and go up and down the shaft, stand on a little ledge when you got to the top and just wait there until the lift had been down to the bottom and then back up again. It was pitch black. In the side of the lift there was a vent through which you could see into the lift itself. We would wait until somebody got into it and then we would blow smoke into it for a laugh or, if a young kid got in, we would make ghost noises to try to make them cry.

It all came to an abrupt end one day, however, as one of my mates fell down the shaft and was killed instantly. It was a real shock and nobody went near that lift again.

I loved school but hated the lessons. I only saw them as getting in the way of football or having a laugh.

Money was always tight in our house and Mum did her best, especially after Dad had left. I was playing in goal for the school when I was told that I had been selected for a trial with Bolton Boys – somebody must have taken notice. Up until that point, I had been playing in goal wearing no gloves.

'Mum, I got a trial for Bolton Boys and I need some gloves.'

'Okay. I'll do my best,' she said.

The trial was on a Wednesday and she promised me that she would get them for kick-off. I waited anxiously and as I was warming up, I saw my mum walking towards me as quickly as she could.

'Philip,' she shouted as she came across the field.

Embarrassed, I just carried on with the warm-up while everybody else was looking at me.

As she got nearer, I told her to just drop them at the post. She did. When I had a minute, I walked to the plastic bag at the foot of the post thinking that soon I would look like Peter Shilton with new gloves.

I opened the bag and found a brand-new pair of rubber gardening gloves.

'What the fuck?' I thought. 'It must be a mistake. She must have given me the wrong bag.'

I looked at her stood on the halfway line as she waved at me. No, it was no mistake; she didn't have any more bags on her. I tried them on.

'Fucking hell, what am I supposed to do wearing these – weed the fucking goal area?' I thought.

Anyway, I put them in the bag and left them behind my goal. After the game she said:

'Why didn't you wear the new gloves?'

'Too big, Mum,' I said, as I didn't have the heart to tell her otherwise.

I would catch the bus every day to Sharples High School and get off at the Pineapple Inn on the corner of Blackburn Road and Mossbank Way. I would then meet my mates and walk the last half a mile to school through the allotments. I would always pass a shop on Blackburn Road called Frank Peacock Sports. This recently opened shop intrigued me and I used to love looking through the window to marvel at the football strips on show, including the new Ray Clemence England strip – a bright yellow shirt with two black lines down the sleeve.

I used to dream about that shirt at night and I knew that there was no way that Mum could fork out the money for things like that.

Anyway, the next time I went past, I promised myself that I would go in and have a look. I stepped into the shop and saw the owner, Frank Peacock, a local celebrity cricketer.

'Morning,' he said. 'Can I help you with anything?'

'No thanks, just looking,' I replied, as he got on with his business.

I looked around and saw the Ray Clemence shirts stocked on a shelf – boys, medium and large. 'If only,' I thought.

Frank then walked into the back room.

'What are you doing?' I thought to myself as I picked up one of the shirts and shoved it into my school bag. My head was pumping as I reached the door.

'See ya,' said Frank, as he walked back into the shop.

'Yer, see ya,' I replied.

As soon as I got out of the shop and onto Blackburn Road – the place where the Smithills lads had given me a hiding – I sprinted round the corner and up the back lanes until I reached the allotments, the last landmark before school. I looked into the bag. My heart was still pumping.

'Had I been followed?' I thought as I looked nervously back.

I ran into school. I could not concentrate all day. I was wondering when the police or Kenyon would turn up to my classroom, followed by an irate Frank Peacock.

I watched the classroom doors all day.

'Oh fuck,' I thought. 'They'll be waiting outside for me.'

I started to panic and began to think of an excuse. Perhaps I should just stash it somewhere. I decided to take my chances. The bell went off at 3.30pm. I walked slowly down the school drive, mingling in with the other kids. There was no sign of anyone. I now knew that I had got away with it.

'Where did you get this football shirt?' Mum said.

'Oh the school have lent it to me,' I replied, indicating that it was part of the school strip.

In bed that night, I thought about the shorts and socks that went with the shirt. Two weeks later, I was in goal for Sharples High School looking like an England international.

It wasn't the first time that I had stolen things as a child. When we lived in Grasmere Street, Mrs Walsh next door always sat outside on a chair and would take great delight in hitting you with her walking stick if you made too much noise.

Be that as it may, I would pop in every Saturday morning and ask her if she wanted any errands doing, such as running to the shop. When she went into the kitchen, I would open up her purse and nick a fiver, a lot of money for a ten-year-old boy, and I would be off to Burnden Park on my own to watch the Wanderers or the reserves, whichever of the two were playing at home. This went on for a while. Until she clicked...

On the way back from Burnden Park, after having seen the Whites beat Chesterfield, they were waiting for me. Mum, Mrs Walsh and her son, Tommy.

I was briskly frogmarched all the way into Bolton town centre and straight into the Bolton Central police station. I escaped with a warning and a severe bollocking from a bobby. Needless to say, it put the wind up me.

I knew it was wrong then, but we were living on the poverty

line like most of the people in the neighbourhood. I suppose we were worse off than most and even at Christmas I don't know how Mum managed to provide us with the one or two presents that were waiting for us on Christmas morning, when we would be up at five or six sneaking downstairs, tackling the cockroaches head on, and seeing what was under the bare plastic Christmas tree, which had one or two lights on it and lots of empty chocolate wrappers hanging from a piece of string – because the contents had been devoured as soon as mum had hung them on.

One Christmas morning I got up to find a scooter wrapped up. All the other lads had bikes, but I suppose that a push scooter was the next best thing.

I unwrapped it at six o'clock in the morning and decided to try it out in the front street. Outside into the cold I went, wearing my pyjamas and slippers, and started to push off down the street. It was freezing cold and there was snow and ice on the ground.

When I reached the bottom of the street, I lost control and banged straight into 'Jackie Charlton', who was still lit.

'Still can't get past this defender,' I thought to myself as I picked myself up and nursed my wounds – grazes on both of my arms and a big tear in the knee of my pyjamas. Even worse, though, was the fact that the scooter was damaged beyond repair.

I knew that I would be in big trouble, so I carried the scooter home, wrapped it back up and strategically placed it back under the tree, and went back up to bed. Of course, Mum hit the roof when she got up and discovered what I'd done, but I still swore blind that I didn't know anything about it and continued to blame my sister Shirley for weeks on end.

The lure of Frank's shop became obsessive until one day the inevitable happened. I was walking past when I saw a new shirt in the shop window. It was a fancy red one with a white band around the chest.

On closer examination, I discovered that it was the new Middlesbrough shirt and it looked great. In I went, oblivious that Frank was watching me. Perhaps he had started to notice that his stock was going down, particularly ping-pong balls, especially the Halex 3 Star, table tennis bats, shirts, shorts or anything else that was in easy reach.

As usual, I waited for Frank to disappear pretending that I was just looking around.

Into the school bag went the shirt and as I walked quickly towards the door, I felt this hand grab me on the shoulder.

'Gotcha, yer little bastard,' he screamed. 'I fucking knew it was you,' he said as I protested my innocence, telling him that it was the first time I had done it.

The police soon arrived from Astley Bridge police station, a mere 500 yards away.

I was put in a cell and started to cry, thinking that I was going to be locked up forever with the key thrown away.

Mum had to pick me up. I felt sorry for her. It must have been so embarrassing for her, but once again I only received a warning.

I also felt sorry for Frank, but my pals thought that I was a hero because I'd spent some time in a cell – something that most of them had already done.

Chapter Two

I already had other interests. I had started seeing my first
girlfriend, Alison Fay, who had quickly become the love of
my thirteen-year-old life. I loved playing table tennis for Bolton
Lads' Club and I always loved playing cricket. It was not
uncommon for me to knock some runs and take some wickets,
either in the back cobbled streets or in the schoolyard, where we
would wait until the janitor, Mr Brindle, had gone home and
would scale the iron railings and play cricket with the wickets
chalked on the wall. One day, we scaled the fence and tried to
claim the best spot, but somebody had beaten us to it.

A new set of wickets had been chalked on the wall. I found a
rag, dipped it in a puddle and started to wipe off the markings
when suddenly I heard: 'Hey what are you doing?' I looked
round and saw an irate Abdul Patel and his army as they climbed
over the railings with bats and balls in their hands.

Some Asian families had recently moved into the area and they
often bore the brunt of some of our neighbourhood pranks.

Some we got along with, including Mustaq Chandia who was in my class at school and who had recently had the front of his terraced home smashed in when one of the other lads in the area, Phil Settle, thought that it would be fun to nick the electric milk float one morning when the milkman was delivering his round. But Phil lost control and smashed straight through the front of the house. Mustaq's family had a lucky escape as they were sitting inside next to the window. The affair made the front page of the *Bolton Evening News*.

'Why are you wiping away my wickets?' Abdul yelled in my face.

'It's not your land is it?' I replied. 'Go back to your own fucking country,' I said, moments before I received a cover drive on the back of my head with a Slazenger size 5 cricket bat. There was blood everywhere, but I was okay after four stitches in the back of my head.

When I returned from the casualty department with Mum, who thought that I'd fallen, I made my way back to the school-yard. When I got there, I found that my mates were playing Abdul and his mates in a kind of England v. Pakistan test match. I was allowed to join in for the second innings, but it was a tense affair, particularly when I had to bowl to Abdul.

I threw one down; it missed his bat and clipped the top of the wicket with chalk dust flying everywhere.

'How is he?' I shouted, as I thought that I'd got my revenge.

'Not out,' he replied, standing his ground.

'Fuck, he was out,' I said to Dave, one of my friends.

Then I noticed a puddle and dipped the tennis ball in it. Next ball, I pitched one right up and beat his bat again. This time the watermark was on the wall and he had to walk.

Test matches were regular fixtures against the Asian kids on Chalfont Street School playground, but I was already playing more serious cricket by representing Astley Bridge Cricket Club Under-14s.

My first season was enjoyable and I finished up by being voted the Player of the Year, but the first fixture of the next season, against a local side called Tonge, didn't go so well.

I was due to open the batting and, as I walked out wearing my white school shirt and a pair of cheap white trousers which Mum had bought for me from an Asian shop called Talib's Fashions on Bridge Street, I felt like Geoff Boycott.

'No I can't be Geoff Boycott,' I thought. 'He's a fucking Yorkshireman.' No, I was going to be David Lloyd of Lancashire.

I stepped to the crease to take my guard, looked up to the umpire and nervously muttered 'middle and leg please' and, to my horror, I noticed that the umpire who was replying 'A little to your left' was none other than Frank Peacock. 'Oh fuck,' I said to myself. I couldn't concentrate.

The first ball of the first game of the season came down. Something caught my pad strap as the ball went through to the wicketkeeper. I knew that it was the ball and that my bat was nowhere near.

'Howzat!' the opposition cried in unison.

I looked up and Frank was holding up his right index finger. It was never out, but I suppose that it was Frank's revenge. Nevertheless, I couldn't wait to get off the pitch.

I had been a member of Bolton Lads' Club now for a few years. Mum disapproved of my membership. I think it was because some of my cousins from my dad's side were members.

I enjoyed playing table tennis with my Mark Five bat that I'd nicked from Frank's shop – a week after acquiring it, I had the cover to match.

When we had moved across to Nottingham Drive in Hailiwell on the new council estate, the thrill of playing in the derelict terraced houses or making dens in backyards where we would light fires and sit by them at night was no more. I missed playing on the coal trucks on the railway sidings behind Warburton bakery. Even though most other people had moved along with us, I still walked back over to the old houses and up and down the now-deserted streets with everything boarded up ready for demolition.

The old terraces, with generations of history, were ready to be wiped away, only the memories were left. It was a place where working-class Boltonians would stand at the front doors of their houses wearing flat caps, smoking and watching the world go by. It was a place where children used to run up and down the streets or push prams. It was a place where fathers and sons would play mass football matches in the front cobbled streets or the narrow back alleys with goals at either end, watched by wives and mothers from the bedroom windows. It was where Hilda Ogden look-alikes would scrub their doorsteps every day or bitch about which 'dirty cow' had the dirtiest curtains. And it was where the doors would be left wide open all day as neighbours would pop in for coffee and gossip.

But the new house and estate had their compensations, such as an indoor loo, a bath and my own bedroom with a flat bunker roof just outside the window, which was great for access after bedtime.

I also met new friends and new players for the football games on the school field just around the corner.

My Auntie Dorothy and Uncle Alan had also just taken over the social club in the small precinct about 500 yards away over Brownlow Way.

She offered me a job collecting bottles and moving the chairs and tables after a bingo session and paid me a pound, which enabled me to open a bank account at TSB just around the corner.

The job lasted for a month before she caught me passing bottles of stout to my friends outside one Saturday night as we prepared for a party at my house whilst my mum had disappeared into the Cotton Tree.

What had pleased me most was that my friend Dave Colgan

had also moved to the area. We had lived opposite each other in Grasmere Street and his family were the first people there to have a telephone installed in their house: it was an event that brought everybody around Grasmere Street to their house to have a look.

Not long after, they were the first to have a colour TV and, once again, people flocked just to have a look at this new invention.

It was great for me, as I could now see the colour of the football pitch and the smart-coloured strips of the players.

Dave was also a bit of a trendsetter. He was soon courting a girl called Gail; I, on the other hand, was more interested in playing football.

At fifteen and in my last year at school, I hadn't a clue what I was going to do.

The dream of becoming a footballer was just that – a dream. I had now stopped going to the lads' clubs. I think that I had grown out of them by that time and besides, I had started the Duke of Edinburgh Award Scheme with Mr Marshall, a teacher at a school in Bury, a couple of years earlier. We used to go away for weekends.

Dave was also a year older than me and had got involved with a new set of lads who he was now working with. I envied him because he always had money in his pocket and he would often walk past in his suit when I was taking a corner on the pitch.

'Where the fuck are you going?' I would say.

'Scamps,' he would reply. 'Wanna come?'

'No, got school in the morning,' I would answer, before delivering the ball into the position of maximum opportunity.

A few weeks later, I did go out with Dave wearing a borrowed suit.

'Where are we going?' I said.

'Wait and see,' he replied.

We walked into Bolton town centre and went straight to a dance studio where we met his new mates. I was quickly welcomed into the new gang.

'Dave what the fuck are we doing here?' I said, confused. I thought that we were going to the Swan, where I knew that they weren't bothered about age limits.

On the door of the studio was a sign advertising *Saturday Night Fever* dance lessons.

'Come on,' said Dave. 'I'll pay for you.'

'I'm not going in there, you fucking poof,' I said. 'Dancing? What's that all about?'

'Just watch,' he said.

For the next hour, I was pissing myself watching as all the lads were dancing under instruction to the sounds of 'Night Fever' by the Bee Gees. When it was over, we walked back down the stairs with me still in fits of giggles.

'Lads don't dance,' I said. 'Lads play football or fight.'

But I was soon to become embroiled in a new stage of my life.

We got into Scamps after Dave had persuaded the doorman that we were all eighteen. Once we were in, I watched dumbfounded and completely out of my depth as the lads hit the dance floor with girls all around.

'I'll have some of this,' I thought and was soon a paid-up member of the lads' dance club. We became regulars at Scamps and good friends with the doormen. I had a lot of bum fluff on my upper lip and soon learned how to apply mascara on it so that it looked as though I had a moustache. I thought that it made me look older.

The rest of the lads had jobs working for Francis Lee, the ex-Manchester City and England star who owned a big toilet paper warehouse in Bolton, and all of them were earning some good money. I still hadn't a clue what I was going to do when I left school, but I thought that I could get a job at Francis Lee's with my mates.

My sister Shirley, who was two years older than me, had applied to join the Army in the Women's Royal Army Corps. I had taken a part-time job working in a small bakery in the precinct so that I had some money for Saturday nights.

Shirley was accepted into the Army, which pleased me because I could now have the bigger bedroom. I could also sell her guitar, which would bring in a bit more beer money.

I managed to get a day off school from Mr Kenyon so that I could go to the job centre in Bolton to see if I could find a job. I looked at the board and something caught my eye. 'School leaver required for help in a wood yard in Farnworth.' I approached the advisor and told him that I was interested in the position. He phoned the contact and arranged an interview for that afternoon.

I caught the bus to Farnworth and arrived unprepared for my very first proper interview at Gordon Clarke Timber Merchants. Duties included selling timber to tradesmen and being the general dogsbody.

I turned up and asked for Terry the yard foreman. He introduced himself.

'What is six times five?' he spluttered as he took another puff on his cigarette and adjusted his glasses.

'Er ... thirty,' I said, hoping that I had given the correct answer.

'Well done, lad,' he said. 'When can you start?'

'Well, I leave school in two weeks. What about the Monday after?'

'Okay,' he said. 'See you then.'

And that was it. A one-minute interview and I had got a job. Starting at £18 a week before tax.

Chapter Three

Mum was pleased when I announced that I was going to be employed. As she had now got a job cleaning houses for the council, things were looking up.

I was also looking forward to leaving school. I was never any good academically; football was always my priority, yet I still managed to leave with five CSEs.

We had planned a few tricks for the teachers on our last day, but when we turned up, there was Kenyon waiting outside, turning away people who he thought might cause trouble, myself included.

What a way to end five years of secondary education, it was a real anti-climax.

I left school on Friday and then started work on Monday. Having to get up at 6.30 every morning to catch two buses to Farnworth was real eye-opener.

I had to clock in bang on 8am and clocked off at 5pm, but I felt that I'd grown up now as I headed off to the bus stop carrying my flask of tea and salmon paste sandwiches in my bag, which were normally eaten by the time I'd reached Bolton town centre to catch the second bus.

I enjoyed the work as I was paired off with Des, another lad who was a year older than me, and it was down to us to run the outside shop that had timber stacked everywhere. On the other side was the small indoor factory where the older guys worked the machines and massive cutting saws. I hated going in there because of the noise and the sawdust that filled the air. You had to wear earplugs and glasses and I don't think I would have liked to work in there all day. Des soon showed me scams to make a little extra money.

Our job was to get the timber for the tradesmen, then load up their trucks, then report to Terry to let him know what they had purchased and he did the rest. But for a fiver in our back pocket, we would tell Terry that they had got a lot less than was on the truck.

At least I had a few more quid in my pocket and it was a real treat on a Friday when we received our pay packets. We would always go to the Railway Inn at Moses Gate in Farnworth at lunchtime for a couple of glasses of mild and a real sandwich.

I gave Mum a couple of quid for my board and paid for my weekly bus pass. After a weekend on the piss with the lads, come Sunday afternoon I was skint and had to wait until the following Friday before I had money in my pocket again.

There was also an old brick chimney in the yard, which was about 100 feet high. One morning, an old Land Rover pulled into the yard with a set of ladders strapped to the back.

'Alreet lad,' this guy said as he climbed out with his right hand adjusting his flat cap. 'Werst gaffer?' he said in a typical Lancashire accent.

'In the office,' I replied and went on with my business.

It was Fred Dibnah and his assistant Donald, who was about seventy.

For the next few weeks it was great to listen to Fred and Donald's stories during the tea break. This was some time before he became a TV celebrity, but he was always well known in Bolton long before his TV documentary fame.

After lunchtime one day, Fred had been to the pub for a few as he always did, when another one of the foremen, called Arthur, said to him: 'Fuck me Fred, you're not going back up there with a few pints inside you are you?'

Fred replied: 'You fucking go up there without a few pints inside you.'

Everybody fell about laughing as he climbed his ladders. It was a joy to watch him work, as first he made a big hole at the base of the chimney, where he placed a skip and he then would climb the ladder and sit on the top of the chimney as he dismantled it brick-by-brick, by throwing the bricks down the chimney, which would be caught by the skip with an almighty thud.

He would sit there whistling away while Donald stood at the base leaning on the Land Rover looking up and drinking tea.

One morning before tea break I was talking to Fred and he said: 'Donald's had gout you know and I'll be looking for a new apprentice, would you be interested?'

'Who me?' I replied. 'Fuck that. I ain't going up there, I'm scared of heights.'

Fred laughed and called me a few names as well as branding me 'a fucking soft bastard'.

On some occasions, Arthur or Terry would let me have a day out helping our delivery driver Howard and we would deliver wood, timber or even plasterboard to houses or firms in the Bolton area. It was great to get out for a day riding in his Bedford flatbed truck.

I got on well with Howard and found out that he had recently just got out of the Army. He had just turned twenty-one and had come out with his HGV3 licence. His stories interested me, as

Shirley had now been in the Army for six months and was due to be posted to Cyprus.

However, I was still having a good time with my mates at the weekends. Sometimes we went to Blackpool on the train or, if not, we would just stay in Bolton, where we would hit the pubs before having a good dance to all the old disco hits at Scamps.

It was the same routine. All meet at Dave's for seven, where we would congregate in his bedroom, much to his dad's annoyance; with the music blasting away he would come up at regular intervals and would always say: 'Turn that fucking music down, I can't hear the television.' We would turn the music down for a few minutes then put it back onto full blast just to annoy him.

We would then open a bottle of vodka, which we all chipped in for, as well as a bottle of lime and we would drink the lot to get us tipsy before we went out. We figured it would be a cheaper night out if we were already on our way. After that, we would all walk the couple of miles into town wearing our three-piece suits, looking just like John Travolta and we would go into the pubs along Bradshawgate before ending up at Scamps until 2am. We would then congregate with all the other revellers at the Bolton Supper Bar, a fish and chip shop fifty yards away from Scamps where the entertainment would continue, usually with a fight or a couple arguing.

One night we were queuing for our fish and chips when in walked Fred Dibnah and his wife Alison, after whom he named his beloved steam engine. They had obviously just been to a ball as Fred was wearing a black suit and a dickie bow tie. I'd never seen him looking so clean. His wife was wearing a black ball gown and when they had got their order they went and jumped into his Land Rover with the ladders still strapped to the back and 'F. Dibnah Steeplejack' painted on the side. Even Fred travelled in style.

We would then walk home, strategically picking our points where to spew up on the way.

I enjoyed working at the wood yard, especially being around older men and listening to their stories. At the time I was still playing for Bolton Lads and relishing the chance to play whenever I could.

As the new boy, I was the one who had to ensure that the tea urn was boiling when it was time for the tea break, otherwise I would have been in big trouble, as the guys lived for their tea.

I also loved a laugh and to play practical jokes, especially when we lived in Grasmere Street. We would tie a washing line around a door handle and run it across the street to the house opposite and tie the other end. Then we would simultaneously bang on both doors and fall about laughing, as nobody could open the door when they were both pulling at the same time.

Along with knock-a-door run, another favourite, which resulted in us being chased for miles by an irate occupant, involved collecting dog shit from the cobbled backstreets, which we scooped up into newspaper, and placing it outside the door of an Asian neighbour – who we knew always wore flip flops – before setting it alight.

We would then knock on the door, wait around the corner until he answered it and we would be in fits of laughter as he stamped on it trying to put out the flames.

Sometimes he would chase us for ages. It was all a little reminiscent of Butch Cassidy; we never seemed to shake him off.

But at the wood yard I always seemed to be the recipient of the practical jokes. Whether it was being sent to the hardware shop for Tartan Paint or skyhooks, I fell for it every time.

I had been at the wood yard now for three months and Howard was still selling the Army to me. I kept thinking that if I joined the Army I could go and get my HGV3 licence and then get a job delivering like Howard.

One lunchtime, I went down to Great Moor Street Army Careers

Office just to have a look. Howard had been in the Royal Corps of Transport, and I was interested in finding out about it.

I walked in and was confronted by a sergeant behind a desk.

'Can I help you with anything?' he said.

'Yeah. I'm interested in joining the Army.'

'Have a seat son,' he bellowed and we proceeded to talk about the Army.

'RCT? What do you want to join them for?' said the sergeant. 'You want to join a decent outfit like mine, the Royal Army Ordnance Corps, especially if you play football.' From then on he convinced me.

I arranged with him to go back a week later to take a written exam, which I passed quite easily.

Mum was a little worried when I first told her, especially as it was at the height of the Irish troubles, but I think that she was quite pleased.

Howard, on the other hand, was horrified: 'Why are you joining the fucking blanket stackers?' he protested.

'Because the sergeant said that it would be better for me,' I replied. My mates were also horrified that I'd decided to join the Army.

Three weeks later, I had to travel to the Manchester recruiting office to swear in and collect the Queen's Schilling – now a crisp five-pound note – which soon disappeared after a pub lunch in Manchester.

Shortly afterwards, a letter arrived with orders to report to Sutton Coldfield selection centre in Birmingham, attached to it was a rail warrant for 14 October, a day after my seventeenth birthday, which was now six weeks away.

A lot of thoughts were going through my mind, including, 'Birmingham, where's that?' I think I'd only been out of Lancashire three times before.

The night before I was due to leave I packed my suitcase. It was an old leather one, which had to be held together with a belt. In it, apart from my suit, I put one pair of trousers, a couple of T-shirts, a jumper and some new nylon Y-fronts, which mum had bought for me from Talib's Fashion, that bargain-basement Bolton institution that clothed a fair number of us working-class families.

Mum came down to the station with me at seven and we said goodbye. I didn't know how long I was going to be away.

I caught the train to Manchester and got the connection to Birmingham New Street station and into the real world on my own with all my possessions with me. I then had to catch a connection to Sutton Coldfield and, when I arrived, I was joined by another fifty recruits.

As we waited outside, a couple of Army buses pulled up and out stepped a sergeant.

'Right then, you lot. My name's Sergeant Wembant, spelled B-A-S-T-A-R-D, get on the buses.'

I started to giggle as I got on the bus.

One lad mumbled: 'Who the fuck is this joker?'

I spent three days at the selection centre and made some new mates. We all had to do numerous written tests and physical tests as well as a medical examination, where a doctor put his hands on my balls and asked me to cough.

On the third day, we were told our results and which jobs and regiments we could join. I was pleased because I was going to join the RAOC (Recruit Army Old Crap) as a driver.

We were then told where in the country we were supposed to report. I was to catch a train to London Euston, take the underground – 'the what?' – and make my way to Waterloo before getting a connection to Brookwood. I would be met there by an Army vehicle that would take me to Blackdown Barracks at Deepcut in Surrey.

Chapter Four

All the way down to Euston I got that homesick feeling and wondered whether I had done the right thing. 'Where do I go from here' I thought, as I arrived in the capital?

I was now on my own. I had been to London once before and that was on a school trip to watch the Rugby League Cup final at Wembley between St Helens and Leeds.

I tried to read the map of the underground on the wall: 'Fucking no chance,' I thought. 'And where will I get a ticket?' The best thing was to ask. By hook or by crook I managed to get to Waterloo and catch the connection.

I saw the Houses of Parliament for the first time as well as the River Thames. Once the train had left London, I noticed the old Brooklands race track on my left-hand side; I had seen it on *Blue Peter* a couple of years before.

As I arrived at Brookwood, I noticed that there were about ten other guys waiting to get off the train. All of them were in the same position as me. We had travelled separately, but before we got off the train we all knew each other's names and where we came from. After all, we were all going to be in the same platoon during basic training.

We were waiting outside the station when, yet again, an Army coach pulled up alongside and a corporal jumped off shouting: 'Blackdown Barrack. Get on now.'

We all jumped on the coach with fear and trepidation and there was silence on the bus as we made the short journey to Blackdown, speculating on what our new lives would be like.

As we were pulling up, I noticed squads of men running around in red T-shirts, Army trousers and boots.

We stopped at the guardroom, where a young private pulled up the barrier and waved us through.

I looked through the window as we were about to stop and saw soldiers saluting an officer as he walked by.

'Get off the bus,' shouted the corporal. We got off and were told to stand in a line at attention. We then waited in silence as Sergeant Neal walked around the corner followed by two lance corporals.

'My name is Sergeant Neal spelled C-U-N-T,' he bellowed. 'Welcome to Blackdown Barracks. I have some good news for you. We are still awaiting other recruits, so tomorrow you will be going home and will be reporting back in three weeks' time.'

This was music to my ears. My mind was racing. If I leave early in the morning I could get home and meet my mates in the pub. The following morning, away we went again. This time I knew which way to go. We all travelled back to London together then split up as we caught our different trains. When I arrived back in Bolton, I didn't go straight home but to the pub, where I knew my mates would be, with £20 in my pocket, which was paid to me by the pay sergeant on my departure.

Dave saw me first: 'Fucking hell, he's been kicked out already,' he shouted as all the lads cheered as I walked in carrying my broken suitcase. After a few beers I was wondering whether to go back; I'd already been away for five days and had been homesick.

Three weeks later, I made the return journey knowing that this time it would be different and that I didn't know when I would be home again. I also had three months' basic training in front of me, which I knew was going to be hell. But I was determined to give it my best shot.

Once again I embarked on the same journey, seeing the same sights as before. I arrived back at Blackdown just in time for tea in the mess hall.

I was shown into the barrack room with ten beds in each room. I soon noticed that I was the youngest in the platoon at just seventeen; some of the other recruits were in their twenties or even their thirties.

Most of them had the same background as me – they were either from broken homes or without prospects in Civvie Street.

I was 24543857 Private Stant of Gibraltar Platoon in the RAOC. We were woken up in the morning by the corporal shouting and bawling: 'Get up and be outside in fifteen minutes.'

'Fuck me. It's five in the morning,' I thought as I looked at my watch. Everybody rose slowly and I knew that this was going to be a regular occurrence. When I got outside, there were sixty new recruits all lined up as I joined them. We were marched everywhere as a squad, even to the cookhouse.

New recruits are stared at by other trainees wearing uniform and I couldn't wait to get into it.

After breakfast we were marched to the barbers for the traditional number one. We all waited one by one. I sat there in line as all the wisecracks came out: 'A little off the side,' one joked to howls of laughter.

'You won't be laughing from now on,' bawled a corporal as we broke into whispers.

I sat there listening quietly as the lads introduced themselves.

They all said where they were from and dished out big bravado lines like: 'I can't wait to fight the Paddies.'

'Fuck that,' I thought 'I'm only in here to get my HGV licence and then I'm getting out.'

I'd signed for three years, but nobody told me until a few weeks later that your time doesn't start until your eighteenth birthday. That meant that I had to do a 'year for the Queen' as it was called.

The first day saw us issued with equipment and clothing, all of which we had to sign for, which meant that if we needed replacements we would have to pay for them out of our wages.

By the end of the first day I was tired of marching and couldn't wait to get my head down. As I lay in bed that night, the realisation suddenly hit me. Here I was, miles from home, in a place where everybody seemed to talk differently to me and where guys were years older than me. I had no mates to back me up now if there was any trouble.

I started to cry under the sheets: 'Now fucking get out of this one,' I thought to myself.

The next day saw the same routine: 5am lots of banging, be outside in fifteen minutes, march to the cookhouse.

After breakfast we were shown how to dress and what was expected of us. I put my beret on and looked like Frank Spencer. We were shown how to make bed boxes with our blankets and pillows and how to bull shine our boots by burning off the pimples of the new DMS boots I had been issued and how to apply the polish with water to get a really good shine.

I was also issued with a new Army suitcase, which meant that I could throw away the old one. It was the second day and already two recruits had quit. The rules were that you had three weeks to decide if you wanted to stay or go, but after that there was no way out. I soon found out that it took three weeks to get your papers released, so I figured that it was better staying on.

We were also shown how to iron and which clothing needed creases and where. We had to clean the barrack block from head to toe, which was expected every night ready for a 5.30pm inspection.

I came to dread the inspections, whether it was the block or yourself or your equipment, which could be thrown at you at any time.

On the fourth day, we were woken as usual at 5am, but this time with the orders 'outside in five minutes'. Of course nobody could be outside and ready in five minutes; only a few of us made it and one of the reasons that I did was because I still didn't have to shave: it always saved me a few minutes.

After the usual abuse, we were told that because we had not been out within the five minutes we were going to be up an hour earlier the next morning.

Sure enough, next morning at 4am, we were woken with the usual shout to be outside in five minutes. Same result: not everybody made it and we were told we would be up an hour earlier the next day. This carried on all week until we were made to stay up all night.

Looking back, I think it was a character test to see whether you could deal with pressurised situations. The outcome was that a further five recruits quit that week, but I was still there and was more determined than ever to stay and see it through. Besides, I'd heard that once you had completed basic training, it would be a piece of piss.

I used to hate drill. I could never quite get to grips with staying in line. Most mornings we would be on the parade square being taught how to march and how to do all the turns. At the bottom of the square was a statue that all the staff called 'Mr Smith'. It was a statue of an old soldier and if you fucked up or went out of time when marching, much to the amusement of everybody else, you had to run down to Mr Smith, stand to attention and shout:

'I'm sorry Mr Smith for fucking up.' This made you concentrate more and, as time went on, I had to make my apologies less and less. I was no more the 'shagging, fucking, thing you' I was Private Stant.

I always kept myself clean as I had been witness to a regimental bath. One of the lads was renowned for being dirty and for never having a shower. So, one night when he was asleep, a bath was filled with bleach and disinfectant. He was woken up abruptly by ten recruits and thrown into the bath where he was scrubbed with wire wool and bristled brushes. Afterwards we were always clean and smart because, like most things in the Army, if one of you gets into trouble, it is taken out on the whole platoon.

Basic training was mentally and physically hard, but I always loved the PT sessions, where we would run for miles as a squad. I was always at the front and felt good as the overweight and older recruits lagged behind and were screamed at for being fat and lazy.

After a couple of weeks we were introduced to Heartbreak Hill, a few miles outside the barracks. It was a really steep hill and recruits had to run up and down it.

On the way up, I was at the front with the PTI (physical training instructor). I was determined to beat him to the top, when he stopped me yards from the top and said:

'Nobody beats me to the top of this fucking hill, understand.'

'Yes corporal,' I said. As a punishment, we were made to run up and down it ten times.

We were also trained on how to use the 762 self-loading rifle (SLR). After a few weeks, I could strip it down and clean it blindfolded; the same applied with the sub-machine gun 9mm (SMG). The SLR held thirty rounds, and in a magazine was capable of 1,000 rounds a minute and was accurate up to 1,000 metres.

I loved it when we went to the ranges. One group would be firing at wooden enemy targets and the other groups would be sat underneath the targets in a bunker called 'the butts' where you had a pointer on a stick to indicate where the last round had hit. We practised on what was called 'grouping', which was to get five rounds into the target as close as possible to each other.

The training was getting harder and, after a month, we lost more recruits who were either kicked out or 'back-squadded', which meant that after a certain time in your training, if you were not up to standard then you had to join the new platoon below you who were just starting basic training and you would have to start all over again from scratch. That provided me with my motivation, because there was no way that I was going through that hell again.

Other punishments were change parades, where you would have to get changed into certain clothing, like your camouflage gear, in five minutes, or even your NBC – nuclear, biological and chemical – warfare suit complete with respirator.

I hated the NBC training. The first time we used the gas chamber was a worrying moment. I'd heard all these stories about it.

We filed in ten at a time all suited up. The sergeant then lit four CS gas capsules and the chamber soon filled up with gas. I was sweating inside my suit and wanted to take off my mask and get back outside. But I knew the drill. You had to wait for a tap on the shoulder by the sergeant and then you would take a deep breath before whipping off your mask, stating your number, rank and name, before putting your mask back on.

The chamber was now full of gas and you could barely see in front of your nose. As I got the tap on the shoulder I took a deep breath, whipped off my mask, but for a split second I'd forgotten my Army number, which forced me to breath in a lungful of CS gas. Straightaway, and to a load of chuckles from my new mates, I was violently sick. I couldn't see as I had water streaming from my eyes, nose and mouth. I was pushed outside into the fresh air, but by now I thought I was dying and I was still spewing for England. I had recovered after ten minutes, but I still had to go back in and complete the initial test, besides I didn't want to be back-squadded. I went back in and completed the test and, after a few weeks, we were taught how to eat and drink in a chemical environment.

The training was hard but for the most part enjoyable. It was the Army bullshit that pissed me off. The constant inspections, cleaning boots, buckles and belts. Toilets, showers and baths had to be gleaming, as were the floors, which had to be waxed every night. And then there were the personal inspections, where you would be in trouble if you had a piece of fluff on you or, woe betide, a button undone on your shirt, or worse still, a speck of dirt in your locker or even on your boots.

My boots, which I'd spent all the little spare time I had buffing to a high standard, was the things that always let me down. You were issued with two pairs, one for training and one that you prepared for your passing-out parade and which you would wear with your smart No. 2 dress uniform. The 'best boots', as they were known, looked like glass after a few weeks, but they were very delicate and if you dropped one, all the polish could crack off ruining weeks' worth of bulling.

The corporal doing the inspection in the morning, Corporal Appleby, a Geordie, would often inspect my boots and would then take great delight in asking me to pick my window. 'That one please, Corporal,' I would often say and watched in horror as we all stood to attention by our beds – with other lads thinking 'Thank fuck its not my turn today' – as he opened the window and threw the boots to the ground below. He would then yell obscenities in my face, with the veins in his neck bulging. I soon learned how to deal with this by thinking that I was somewhere else.

The training was varied during the day, but it always started off with drill on the parade ground followed by PT, which was either a run or the assault course. Wednesday afternoons were sports afternoons in the Army and it was often said by Army personnel that they hoped the Russians didn't attack on a Wednesday afternoon as everybody in the Army would be playing sport.

Our platoon officer was a young lieutenant called Lieutenant Davies, who was fresh out of Sandhurst, just down the road in Camberley.

One day he said: 'Does anyone here play football?' My hand shot up along with those of a few other lads. 'Yes sir.' We were picked, along with some more recruits from other training platoons, to play against the permanent staff of Blackdown Barracks in a friendly practice match.

I played up front and ran the defence ragged, much to the cheering of the watching recruits. This was time to get my own back. Time after time I would be brought down, but I gave my all, including a crunching 50–50 with Lieutenant Davies.

Even though we were playing in Army-issued plimsolls, vests and shorts, we were winning 3–2 with a few minutes left and I had scored three goals. I had the chance to make it four, but missed the goal from five yards out.

The referee, who was a sergeant in the Physical Training Corps, suddenly stopped the game. I was then frogmarched at double time off the pitch by two corporals – much to the amusement of my mates on the touchline – under the instruction of the sergeant referee to take me immediately to the medical centre where I was subjected to an intense eye examination.

I had made my mark, however, and was then selected to play for the battalion team. It was quite an honour playing with these regular soldiers, as I was the only recruit in the team. All the team were permanent staff at the base, including Lieutenant Davies.

A week later, I was picked for the side, but our goalie didn't show up. I volunteered to go in goal and that was where I stayed until I left the base.

We were a month short of finishing our basic training and were given a few days off at Christmas. When I went home, I couldn't wait to get back to my new life. I had suddenly found that because I was playing football for the battalion I was no longer the young recruit who was always getting picked up on anything at inspections: I had gained some respect. There were no more bawlings from Sergeant Neal and his storm troopers.

The last month went quickly. We finished the last couple of weeks with a five-day exercise on Salisbury Plain, where we had to put into practice all the things that we had learnt in basic training.

I had passed all the weapons tests and fitness tests. I had even finished basic training as a marksman with an SLR along with a few others, which gained me the cross rifles, a badge that was proudly sewn onto my best No. 2 uniform.

I passed out in early February with twenty-four other ex-recruits, out of the sixty-four initial recruits, and was now a fully trained soldier.

Mum came down for the passing-out parade. As we marched perfectly behind a brass band, I felt really proud that I had grown up so much in just a few months. The Army was my family now, and although Mum missed both me and my sister, she knew that for kids growing up on a council estate with few qualifications and little hope of paid employment back home, it was a golden opportunity that was not to be sniffed at. I knew that we would then have a weekend pass before having to report on Monday morning to the Army School of Mechanical Transport at Leconfield, an old Second World War airbase near Beverley in Humberside, to do my driver training. Hopefully, in a couple of months' time, I would have my HGV3 as well as my driving licence.

Chapter Five

In Civvie Street, you have to be twenty-one before you are allowed a heavy goods driving licence, but in the Army it is eighteen. I arrived in Bolton late on the Friday night and I was out straightaway to meet my mates.

'Fucking hell, they're not going to let you loose in one of those Army trucks are they?' Dave said as I tried to catch up with them on the drinks, and followed up by saying: 'We'll be in trouble if the Russians attack and you're going to protect us.'

Everybody laughed, but I knew that I was now different to my mates. I was now a fully trained soldier and I had to live by a different code. I also knew that they were all proud of me.

I arrived at ASMT on the Monday morning and reported to the guardroom, where I was shown to my new barrack room, with new mates from different corps and regiments who were also here to do their trade training.

It struck me that all the barrack blocks had strange and funny names. I was put in Juno Block, the other blocks had names like Caen, Gold and Ouistreham. Somebody pointed out that all the names of the barrack blocks were relevant to the Normandy landings in the Second World War.

At the ASMT you had all kinds of Army tradesmen, from drivers to mechanics, troops who would learn how to service a pushbike as well as a chieftain tank, and troops who learned how to operate forklift trucks and eager beavers (a cross-country, four-wheel-drive forklift) as well as tanker drivers.

It was totally different to basic training. It was far more relaxed with only occasional inspections. No more shitty guard duties or peeling spuds in the cookhouse.

After a week in the classroom, I was paired up with my driving instructor who was a civilian and who was employed by the Army, as most of the instructors were.

Mr Jones would be my instructor all the way through until I had passed my HGV3. For the first week, I learned in a Ford Escort and spent my time on the airfield, which was made up into a road with road signs all over it. There were also traffic lights and roundabouts, so that I could practise in safety before being let loose on the local roads. During that first week, I often wondered about the Lancaster bombers that had taken off from this base all those years before as they made their way to various targets in Germany.

There wasn't much to do at night apart from going over to the Navy Army Air Force Institute (NAAFI) to have a pint and put some money into the jukebox. At weekends, however, the lads that didn't go home from our block would go into Beverley for a few drinks and then onto the Beverley Hills Nightclub in town.

Beverley is only a small town and it soon became clear that the locals didn't like the squaddies pinching their girls. It became even clearer one night when, dancing to 'Hands Up' by Ottawan, there was a big commotion behind me. I looked round and there was Jack, an Army air corps recruit, beating the shit out of a couple of civilians who had obviously made some remark.

Of course, all the Army lads joined in and were forced to make a quick exit when the police were called.

When we got back, everybody was saying what a good night it had been. Get pissed, have a fight, and if you didn't it would be classed as a boring evening. I soon found this out, even if it meant that you got a hiding yourself.

The idea was not to get caught, because you would be in serious trouble with the Army for fighting and for bringing your regiment into disrepute.

I found this quite funny, especially as the Army had just spent thousands of pounds on training me how to fight. The fact is, yes they had, but you also had to be disciplined. We were trained soldiers, not thugs. Still, the mentality tended to be: 'Oh fuck it, let's have a scrap anyway, let's just not get caught.'

Things on the driving front were progressing well and, after a month, I was given a truck to drive. In the Army you didn't do a car test, because if you had proved that you were competent in a car, you would then learn to drive trucks and take what's called a dual test in a truck. If you passed, you would get both licences automatically.

It was a big step up for me from driving low down to suddenly being high up in a Bedford TK Army truck. Again I spent time on the airfield before I was allowed on the roads and driving to new places like Bridlington, Scarborough or even York.

I soon knew all the cafes in the area. My instructor, typical civilian I thought, always had to have his tea break or lunch break at certain times, both in the morning and in the afternoon which, despite being used to a life of routine, pissed me off enormously – all I wanted to do was to drive my truck.

My test was at 11am, meaning that I had two hours' practice before the test, which was to be carried out by another Army-employed civilian examiner. I was nervous and I was shaking even more at 10.15am on our way back to the camp to meet the examiner. I found myself staring at a flat Labrador that had somehow found its way under my rear wheel.

I was oblivious to his owner's screams and my instructor yelling: 'You fucking idiot, didn't you see it? You will never pass your test as long as you've got a hole up your arse.' After another hour of apologising, excuses and scraping some of the dog off my truck, we arrived an hour late for the test.

As my instructor jumped out of my truck after telling me to wait for my examiner, he walked round to my cab door. My beret fell off as I wound down the window.

'If you fail today get yourself another instructor,' he barked at me. As he walked off I was fuming:

'I should have run you over, you fucking civvy,' I shouted.

He turned quickly and stared at me with one of those looks-could-kill glares.

'And why do you need a briefcase to carry just your sandwiches,' I continued.

He started to walk towards me and then must have had second thoughts before turning back and walking away. I was glad; otherwise I would have been in serious trouble.

Twenty minutes later, I was in Beverley town centre with my test well under way. At the end the examiner asked me a few questions and was pleased to tell me that I had passed.

In the space of five months, I was now a trained soldier and, at just eighteen years of age, had an HGV3-class driver's licence, which I thought I would never eclipse in my wildest dreams.

I had achieved something with my life.

'That's it,' I thought. 'I am happy with what I've achieved and as soon as my Army days are over I will become a driver just like Howard, my mate from the wood yard.'

In fact I didn't want to leave Leconfield. I had enjoyed it that much and now, for the first time in my life, I felt I was somebody.

After I had passed my test I knew that it was time to report back to Blackdown Barracks, where I would have to wait until my orders came through and I would be joining my new unit, once again with new mates.

I would have to wait two weeks before the orders came through with my permanent posting.

Back at Blackdown I was put in Trade Platoon, along with troops who had also completed their trade training and were waiting for their permanent postings.

Every day I was thinking Germany, it must be Germany. Hong Kong, could it be Hong Kong? I hope it's not fucking Northern Ireland. Some of the lads bragged that they wanted to be sent to Northern Ireland, but it was just bravado. It was 1980, and British soilders and Royal Ulster Constabulary officers were dying every few months. What about Cyprus? Our Shirley was posted to Cyprus, so why not me? Belize? Maybe Belize? No, probably Germany.

I had been told: 'For fuck's sake I hope you don't get a Field Force.'

One of the lads said: 'You're on exercise for eight months of the year.'

That I didn't fancy, particularly when I thought back to our five-day exercise at the end of basic training; it had been a nightmare, especially the ten-mile yomp back to the barracks. No, I fancied a depot where they didn't do field exercises and where I could play football.

We all lined up on Friday morning waiting to be called in with our orders. Lads were coming back out smiling; most of them got Germany, one lad got Cyprus. 'It must be Hong Kong,' I thought to myself as I marched in last, saluted and nearly spewed up when I was informed: 6 Field Force, Aldershot.

The reality suddenly hit home. 'Fucking hell. Three years at Aldershot, the home of the British Army.' Three years in an austere garrison town with little opportunity for extra-curricular activities was not a pleasant thought.

All the lads had been coming out with flight coupons and I was coming out with a fucking bus ticket for a twenty-minute journey.

'Was it a Labrador I'd run over or a fucking black cat?' I thought as I marched back through the door and outside where all the lads were backslapping and praising each other.

They could tell by the look on my face that it hadn't been good news for me. They did console me in the NAAFI that night, but I knew that they didn't give a fuck because they had mostly all got what they wanted.

On Saturday morning I sat at the bus stop after saying goodbye to the lads as they went their separate ways, with my Army suitcase and kitbag, still in disbelief at my luck.

I had joined the Army to see interesting places and to meet interesting people and kill them.

'Fucking Aldershot,' I kept saying to myself, but little did I know that it would be the best posting I could ever have.

Chapter Six

I jumped on the bus, which was empty. It was a Saturday morning and we were soon entering Aldershot. You are greeted there by a big green sign that reads: 'This is Aldershot. Home of the British Army.'

The bus drove all the way down Queens Road and past the military stadium where the Army played their matches.

I got off the bus at the crossroads next to a church and walked the last half mile to the barracks. As I walked down, I passed the para-training depot. I recognised it instantly because it has a Second World War Dakota airplane sat outside.

My new barracks were directly opposite and, as I walked up the road towards the guardroom, I passed the place where I would be working for the next three years. MT (Motor Transport) Platoon 6 Field Force RAOC.

I reported to the guardroom and was shown to the block. This place was a little bit different, as 6 Field Force was made up of a few regiments and corps. The blocks were square shaped and three stories high. There were four beds to a room, which was a bit better and, after you had re-arranged a few lockers, it had more privacy.

I looked out of my window. The next block was the home of the feared 9 Para Squadron Royal Engineers. The block in front belonged to the Royal Signals and the block to the left housed the Slop Jockeys – chefs from the Army school of catering. Well, we still had to eat even when we were in the field, didn't we?

I unpacked and lay down on my bed. There was nobody else about. I assumed that everybody else was in town getting pissed or had gone home for the weekend.

Soon after a Lance Corporal walked in: 'Are you Stant?' he said.

'Yes,' I replied.

'Then report to the MT at 0600 hours on Monday morning kitted out. We are going on exercise to Salisbury Plain for a week. Welcome to 6 Field Force.'

'Shit,' I thought. 'Oh well, better check out my kit for Monday morning then.'

Not long after, another guy walked in carrying a football.

'Have you seen any of the lads?' he asked.

'No, I've just arrived.'

'Right okay,' he said and introduced himself. He was a private, Terry Diggle, or 'Digsey' as he was known. He was on his way out when I said:

'Hey Digsey, are you playing football?'

'Yeah,' he said. 'If I can find all the lads … why, do you play?'

I didn't need a second invitation. Within an hour, I was as happy as a pig in shit playing football with my new mates. Most of the lads played for the unit team and, by the end of the session, I had made enough of an impact to be invited to play for them. I had only been there a couple of hours, but I already felt at home.

My room-mate, who had been on weekend leave, arrived by Sunday night.

'Keith Yates, MT Platoon,' he said.

Yatesy and I got on well and, in the next several years, we would have a few scrapes together and would become like brothers.

I reported as instructed on Monday morning and met the rest of my new colleagues.

I was assigned to drive the Bedford MK, which carried the mobile shower unit. It was a nice little job that would mean that I would be on the edge of the exercise. My partner in the cab would be Lance Corporal Archibald. Archie was from the old school and he soon made it clear that he wasn't happy about working with a new guy like me, whom he called a 'sprog'. But I got through the week okay. Archie and I got on better when he found out that I would be part of the football team.

I soon settled in at my new unit and would often be driving all around the South East, which I loved. I hated duties, which for me would mean duty driver, a twenty-four-hour driving shift.

I hadn't been at the unit long when it was announced that, the following month, we would be going to Jurby, an Army training facility on the Isle of Man for adventure training. Joining us would be the new Sergeant Major Jimmy Boyle, who had a fearsome reputation.

Adventure training I loved. It included rock climbing, canoeing, abseiling, as well as other things. But the best bit was the football match that had been arranged against a local side and Jimmy Boyle was going to be the new manager of our football team. I had to play in a pair of Army-issue pumps as I didn't have any football boots with me, but I scored the winning goal in the last minute to complete my hat-trick. I felt like a hero and there were plenty of drinks coming my way in the bar afterwards.

Back in Aldershot, the unit team played in the local Army league on a Wednesday afternoon. I couldn't wait for Wednesdays.

At weekends, a few of us would go into Aldershot. It was like a Wild West town, especially on Saturday nights, with all the different regiments and corps stationed there, eyeing the local women and vying for space at the bar.

The paras and marines referred to us lower-ranking soldiers as 'Crap Hats' after the colour of our berets. Each regiment or corps had a pub that they liked to congregate in and they took a dislike to any Crap Hat that walked in. The Globetrotter, in town, was renowned for paras and if you wanted a fight all you had to do was to go in there and you would instantly be recognised as not one of the them because of the clothes you wore. All paras seem to wear maroon T-shirts, green bomber jackets and jeans as well as the customary shaven head and moustache.

If it had been a boring night, we would go to the Globetrotter late, when everybody was pissed, as a dare to take the piss out of the paras. More often than not you got kicked to shit, but at least it hadn't been a boring weekend.

After one such weekend, we were walking through the door of the block when, across at 9 Para Squadron's block, there was a commotion going on. There was lots of noise, shouting and banging when, suddenly from the middle floor of the block, a wooden locker was thrown out of the now-shattered window. It banged on the ground with a hell of a noise followed by laughter and whistling from the 9 Paras looking out of the broken windows.

'Fucking idiots,' Yates mumbled. 'Why throw a locker out of the window?'

All of a sudden, bang. The doors on the locker smashed open and a dazed, pissed-up para hauled himself out screaming:

'You fucking bastards, that's not funny.'

'Fuck this. I'm going to bed before I'm next,' I said.

The others quickly followed, as 9 Para were known to go into other blocks after a night's drinking just to kick the shit out of some poor Crap Hat.

Things were going well on the football front. Whether we won or lost, I usually scored a hat-trick, some days five and a few times six. I got on well with Jimmy Boyle and I was spared disciplinary procedures on numerous occasions.

It wasn't long before I was selected to play for the corps, which was considered a great honour, not just for me but for 6 Field Force. I wanted to call mum and give her the good news, but back then there was just one phone box and you'd have to queue for ages. Besides, mum didn't have a telephone at home. If you wanted to get in touch, it was by letter. Our greatest honour was reaching the final of the RAOC Cup, called the Richards Cup. At this time I was selected for and passed my HGV2 driver training, so things were going well for me.

No minor unit, as we were classed, had ever won the Richards Cup. Our commanding officer, Major McDougal, was chuffed to bits that his unit had reached the final, which was to be played at the home of the RAOC, Blackdown Barracks.

We were due to play Central Ordnance Depot Bicester, who were a big depot and, therefore, had lots of players to choose from.

We were the underdogs, but at least we had the shortest travelling time. All our unit was going to be there as well as coach-loads from Bicester.

All our troops clambered into the back of trucks and were ferried in convoy to Blackdown. The pitch was roped off where all the Bicester supporters (or troops) were positioned.

Our lot was on the other side, sat on a grassy bank. There must only have been a few hundred there, but to me it seemed like thousands.

As I warmed up, I wondered where Yatesy was. I then heard

the beeping of a horn. There was Yatesy, flashing his lights with more of the lads hanging over the side of the truck, on the front of which was a banner that read: 'Stant strikes more than British Leyland.'

We got off to a bad start. We were a goal down after five minutes, but just before half-time I ran onto a long ball, held off the defender and fired the ball past the keeper. 1–1.

The second half was a tense, scrappy affair and when the ref blew for the end of the ninety minutes I was knackered. No matter what happened now we were winners, because to take COD Bicester to extra-time was a great achievement in itself.

Chances came and went for both sides in extra-time, but all the players were knackered and settling for penalties. With less than a minute to go, I chased the ball over the top of two defenders, got in the middle and let fly from just outside the box. It was like slow motion: I lost sight of the ball, but then saw it again as it emerged from the underside of the keeper and into the net.

I turned round and saw the whole of the grassy bank rise to their feet cheering, but I was so tired that I just fell to the ground like Arsenal's Charlie George in the 1971 FA Cup final against Liverpool and waited for the lads to jump on me.

The CO was chuffed when we were presented with the trophy, but there was only one thing on everybody's mind and that was to get back to our unit bar and get pissed. The cup was passed round the club full of everything alcoholic. Even the CO was pissed as all the Army singsongs came out. Once again I was a hero.

I started to think about where I would be if I hadn't joined up. Could life get any better than scoring the winning goal in an important cup final in front of a massive crowd – well, it was to me anyway. Even Staff Sergeant Grumley (my boss) bought me a drink. Soon I was the CO's new driver. My duties included picking him up and taking him home to nearby Wokingham.

It was a cushy but boring job: I spent most of my time waiting for him as he came out of meetings. After one of them, he said:

'Pick me up at two please, Stant.'

'Yes sir, see you at two,' I said.

I then went back to the block, but fell asleep on my pit. I woke up.

'Fucking hell.'

It was 2.40. I quickly ran to the Land Rover and jumped in, but as I was approaching Queens Road I saw him walking. I stopped the Rover and he jumped in. He didn't say a word, but I knew I was in the shit. After all, you can't let your CO walk three miles back to barracks after an important meeting.

I started to imagine how he felt as all the other COs jumped into their waiting vehicles with their driver opening the door and saluting them, and him waiting there, briefcase in hand and clicking his heels. He must have been fuming at being embarrassed like that. An hour later, I was summoned to see CSM Jimmy Boyle.

'You're being charged,' he said.

I was also off the job and back to normal driving duties, which I wasn't too bothered about. I was more interested in how much I would be fined by the CO.

The next day, CSM Boyle summoned me back to his office. I marched in and he shut the door. What I didn't know was that the CO had gone home that night and told his wife, who I got on with quite well, and she had given him a bollocking for insisting that I was to be charged.

'You lucky bastard,' Boyle said. 'You must be the only soldier who has had a charge dropped after the intervention of the CO's missus.'

Word soon got around that I had been saved by a woman.

We had recently had a new admin officer, Captain Peter Turrell, who was also a football nut. He started to help and play for the team. I soon had two allies in senior management with him and Jimmy Boyle, but Jimmy had had his orders through and he was soon going to be heading off to Antwerp as Regimental Sergeant Major. Captain Turrell would take over the team following his departure.

I knew that I would miss Jimmy: I had a lot of respect for him, but I wasn't sure about his replacement CSM Kevin Townsend. Captain Turrell loved his football and took a great interest in me. I was now scoring goals for fun, both for the corps and my unit.

In two seasons for my unit I had scored over 120 goals. Unfortunately, our defence had conceded more. One day Turrell said to me:

'Have you ever thought about playing professionally?'

'No sir. I only dreamt about it as a kid, but I'm in the Army for another eight years.'

This was true. I had only signed for three years, four if you included the year 'for the Queen', but the previous Christmas I was skint and I had approached the pay sergeant and had asked how much back pay I would get if I signed for nine years. It worked out at £400. So I signed on for nine years and got my money just in time for Christmas leave.

Imagine waking up on New Year's Day skint again, hungover and with the prospect of having to do another seven years in the Army. It was a sobering thought.

'Why do you ask sir?' I said.

'Well, I think you could go pro and if you want to, I will try to organise some trials at local league clubs.'

'Me a pro, sir?'

'Yeah, why not?' he said.

'Well I'll leave it with you.'

I walked out thinking that he was off his head. I would never be good enough to be a pro, besides I was in the Army. I did know, however, that I could be bought out of the Army.

A week later, I was summoned again to Turrell's office where he produced a letter with headed notepaper. Aldershot Football Club. Aldershot were in the old Fourth Division and were inviting me to a trial the following Saturday morning.

Eighteen years old and my first trial at a Football League club. Just to be offered a trial was a big deal to me and all my mates were chuffed to bits for me.

I kept on reading the letter over and over again.

'I think I'll frame this letter,' I thought.

I lay there on my bed. Saturday morning at 9.30 sharp it said. The realisation hit me.

'Oh no, not Saturday morning.'

We were all going out Friday night and I wasn't going to miss that, besides getting a trial was like winning the pools and there would be no chance of me getting more than that. Maybe I'll only have a couple of drinks on Friday night and not kick the arse out of it.

The alarm went off. It was the usual Saturday morning feeling: tongue like sandpaper and the room stinking of old farts. I looked at the clock. Fuck me, I'd dozed back off and it was now ten past nine. I was still lying on top of my bed in the same position and clothing that I had dumped myself in at two in the morning.

I grabbed my bag, which I'd prepared the previous afternoon. There was no time to have a shower or to clean my teeth; I would have to run the two miles or so to the Recreation Ground, the home of Aldershot FC. I took a short cut through the married quarters, but had to stop to be sick at the side of the red telephone box.

I looked at my white – well not so white – T-shirt and examined the stains that I'd acquired the previous night. I got to the ground at 9.35 and ran through an open set of gates and found my way to the changing rooms where a coach was giving out instructions to about twenty young hopefuls. I was still only eighteen years old and I must have been classed as that.

I popped my head through the door and said my apologies for being late. I looked round at all the hopefuls, all of whom were wearing tracksuits of some kind and chewing gum ... and there was me, looking like a bag of shit.

'Are you here for a trial?' the coach said.

'Yeah,' I replied, pretending to be chewing gum myself.

'I think your trial starts at the courthouse on Monday,' he said.

Most thought it was funny, but I didn't.

'Wanker,' I thought.

Soon after we were in the park and were divided into two teams. All we had to do was play and nothing else.

Just before kick-off I went to tie my bootlace and, as I tightened it, it snapped.

'Fuck it, this always happens to me,' I moaned, but maybe if I had looked after my boots and not left them in my bag from one game to the next this might not have happened.

Anyway, ninety minutes later, breathing out of my arse, and my side had won 6–0 – I had scored all six of the goals. Despite the previous night's excesses, I felt great. Back home I'd rarely even been picked for teams let alone scored six goals. The boys in the smart kit, whose dads had brought them to the ground in their flash cars, were always more popular.

'We'll be in touch,' the coach said.

I remember seeing him a few years into my pro career and saying: 'I'm still waiting for your letter'.

There was only one thing on my mind and that was to get back to bed. We had another night out later on and I would need some sleep if I was going to be on top form.

Days and then weeks went by and still there was no reply from Aldershot. But then again I didn't expect it. In my view, I had

had a trial for a Football League club and I could now brag about it. Captain Turrell approached me again and suggested that he would get in touch with Reading, a Third Division club about thirty minutes up the road.

'How would I get there, sir?' I asked.

'We will get the duty driver to take you,' he said.

So one Monday morning off I went in the Land Rover looking for Elm Park, the home of Reading Football Club, managed by Maurice Evans.

I arrived at the ground only to be told by a receptionist that they had all gone to the training ground, which was three miles away. After giving me directions, I got back into the Land Rover and sat there looking at Vic Day, our duty driver, considering whether to go back or go to the training ground.

Captain Turrell had arranged the trial with the first-team coach called Stuart Henderson and when we arrived at the training ground I quickly found him and introduced myself.

'I didn't know you were coming today,' he said, 'but you're here now, get changed and warm up.'

I got changed and joined in the warm-up. It felt great training with professionals, even though they were nutmegging me – much to their amusement – at every opportunity. I still had this notion in my head that I was a conman who had no right to be with these people. I didn't know it then, but I was training with the first team, alongside future international players like Neil Webb, Kerry Dixon and Lawrie Sanchez. We played a small-sided game and I must have done enough as Stuart said to me afterwards that he would like to involve me in a reserve game the following week against Chelsea reserves at Stamford Bridge.

'Chelsea, fuck off. Are you shitting me? Stamford Bridge, fuck off, no way. Are you sure or are you taking the piss?'

These thoughts were screaming in my head as Vic drove me back to Aldershot. I couldn't wait to get back to tell the lads and

Captain Turrell. Vic was smiling as well, because he loved watching football and took great joy in telling me what I had done wrong during the game.

We arrived back in Aldershot and I went straight to see Captain Turrell with my good news. After that my staff sergeant brought me back down to earth again.

'Football is for puffs, now get that fucking Land Rover cleaned,' he growled.

'Yes staff,' I replied.

Stuart had been talking to Captain Turrell and I was informed that I had to be at Elm Park the following Wednesday at 12.30pm to travel on the team coach to Stamford Bridge. Captain Turrell also arranged for four of my mates to travel with me.

Suddenly I had to start thinking about my fitness. This was serious stuff now and I resolved to train in my spare time. Wednesday seemed like ages away, but when it came I couldn't wait. All five of us arrived at Elm Park just in time for the coach's departure.

I wondered what the rest of the players were thinking as my mates and I climbed aboard the coach and sat at the back.

I looked around. The coach had tables with lamps and a TV at the front: I'd never seen anything like it before – it was luxury.

'What the fuck are you doing?' I whispered to Scouse as I saw him try to unplug the lamp to put in his bag. 'Fucking put it back,' I said.

My mates were in their element, but not as much as me. I felt like a real footballer, travelling to the game on a luxury coach with a big sign on the front, which read 'Reading FC Team Coach'.

We headed down the M4 and into central London. I was now getting nervous about how I would perform and the importance of not making a fool of myself.

We pulled up after driving through the big blue gates behind the main stand at Stamford Bridge. We jumped off the coach with me carrying my boots. I watched the kit man get the skips off the coach, which carried the kit and the warm-up tops. We then walked down the tunnel and into the stadium. It was fantastic. My mates just sat on seats behind the dugout as I walked onto the pitch. I looked around and to my left saw the famous Shed End.

I thought about all the famous players who had played here, like Peter Osgood, Alan Hudson and Ian Hutchinson, and how many times I'd seen this place on *Match of the Day*. And yet here I was, Phil Stant. Phil who?

I walked back towards the changing rooms. All the strips were hung up, all set out for you. I was used to rummaging around a bin liner for the best socks or shorts.

The strip looked great. We were going to play in an all-yellow strip with me wearing the No. 9 shirt.

The dressing rooms were unreal with a place to get changed and another part where you could have your half-time team talk. There was even Astroturf on the floor.

The team sheets were brought in. I looked at their team, but didn't recognise anybody, even though I was informed that there were a few old pros playing for them.

I took my time to get changed so that I could let this all sink in, just in case it never happened again. I then went out to warm up, still not believing what was happening. I made sure that I got a ball and hit it into the back of the net. At least I could say that I'd scored at Stamford Bridge, even if it was only in the warm-up.

We went back to the changing room for Stuart's last-minute team-talk. We then made our way into the tunnel and waited for Chelsea. There was a lot of shouting, clapping of hands and bouncing of balls. Soon our opposition appeared, they looked smart in their familiar all-blue Chelsea strip.

We then walked out together into the stadium to a few claps and one or two shouts from the 100 or so people in the empty stadium.

'Just get an early touch and keep it simple,' I told myself.

The game kicked off.

'Come near me and I'll break your legs.'

I turned around and was met by the glare of a monster. It was Mickey Droy, the man mountain who'd been Chelsea's giant centre-half for what seemed like forever.

I was getting a few touches and laying it off and, funnily enough, after about fifteen minutes I started to feel comfortable: even the lads were starting to call me Phil. I felt part of the team now and I liked it.

Two minutes before half-time, I spun off Mickey and took a pass first time. I was now one on one with the keeper, forty yards from goal. I ran as fast as I could, but I felt as though I was treading water. I knocked the ball forward, it felt like a medicine ball – that huge, brown leather ball from school PE lessons.

I could hear the defenders chasing me, but I kept running and, as I got into the penalty box. I knocked the ball past their Yugoslavian keeper, Peter Borata, who dived at my feet. I jumped over him and slid the ball into the empty net from six yards and at a slight angle. My new team-mates were jumping all over me: I really felt part of the team now.

I looked towards the dugout. My mates were jumping up and down as I punched the air to salute them. The game ended 1–1, but I didn't care. I had scored against Chelsea at Stamford Bridge. Surely Stuart would ask me back now.

Back in the changing rooms there was a lot of backslapping and shouts of 'well done'. After all, Chelsea were a First Division club.

Stuart congratulated me and also confirmed that he would like me to play again the following week.

'Would I be okay?'

'Would I be okay?' I replied, ecstatic.

As we left the stadium on the team coach, all I could think of was to get off the coach and back into the Land Rover so that I could have a fag. I didn't want them to know that I liked a cigarette.

I took one last look as we turned right out of the ground and wondered if I would ever play there again. Whatever happens now, that had been a magical moment, one that I would never forget.

The only problem would be playing for my unit on a Wednesday afternoon in the local Army league and playing for Reading in the evening in Reading's second eleven.

Most reserve games were played on Wednesday evenings.

There was only one thing for it and that was to play for the unit in the afternoon and then play again for Reading in the evening. And that is exactly what I did.

I loved playing for Reading reserves. It gave me an opportunity to play at more grounds against top players who were coming back from injury.

I also knew that I was only there to make up the numbers. After the Chelsea game, I played in the afternoon for the unit team and then made my way to Elm Park for my home reserve debut against Watford.

A young boy stopped me outside the still-deserted ground and asked me for my autograph. It took me by surprise.

'Are you sure?' I said. 'Don't you want one of the real players.'

'Are you a player?' he inquired.

'Yes, I am,' I replied.

'Then can you sign my book.'

I took his autograph book and signed my name.

'Yes, you are a player,' I said to myself.

But I was worried in case any of the other players saw me signing his book. I was worried that they would think that I was a fraud or, even worse, a big head.

I scurried back into the now-familiar changing room. Once again all the strips were out, all the lads were sat down looking at the team sheets, there was a gap near to the No. 9 shirt. I looked at the team sheet and saw that I was to wear the No. 9 shirt once again, so I sat down where the No. 9 strip was set out.

'You're up against a good one tonight, Phil,' Stuart said.

I looked at the Watford team No. 5, Steve Terry.

'Who the fuck's he?' I said.

'A young defender who's nearly in the first team,' he said.

The game started and quickly this big, loud No. 5 started barking orders at his team-mates. It was clear that he wanted me for his dinner.

I received the ball and turned in the box. Terry stuck out his leg, down I went, penalty. I grabbed the ball. 'I'm fucking taking this,' I said to myself as I put the ball on the spot, half expecting somebody to say, 'I'm taking this, Phil.' But nobody did. I sent the keeper the wrong way. I had now scored on both my home debut and my away debut. Things got even better in the second half as I grabbed a second. We went on to win 2–0.

I was soon a regular, playing two games on a Wednesday. Appearing at grounds like Fulham, West Ham, Crystal Palace and Swindon was a great experience and the more I played, the more confident I became.

Once we played Spurs at Elm Park and their back four consisted of the entire first-team back four of the time. The two centre-backs were Paul Miller and Graham Roberts, who took it in turns to rough me up and call me all sorts of names.

I soon realised that I would have to stand up and look after myself, otherwise players like these experienced pros would just walk all over me.

We were now near the beginning of April, but it soon became clear that I was about to become involved in the biggest match of my life so far.

Chapter Seven

Some Argentineans had taken over a whaling station in South Georgia in the South Atlantic. It was somewhere near the Falkland Islands. The Falkland Islands?

'Where are they?' I enquired.

'Somewhere near Scotland,' one of the lads replied.

South Georgia and the Falklands Islands were British-owned territories in the South Atlantic and nobody I knew had ever heard of them before. We all thought that they were off the coast of Scotland.

Why would the Argentineans do that? 'It's a long way to come,' we thought as we scurried about looking for maps.

We watched the next few days with interest, and all hell broke loose in the barracks as events unfolded. We all watched the TV with anger as we saw the Argentinean army take the Falklands with minimum force.

The marines based at Moody Brook put up a fight, but they had no choice but to surrender due to a lack of numbers.

The whole of the newly formed Fifth Infantry Brigade, as well as most of the Army, was put on standby with all leave cancelled. I knew that that would signal the end of my football for the season at least.

Captain Turrell informed Stuart of the situation and I was invited back whenever I could. I was gutted, but the Army was my career after all.

We carried on watching the TV from the relative comfort of the barracks, knowing that a war was inevitable.

Argentina was in deep economic trouble and, after a coup in 1976, the country was being run by the military-backed president, Leopoldo Fortunato Galtieri.

It was reported that the invasion of the islands was supposed to be launched on 25 May 1982, the anniversary of the revolution. Its main purpose, however, was to divert the public's attention away from the problems within Argentina and to restore the long-lost popularity of the dictatorship. However, because of internal pressure and union demonstrations in late March, the date of the invasions was moved forward to 2 April.

The governor of the islands was Rex Hunt and, after the invasion, he, along with the marines who had surrendered, were flown to Montevideo.

We all carried on watching as some guy called General Menendez was appointed Military Governor of the now renamed Malvinas Islands.

'Fucking cheek,' I thought.

In the coming days, we watched as thousands of Argentinean conscripts were drafted in to boost their numbers to 10,000 troops on the islands.

The US Secretary of State, Alexander Haig, was shuttling backwards and forwards trying to get both parties to agree to a peace solution. I couldn't see that happening. Even a young lad like me could see the politics behind it. Considering Argentina's domestic problems, what better way to regain support than to reclaim the Malvinas, which Argentina had first claimed in 1820.

Back in England, unemployment was at its highest level for decades, and inflation was still high. Margaret Thatcher's popularity was also dwindling, but a fight against Argentina would pull the whole country back together and would also get her re-elected.

Argentina obviously cared deeply for the Falklands, and I'm sure that 90 per cent of England had never even heard of them.

A couple of months previously, 6 Field Force had been renamed 5 Infantry Brigade and our own 6 Field Force Ordnance Company had also been renamed 81 Ordnance Company, part of the 5 Infantry Brigade. A Task Force had been arranged. 5 Infantry Brigade had been put on standby and we were sent to Salisbury Plain for an exercise to prepare us, just in case.

On the exercise, we had been constantly strafed by RAF fighter jets, just to get us used to operating under fire in case we were attacked over there.

Word had got around by now that the war would probably be over in a month and that we were going to go down there to garrison the islands after the inevitable conflict had finished.

'Fucking hell, what about my football?' I thought. It would mean that we would be away for about six months.

After the exercise had finished, we were told to go home for a few days' leave to say our goodbyes to everyone. We had to report back on Monday, 10 May to be ready to travel to Southampton to embark on a two-week free cruise on the *QE2*.

I had been going out with a girl called Jackie, who I had met while on weekend leave nine months earlier and, at Easter, we decided to get engaged. We celebrated by going to Blackpool with all my old mates and their girlfriends, but after seeing me climb a tram shelter on the promenade and do a mooney, before falling off pissed, I think she was already having second thoughts about me.

During my time off up there, I decided to go round and see as many people as I could. I stayed at my mum's house, who by now was cursing Margaret Thatcher.

My Auntie Dorothy and Uncle Alan had now moved from the social club in Hailiwell and had taken over a pub in Bolton town centre called The White Lion.

I often popped in for a drink and they always teased me about the time they had caught me passing bottles to my mates at the social club.

As we walked in, the pub was packed with the usual regulars, who were now joined by me, my mates and our girlfriends.

I knew that it would be the last time I would be in here for a while, but the drinks were flowing and the music was playing. In the corner on the wall was the TV, but nobody was watching it or paying any particular attention to it.

Suddenly, somebody noticed a newsflash. The room went silent as it was announced that *HMS Sheffield* had been hit by an Exocet missile from an air attack by a French Super Etendard Fighter.

I immediately had a mental picture, as we had been issued with aircraft recognition cards: as well as the French-made Mirage fighter jet, I could also remember the Etendard.

Everybody in the room was looking at me and I felt uneasy. Those poor guys wouldn't have known what had hit them. There were obviously going to be casualties, but it was only speculation as to how many had been killed.

It had also been reported that a Harrier plane had been shot down. Perhaps this wasn't going to be the walkover that everybody had been predicting.

Back at the barracks I began checking all of my equipment, which included new Arctic clothing to combat the cold. My backpack weighed a ton and was soon hurting my back. I sat on my pack next to Yatesy and lit up a fag. I was pleased that he was with me; he was my best mate.

We had had some scrapes together. We sat there talking as I again started to clean my 9mm sub-machine gun. If I was ever going into a war situation, I would have been glad to have had Yatesy with me. We were known within the unit as Laurel and Hardy, as we were always messing about, but we would do anything for each other.

We got the order to board the trucks, climbed aboard and made our way down the M3 to Southampton docks. When we got there, we were put in a storage shed and were told to wait our turn before embarking on the ship. The place was in chaos. Military personnel, families and civvies were all running about.

The ship itself was the biggest thing I'd ever seen, it was massive. It had just been commandeered by the government and was being transformed into a troop carrier. We eventually boarded and I found my allocated bunk. There were six in a room that was normally reserved for two people. There wasn't much space, especially with all our backpacks – each of which weighed about 60 pounds – blocking up the place.

We dumped our stuff and fought our way to the upper deck where we could see for miles. There were thousands of people lining up against a fence, waving and cheering their husbands, fathers and sons off.

The ship was soon moving and we were on our way to God-knows-where. I'm sure that all of us were thinking: 'When the fuck will we be back?'

We watched as Southampton disappeared over the horizon, then it was time for a wander around the ship. We had to be on parade first thing in the morning, when we would have to congregate on the lower deck at the rear of the ship.

The ship itself was fantastic. We wandered around the shopping mall: there was even a post office where we could send mail. We walked into one of the restaurants, which had been allocated to us.

The next morning we were given orders and a daily routine, which consisted of weapons training and fitness training. The big problem came when we were told that we would only be allocated two cans of beer per night. So Yatesy and I quickly went round to find people who didn't want their beer rations. We still managed to get pissed every night.

We endured a strict programme during the day. Because of the number of troops on the ship, time was limited to thirty minutes of physical exercise. The trouble was, there was hardly any space to exercise a hundred troops at a time. This was solved by using the upper deck as a running track; you could actually run all the way round the ship.

The further south we went the hotter it got and sometimes I was placed on watch in the bridge of the ship.

Rumour had it that we were being followed by a British submarine for protection.

After a week, we stopped at Freetown in Sierra Leone.

'Sierra Leone? Where the fuck's that?' I'd never heard of it.

'It's on the coast of Africa,' one of the lads said.

'I've never been to Africa,' I thought.

We docked at Freetown with orders that nobody was to leave the ship. What I would have given for a few minutes on terra firma.

The docking of the *QE2* at Freetown was obviously a big deal for the locals. They came out in their hundreds just to have a look at this massive ship.

Fences were erected about 50 feet from the ship. Most of the troops had made their way to the upper deck and were watching the locals with a puzzled look. The ship was also surrounded by locals in canoes, who offered us their wares, among them carved wooden figures.

One local man suggested with his actions that he would like something to wear on his feet. One of the lads got some rope and sent down one of his Army plimsolls to the canoe at the back of the ship and indicated that he would get the other when he sent up his carved figure. The local man smiled, sent up the figure and waited for the other plimsoll. All the lads were in uproars of laughter when one of them shouted:

'Fuck off! You're not having the other,' and walked away.

The local man was going mad and nearly fell out of his canoe as he shouted back obscenities.

However, the couple of days in Freetown broke up the tedium of the journey.

Before we set sail for our next stop – which would be Ascension Island, a few days' sail away – we were still intrigued by this now-massive gathering of locals who were being guarded by local policemen holding wooden batons.

Jock, one of the Scottish privates, had had enough and wanted a bit of fun. Didn't we all? Apart from having a few beers at night, the only thing that I was happy about was that I'd listened to the FA Cup final between Tottenham and Queen's Park Rangers on BBC World Service on the radio in our rooms. It was our only contact with the outside world and not at all like today, where soldiers have Internet access and dozens of TV channels and radio stations at their disposal.

It was the first FA Cup final that I had not seen on TV since 1969, when Neil Young scored the only goal of the game during Manchester City's victory over Leicester in the final.

Suddenly Jock threw a coin near the gathering, which by now must have been over a thousand. Pandemonium broke out as everybody started to fight for this coin. It was great entertainment as all the lads suddenly caught on and were digging deep into their pockets for any loose change to throw over the side and onto the docks.

In a matter of seconds, coins were being dropped from all along the side of the ship, much to the amusement of the squaddies. Fights broke out all along the dockside; even the police started hitting people with their batons, just so that they could take the money.

Jock had been to his room and then threw over his Celtic football shirt: it was great to see a young lad emerge from the scrum with the shirt. He quickly put it on and was dancing with joy.

After that we walked round the ship, still feeling pissed off because we couldn't get off, but after that day's events we all felt slightly better.

Just before dark, we went back to the upper deck and looked over the side. The mass gathering was now all on its knees praying, led at the front by someone who I took to be some kind of priest.

Once again somebody threw a coin towards the crowd and, once again, the locals started scrapping for this bit of silver. For a ship full of bored, worried and homesick soldiers, it was definitely the highlight so far.

We set sail for Ascension Island. The island was small and volcanic, just 35 square miles large and situated in the middle of the South Atlantic.

We stopped there a couple of miles offshore and waited for two days while we were re-supplied.

We also took the time to black out the ship and covered all the windows and portholes with black bin liners. As soon as we left Ascension we would be entering a war zone, even though we were probably only halfway there.

Most evenings, we would all gather around the radios in the cabins and tune in to the BBC World Service for the daily war update.

We were heading for South Georgia, a set of islands two days' sail away from the Falklands, where we would be transferred: it was deemed that it would be too much of a risk to take the *QE2* any closer.

Day by day we listened as events unfolded. It seemed as though peace proposals were being rejected daily. We heard how Argentinean Skyhawks had been shot down and how Special Forces had destroyed eleven Argentinean aircraft in a night raid on Pebble Island.

On 21 May, the British had managed to make an amphibious landing at Port San Carlos, which was soon renamed 'Bomb Alley', on the northern coast of East Falkland, where a beachhead had been established.

We heard that *HMS Arden* had been sunk by an Argentinean air attack in Bomb Alley and the next day *HMS Antelope* was attacked and sunk after an unexploded bomb detonated. During the next two days, seventeen Argentinean aircraft were destroyed.

Then *HMS Coventry* was hit, claiming nineteen British lives, and the Atlantic convey – which carried stores, a lot of them ours – was also hit by an Exocet: twelve more servicemen were killed.

After listening to all this within the space of a few days, I knew that there was no way that this war would be over by the time we got there.

We were now way down in the South Atlantic. The sea was rough with big waves; up and down went the big ship.

It had been nice and hot near Ascension, but the further south we went the wind chill made it very cold. We could see icebergs, which were miles long, but the last few days were all about checking our personal kit and weapons. We were allowed to test our weapons over the side of the ship, using rubbish thrown overboard as targets.

We soon arrived at Grytviken, a tiny whaling station on South Georgia, which had been retaken by the British on 25 April by a small commando force, a feat that included disabling the Argentinean submarine, the *Sante Fe*, which was just about staying afloat at the side of the dock.

The *QE2* stopped. We were about half a mile from land and I could see the whaling station where the notorious Captain Astiz and his forces had surrendered.

I knew that it would take a day or two to disembark the *QE2* onto other ships with all the stores and equipment, so all we could do was to sit, wait and be patient.

My first thought about South Georgia was how beautiful the mountains were and what a fantastic sight the glacier was.

The sea was like a millpond as I looked at the islands. Again I could see the *Sante Fe*, as well as the wreckage of the wasp helicopter, which had crashed killing several Special Forces personnel.

Troops disembarking the *QE2* were transferred onto trawler ships, which could come up close to the *QE2*, and then transferred again to another ship, to take them the last few days' journey to the Falkland Islands. I watched from the top deck as a trawler pulled alongside us.

The water was now getting choppy and it was hard for the troops as they came out of a door at the side of the *QE2* ready for a small jump onto a gangplank and into the trawler.

It should have been easy, but the freezing cold and a 60-pound pack on your back, a rifle in your hands and waiting for both vessels bobbing in the water to come level before taking the small jump, made it a very difficult operation. We were also doing it one man at a time. It was going to be a slow process, especially in the dark with no lights because of the blackout.

The trawler slowly inched by our side, then I saw quite a few men, wearing white boiler suits or T-shirts and shorts, getting off it and jumping onto the *QE2*.

I didn't know it at the time, but these were survivors from *HMS Arden*, *Antelope* and *Antrim*.

The next day, the cruise liner *Canberra* pulled nearby containing more casualties. The *Canberra* had been one of the first ships to come down to the area carrying commandos, as well as the *Norland*, which carried the Paras.

We had our orders to disembark at night.

'Fucking hell. Not at night,' I moaned.

I wasn't sure that I fancied this with all the weight on my back; I could hardly stand as it was.

We all waited patiently in line down the corridors. We met survivors, who were now to stay on the *QE2* as a cruise home, and listened to their tales.

We were to be transferred along with other regiments to the Royal Fleet Auxiliary ship the *Stromness* via ... this trawler.

I got to the door in the pitch black and heard a voice, saying: 'Wait till I tell you to jump.'

The ship was bobbing up and down and I could just about make out the gangplank on the trawler below.

'Where are you?' I said.

It was pitch black and I couldn't see anything, but I could hear voices whispering from the darkness below. I made the small jump and was ushered down some steps onto the deck to become another sardine squashed among all these troops.

Chapter Eight

All of us stood around. I could just make out the blackened faces.

'What now,' I thought as I looked up, barely making out the big ship above us that I had just left.

I watched as more black silhouettes made the jump, all of them timing it just right.

I thought about the relative comfort that I was about to leave behind. The meals, the few beers at night, God knows when we would get another one. The evenings going to the cinema on board to watch one of the latest films like *Stripes* with Bill Murray or *Escape to Victory*, which I liked because it was football, even though one of the players in the film was Ossie Ardiles, the Spurs midfielder and the Argentinean international who was met with boos and expletives every time his face came on the screen.

Our destination was the *Stromness*, a troop carrier that was being used as a logistics vessel. By the time we boarded her, it was nearly light. The *Stromness* was now a veteran of the Falklands War and had already been attacked, but she had emerged unscathed, apart from a few holes here and there.

When we got on board my worst fears were realised. We were to bunk in the hold of the ship where hundreds of beds were crammed in three-beds high: there was hardly enough room to pass people in the tiny gangways. There was no room to store your kit, so you had to put it in your bunk and sleep with it there. It was very uncomfortable. Now I really felt like a sardine down here in the hold with hundreds of troops.

The other thing that concerned me was that there were only two ways out. One was by a small set of stairs, which led to the deck, the other was by a small industrial lift. Fucking hell, if we get hit, there was no way we could get out. It would be a mass panic and I was at least 50 feet from the stairs.

Before we left South Georgia, we all practised the air attack imminent procedure.

When the alarm sounded – which reminded me of all the Second World War films I'd seen where warships are blown to pieces – 'attack imminent, attack imminent, this is a drill, this is a drill' would ricochet around the quarters. We then had to hit the top deck and go to our allocated positions around the ship.

The first time we did it on *Stromness*, I was right. There was a mass panic with everybody fighting to get out. It took ages, but after a few more practices we got into a routine. I was still shit scared in case we got hit, though.

My allocated position in the case of any attack was right on the bow of the ship with Geordie Dickson. We had also been given the responsibility of the light machine gun (LMG). So now, as well as our own kit and weapons and ammo, we also had to take it in turns to carry this weapon and its ammo.

Imagine trying to get through the crush of bodies to get on

deck with all this weight and making it to the bow of the ship where we had to mount the weapon on a pole.

Down in the hold there was a single TV set and a video to take your mind off things. The most common video was one of Billy Connolly and it always raised a few laughs.

The next morning, after grabbing what sleep I could, I made my way up to the deck. I looked out and to my surprise saw what seemed to be a thousand ships.

We had now joined the task force and it made me feel a little safer. However, the sea was now very rough; I looked at the bow and the waves were just crashing over it, right where Geordie and I were supposed to be positioned.

'Fuck me. We're going to get soaked,' I thought.

I went back down and sat on my bunk with all my kit on, including my steel helmet, when I heard 'red alert, red alert, aircraft attack imminent, aircraft attack imminent, this is not a drill, this is not a drill' followed by the alarm sound.

Here we go, now it was real panic. Because it wasn't a drill, it seemed as though there was a greater sense of urgency.

'Please just let me get on deck, I don't want to get hit while I'm down here,' I thought.

My heart was pumping and the adrenaline was flowing all around my body. At least, thanks to radar, we had warnings before any attack.

After a fight and a lot of swear words I finally got to the deck. Once there, I was hit with a blast of fresh air, which was quite nice. I ran as best as I could with all the weight down the side of the ship; because it was going up and down, it made it more difficult. The deck was wet with seawater spray and I slipped, dropping the LMG in the process.

'Thank fuck I'd left the safety catch on,' I thought.

I eventually made it to the bow and attached the LMG to the anti-aircraft pole.

'Where the fuck have you been?' said a waiting Geordie as we struggled to hold onto something. Suddenly the planes came into view.

'Please don't go for us,' I thought as I saw their bombs hit the water.

Missed, you fuckers. Then the harriers appeared and soon it turned into a dogfight. I'd seen this before on TV, but this time it was for real.

I was ready just in case, with weapons cocked, safety catch off. I wouldn't need to use the sights on the gun as we had filled our magazine with a tracer round every four rounds in the mag. Tracer rounds light up after 100 metres, which can give you a guided aim, especially at night.

We saw the aircraft coming towards us, it was a Mirage. I could tell because I had read the aircraft recognition cards every spare minute.

I knew that we would probably have maybe one second or even two to hit the Mirage. It came closer. Everybody around the ship opened fire with small arms, including me. I was screaming as I fired the LMG in one long burst, or so it seemed, but the plane had got away.

That was it, two seconds of real action. The adrenaline was still pumping. We waited at our positions until it was announced over the tannoy to stand down.

I went back down to my bunk. Everybody seemed to be laughing and joking and even backslapping, but I knew that this was far from over.

I sat on my bunk and immediately refilled my magazine and dismantled the LMG to clean it and oil it. I could dismantle my weapons and put them back together blindfolded.

Later that day, the alarm sounded again and we made our way to our positions, but even though we could see the enemy aircraft, they never came directly at us, much to my relief, as I thought I'd much rather be attacked on land than in the middle of the freezing cold South Atlantic.

Word was filtering through that 2 Para had made a major breakthrough at a settlement called Goose Green. It turned out to be possibly the longest and toughest battle of the war.

Seventeen Paras – including Colonel H. Jones, who was posthumously awarded the VC – were killed; about 200 Argentinean soldiers were also killed, with a further 15,000 prisoners taken. This gave everyone a huge lift. All we wanted to do now was to get onto terra firma and play our part. It was also reported that of all the prisoners taken, only about a third of them were in any condition to fight.

We arrived and dropped anchor in Bomb Alley. We had joined other ships. Our unit was going to be the last to disembark onto the landing crafts, which would take us to shore at San Carlos. Until then, I was positioned at the top of the bridge on the highest accessible point with Geordie, because we had the LMG. We could see for miles. I looked to my left and could see some floating buoys used as markers to indicate where the *Antelope* had gone down. In front of us were a set of hills and behind us the same. I couldn't help but feel as though we were a sitting duck.

I knew I would be up here for hours, but I still wished that they would hurry up.

We just waited and waited. One part of my head wanted an attack, just to give us some excitement; the other part wanted me to get off the boat as quickly as possible. All the way down on the *QE2* we listened to the BBC World Service, Bomb Alley was mentioned nearly every time and here I was right in the middle of it, a bleak and thoroughly unpicturesque gap between two tall hills, a world away from the peace and beauty of South Georgia.

Then the all-too-familiar alarm and announcement went off again. 'Oh fuck.'

We waited for about ten minutes, the usual warning time you had. All the ships in Bomb Alley were on alert and bracing themselves.

I saw them coming just to the left. I opened fire along with everyone else. Two Skyhawks. We had less than a second, as they came over the hill in front of me and disappeared behind the hill before we had even heard them.

It is only when the aircraft had gone that I heard the engines, or so it seemed.

They'd dropped their load. One went into the sea and one exploded into the hillside. I checked my weapon and put the safety catch back on. The smell of cordite was overwhelming.

I took off my gloves and warmed them up on the hot barrel of the LMG. Thank fuck we now got the shout to get on one of the landing craft, which would take us the short distance to San Carlos.

We were all packed in the landing craft and couldn't see out. We were just bobbing up and down and getting pissed-wet through from the splashing waves. It was like somebody was outside throwing buckets of water onto the craft.

The engine slowed. At least we would be getting out with no enemy fire, as by now we had established a firm beachhead, which was a hive of activity.

We were all told to dig in and await further orders. Some of us were lucky, we just took over the empty trenches vacated by 3 Commando Brigade who had left the day before. Some of the lads, however, had to dig their own.

A couple of us put a brew on and it was nice to have a cup of tea, a well-earned one, I thought. I looked around and the first thing I saw was an old barn at the end of the wooden jetty we had just walked down. I hadn't noticed it before, probably because I just wanted to find myself some cover in case of attack.

Top: Me as goalie (centre) for Chalfont Primary School.

Middle right: Mum and Dad.

Bottom left: With Carole and the kids.

Bottom right: Me and Shirley in 1962.

Top: With the civilian team in Germany.

Middle left: Fisticuffs with Steve Richards and Paul Durkan refereeing in 1988.

Bottom left: My league debut goal against Newport, 1982.

Bottom right: Playing with my cousins in Blackpool.

On the assault course the day we put Jim Rosenthal through his paces on
On The Ball.

PAGE 26   DAILY MIRROR, Monday, January 31, 1983

Phil gets ready to soldier on

SOLDIER Phil Stant is today standing by to be called from the glasshouse—and into the heat of a relegation battle.

Reading striker Stant, 20, has spent the last 72 hours locked up in detention at Aldershot barracks for "insubordination."

But injury-hit Reading are so short of players they must now ask his C.O. to give Stant the day off to play at Plymouth tomorrow.

Stant, who served three months in the Falklands war, is just one of four non-contract players to be called up.

The others are furniture removal man Wayne Tully, bricklayer Mark Matthews and sales rep. Des McMahon.

Reading's crisis deepened in the 1-1 draw with leaders Lincoln when Martin Hicks suffered a broken cheekbone, Michael Barnes a broken nose and goalkeeper Alan Judge a thigh injury.

Reading have asked the Football League to postpone the Argyle game because 10 of their 18 professionals are injured.

But Reading manager Maurice Evans said last night: "I don't hold out much hope of them agreeing.

"The crazy thing is that the League will allow postponements for a 'flu epidemic—but not for an injury crisis. It's an absolute nonsense."

GRAHAM BAKER'S THIRD FOURTH SCENE

How the *Daily Mirror* reported the end of my bad behaviour, and six years later, an (almost) changed man with my addidas Golden Boot award.

Above: One of my many run-ins with Steve Richards at a Hereford vs Scarborough match in 1988.

Left: Scoring against Chris Waddle's Burnley at Turf Moor in 1998.

© Lincolnshire Echo.

Top: Fulham vs Stoke City in 1991.

Bottom: Looking less than impressed on being presented with my courtesy car in Mansfield, 1991.

Above: Tussling with a defender at the Cardiff vs Swansea City Welsh Cup Semi-Final, 1994.

Left: Being presented with the award for Cardiff player of the year by our mascot later that season.

Top: In agony after tearing my medial ligament in the 1994 Cardiff vs Middlesborough FA Cup replay.

Bottom: Moments later I scored the equaliser.

Top: Walking out Bury on to the Wembley pitch, 1995.

Middle left: Against Kevin Keegan's Newcastle in 1992.

Below left: Collecting the Third Division Championship for Cardiff, 1994.

Below right: Captaining Lincoln City.　　　　　　　© *Lincolnshire Echo.*

Top: Struggling with Chesterfield's Darren Carr at the Third Division playoff, 1995.

Bottom: Celebrating my goal against Burnley in style with the lads, 1998.

Top: Broadcasting my thoughts to the players (and the rest of Hull), 2000.

Bottom: Facing the pack after a tough game, 2000.   © *Lincolnshire Echo.*

My triumphant salute after scoring for Cardiff City, 1993.   © *Action Images.*

Somebody had written on it in chalked letters: 'Last Stop before Goose Green.' It was obviously a Para, but what a great slogan for a T-shirt.

'When I get back I'll have one printed,' I thought.

After the brew we managed to get a couple of hours' sleep.

As the war progressed I soon learned that there was no time, dates or even an outside world. It was just an existence. You slept when you could, you ate when you could and even shat when you could. War doesn't start at nine in the morning and finish at five at night.

A decision was taken after a few days to move 5 Infantry Brigade using LSLs (Landing Ship Logistics) *Sir Galahad* and *Sir Tristram*. The air war was almost won and air attacks were less frequent. About twenty of our company were due to be shipped at night and moved near a little settlement called Fitzroy, where we would dig in and from where we would distribute ammo and food.

We would have to unload both ships and make a holding area so that we could get the supplies through to the front lines.

At least on board we would be able to have a proper meal in the ship's canteen. For the past few days we had been living off twenty-four-hour Army ration packs, with their measly portion of biscuits, tins of soup, beans and stew and, if you were lucky, a small chocolate. What I would have done for a McDonalds!

Back onto another fucking ship, this time round Bluff Cove and into Port Pleasant, where we dropped anchor and unloaded ammo, rations, even vehicles, all by way of a couple of Mexifloats – the motorised flatbeds that ferried supplies between the ship and the shore. It would take a day or two to unload, I thought.

We sailed at night, again in the pitch black, and again I was worried about being hit. I just kept on cleaning my sub-machine gun, as we had now passed the LMG onto some other troops.

At daylight, I was ordered to the back of the ship where I was to drive a forklift and load the ammo crates onto the Mexifloats for delivery to the shore about 500 metres away. Most of the lads were now off the ship and I could see some of them digging trenches while others helped with supplies. They would swap over after an hour or so.

'I hope there's enough room for me,' I thought.

Once again, I had that sitting-duck feeling, but to be honest I would rather have worked on the ship and maybe get another couple of hot meals than be out on the shore digging in.

My joy was short-lived, however. An announcement on the tannoy came over: 'Would Private Stant get the next Mexifloat to shore as he is needed there.'

'Fuck it.' Pissed off, I got the next float over and landed with all my equipment.

I had to share a trench with Warrant Officer 2 Class Langham (WO2 Langham). I really hated this guy, as I thought he was really stuck up. What's more, it meant no more proper food from the ship's canteen for the foreseeable future.

I was ordered to drive the Eager Beaver, the cross-country forklift, and started to unload the Mexifloat full of ammo crates and move them about 100 metres away from our trenches.

We worked most of the night. It was a nightmare. I had to drive into the sea, which came up 4 feet to the top of the Beaver's tyres and I kept stalling it.

Trying to operate this machine in total darkness, just relying on someone else's word and a small red flashlight was proving very difficult in freezing rain and temperatures. The wind was unbelievable and soon I was soaked. I was already in zombie state, that's what war situations do to you.

A sergeant kept yelling at me to concentrate, but with all the elements against me, one of the crates of 105mm shells fell off my forks and into the sea.

'You fucking idiot,' the sergeant shouted.

'Sorry, it was an accident, it's so hard to do this,' I pleaded.

'Well if you can't work under pressure, fuck off,' he replied.

'Work under pressure, work under pressure, I'll show you, you jumped-up twat,' I said to myself. I did concentrate more and everything went smoothly, despite the conditions and hazards.

By daybreak, I was allowed a few hours' kip while one of the lads relieved me. I got my doss bag out – sleeping bag – and got into the L-shaped trench, which was now in an inch of water, but it didn't matter, I was knackered.

I had only been sleeping for an hour or so when I was woken up by one of the lads. Another ship was pulling into Port Pleasant. These two ships looked huge in such a small stretch of water; I couldn't believe that they were here, virtually docked next to each other.

War does strange things to the mind and one of the lads suggested that it was delivering mail and everybody believed him, even me.

On board were the Welsh Guards. A few troops came off along with the eagerly awaited Rapier SAM – surface-to-air missiles – which were intended to guard our position by being placed on the brow of a hill behind us.

Then nothing, nobody came off, but we could see the troops waiting on the decks.

I couldn't believe what I was seeing. No air cover, no SAM cover, nothing. Now we would be in trouble if an air attack came in. I heard a major screaming at a young Welsh Guard officer to get his 'fucking troops off that ship now', but the young Rodney wasn't saying much. The major I later identified as Southby-Taylor, a commando who was in charge of the Mexifloats.

Why didn't they get off, I kept thinking as I got back onto the Beaver with my SMG strapped to the back of my seat.

What we didn't know was that, hiding in the hills behind us among the rocks, there was an Argentinean observation post that had reported the location of the ships as well as our positions.

I got off the Beaver to have a couple of minutes' break and a fag, a small luxury that briefly took off the chill. I sat on the edge of a small cliff and looked down at the water.

The cliffs were covered in human shit, as we had decided that this would be our toilet. I looked at the ships about 500 metres away. They just sat there in the calm water. It was a clear day, with not much wind. It was cold, but there was no rain.

I looked behind me at the landscape, which was now covered with hundreds of crates of all kinds of ammunition and food stores, as well as the twenty-four-hour ration packs.

I was just finishing my fag when, whoosh, from my left, and this time with no warning at all, came three, or was it four, Skyhawks. My worst fears had been realised: they weren't coming for us; they were attacking the ships.

We had no warning of the attack. The SAM Rapier Missiles were not yet ready to defend our position. The bombs exploded, maybe two, maybe three, into *Sir Galahad*, with two hitting *Sir Tristram*. One was a 1,000-pound bomb, which went right into the arse of *Sir Tristram*, just where I had been the day before.

Sir Galahad immediately exploded in a massive fireball. The noise was horrendous.

I picked myself up, covered in human shit, as I had dived into the cliffs and just stayed there. The attack seemed to last for hours, but it was probably no more than fifteen to twenty seconds until it was all over.

Hardly any shots had been fired from our side, as we had been taken completely by surprise, even though it was an accident waiting to happen.

I looked at *Galahad*. I could hear the screams and shouting. Guys were running up and down the decks. Smoke poured out of *Sir Tristram*. Bright orange life rafts were soon coming over the side of *Galahad*.

Sea King helicopters arrived within minutes. There was

nothing we could do apart from wait until they came ashore. Land Rovers arrived from Fitzroy, which was about two miles away, so we could ferry the injured to a makeshift hospital.

I noticed one helicopter hovering above a life raft. I presumed that it was trying to blow it away from the ship. Flames were now coming from all over *Galahad*. *Tristram* by comparison looked injured, but not too bad.

We were soon joined by field Land Rover ambulances. I also noticed that a TV crew had joined us. We went down to the shoreline and waited, overcome with a feeling of helplessness.

Soon a lifeboat full of survivors was being rowed to our position. We ran into the freezing water to pull it the last few yards. We took some of the lads to our locations where we gave them water. Some of them had burns. One guy was walking round in a daze, covered in someone else's skin.

Soon the ground was covered with survivors and the injured. I noticed that there were a few bodies lying around now. The Sea Kings were now relaying casualties from the ship to our position. I grabbed a stretcher with a lad from another unit who I'd never seen before. He looked like a medic. He said: 'My name's Paul, now help me,' which I did. We ran towards the helicopter, which was just about to land. Two guys were already waiting with a stretcher. The door on the chopper opened and out on a stretcher came a lad with his leg blown off just above the knee, with skin hanging off everywhere. I looked straight down at his leg. He was screaming in agony and was put into a Land Rover.

Paul and I got the next one out and put him on our stretcher. His legs were already strapped together and both of them were broken.

We put him in the ambulance and off it went. I then went round helping anybody I could. Chris Hoggard was one of our lads and he was holding up a drip as one of the dying lads tried to pass him his wallet. By now there were casualties all over the place.

Jock Laing, another one of my mates, was driving one of the Land Rovers over to Fitzroy with the injured and was being sick out of the window at the same time because of the stench of burning flesh.

All the Welsh Guards, including the casualties, were ferried over to Fitzroy Settlement. When it had quietened down a bit, I had time for a cigarette. The events of the previous hour then hit me. I hadn't given it a second thought while everything was going on, but I couldn't get that lad's leg out of my mind.

The air was full of the smell of burnt flelsh. It was then that I realised that I had no weapon. 'Where the fuck's my SMG?' In all the chaos, I'd just thrown my weapon down and run for the stretcher.

I reported this straightaway to Lieutenant Stevens. We soon realised that all the kit lying around had been thrown into the back of a Land Rover and taken to Fitzroy.

Lieutenant Stevens then went to Fitzroy and came back with another SMG and handed it to me. I had a nervy two hours or so in a war zone with no weapon of my own.

Fortunately, we managed to get a lot of stores off *Tristram*, but *Galahad* was still full of its cargo, mainly ammunition.

Later on that afternoon we were attacked again. This time, though, we were ready. Once again I had been assigned to the LMG position, which had now been fixed, permanently manned on a pole.

Skyhawks again came in. We opened up. Some of the lads used rifles or their SMGs, but that was like farting in the wind.

A Rapier SAM – the heat-seeking, surface-to-air, anti-aircraft missile – was launched. It started to chase one of the Skyhawks as it attached itself to the heat of the engine.

I was firing a long burst at the lead enemy aircraft, using tracer as a guide. Other units on the hill were also firing an LMG with tracer. I could see the Tracer going into the back of the plane. I'm sure that it was mine, but it got away. The other Skyhawk was trying to shake off the Rapier missile, and it did.

The SAM just ran out of steam and started to fall to ground. It was coming straight for me. I thought should I stay here or should I go and run over there? Yeah, but what happens if I run over there and it hits there? No, I know what I'll do, I'll run for the cover of my trench. Shit, what happens if it hits my trench? War plays funny mind games, however, and I just stood still.

I had all these thoughts in a split second, but it seemed like an age. The SAM splashed into the water about half-a-mile away. Altogether the engagement had lasted about ten to fifteen seconds at most, but it seemed an awful lot longer than that.

Shortly afterwards, we were stood down. Dusk was falling, so it was time to eat and get a good brew going before dark. After all, we couldn't light the burners after dark for obvious reasons.

It was about three in the morning and I was still wide-awake. Everything was outside. I looked out of my trench. There were no pounding noises tonight. No Argentinean locations being bombarded and I didn't know why.

Some of the lads were leaning out of their trenches, probably going through the events of the day in their minds. I couldn't sleep because all I could see in my head was that lad's leg. It's funny how you don't think of things at the time of a crisis, but now I had time to reflect.

We stared at the burning *Galahad*, which lit up our location like a beacon. I stared at the ship and the still-smoldering *Tristram*.

I was wondering if anybody was still on there alive, still trapped. I thought about how many dead bodies were on board and all this was just 500 metres away from my trench.

I looked at the *Tristram* and thought about how lucky I had been to have got off when I did. Some of the crew, who I'd been working with just over twenty-four hours earlier, had been killed.

I also thought about how there was no chance of me seeing the start of the World Cup, which was to be staged in Spain. Mind games, eh!

Then a massive explosion lit up the sky again. The ammunition magazine had exploded on the *Galahad*, followed by loads of little explosions and whizzing sounds. Heads quickly went down in the trenches. Little did we know that the ship would burn for another two weeks.

After a while it was back to work. I was tired. I couldn't remember the last time that I'd slept. I felt for the lads on the front line.

The next day reports were coming through that an Argentinean Skyhawk had crashed 50 miles from home. I was convinced that it was mine, but everybody else thought that it was their hit. In the end, we all drew a picture of a plane on our helmets and wrote the word 'probable' next to it. It kept our spirits up anyway.

It had started raining again and yet again I was soaked. I had no spare kit to change into as I'd already done that and my other kit was in my Bergan pack, wet through.

My socks were sticking to my feet. My boots were soaked. I couldn't feel my toes and knew that these were the early stages of trench foot. Our trenches were constantly filling up with rainwater. I couldn't remember when I had last changed my socks or underpants.

We walked down to the shoreline to our left where the survivors had landed. Somebody had a brainwave to drag the life rafts up to our location and to sleep in them.

Great idea, we all agreed, and we manhandled them up to the trenches.

The life rafts were bright orange and still inflated, but they had a roof, which could be zipped up: ideal shelter from these Arctic conditions.

'Only one problem,' said one of the lads and pointed out that they would be like a bullseye from above.

'Fuck it. Let's camouflage them,' I said.

So that's what we did. They housed twenty-four people, but it was still a tight fit with all our equipment. At least it was a shelter when you needed a kip.

Later, when I went for my sleep, I had to climb over everybody else who was already there. Now and again I could hear an 'ouch' or a 'fuck off' as I stepped on somebody.

During the day, choppers of all kinds were coming into our location as we netted up crates of ammo and food and hung them under the chopper, which would then fly away and distribute their loads around all the locations.

A report, or signal as they were called, came over the radio. Apparently our location had been identified as the main stores base and we were to expect an attack by the Argentinean equivalent of the SAS.

That night Geordie Dickson (again) and I were on patrol duty round our location while the rest of the lads had a kip. We were just walking past the cliffs when I heard a noise. We both lay down with our weapons pointing at the cliffs, half expecting someone to come over, but I'd definitely heard a noise. It was as though somebody had stepped on some stones and was falling down the cliffs. I imagined an Argentinean crack unit trying to scale the cliffs with a surprise attack.

'Shall we wake the camp?' Geordie said.

'No, let me have a look first,' I replied. Besides I didn't want to wake up the whole unit for nothing. I would look like a right twat.

'Cover me,' I whispered as I crawled to the edge of the cliffs so that I could peek over. Once again my heart was racing.

I was near the edge of the cliff and sweating, despite the weather. I took a deep breath before looking over the edge.

Suddenly there was a big scream as this duck came flying out. I nearly shat myself. Geordie was pissing himself laughing.

'What are you laughing at, you Geordie bastard,' I said.

'You, you twat. Wait till I tell the lads,' he replied. I then burst out laughing myself, probably with relief.

'Attacked first by the Argentineans and now by a fucking duck,' I thought to myself.

Around dawn we were out in our trenches, 'stood to' as it is called. Again a signal came to expect an attack.

'Fucking hell, this is for real,' I thought.

It wasn't quite light yet. What was I going to do if loads of Argies came running down the hill? After all, there were only twenty of us here. I looked around for my escape route. I saw a gap in the side of the hill and quickly decided that that would be my destination if things got too hot.

Once again my brain was doing funny things. I heard a voice. It was Lieutenant Stevens.

'I have a positive sighting,' he announced.

Oh fuck here we go. We all watched the direction he was pointing to. Weapons were cocked and ready, grenades were in our hands. I was looking down the sights of my SMG when I saw the outline of a figure.

'Hold your fire,' the order went up.

The figure got closer. I recognised him straightaway. It was Scouse Shearin, an LCPL from the stores carrying some bog roll.

'What the fuck are you playing at?' Lieutenant Stevens bawled.

'Sorry sir. I was dying for a shit,' he said.

I just heard laughter around the location. Once again we were stood down. Lieutenant Stevens walked past me and gave me a shove, which was not complimentary. I don't think he liked my comment about missing the World Cup. We then handed back the grenades.

We carried on loading the choppers with nets of stores. We had not had an air raid for a day or so, but once again, in the middle of the night, we were all stood to in our trenches.

The air raid red alert had come over the radio. This time there would be no firing. We were going to be bombed by Canberra bombers from 20,000 feet. Fucking hell, when is this going to end? It felt like the goalposts were moving frequently and that there was nothing we could do.

WO2 Langham was not well liked because of his attitude to lower ranks like myself. Us Toms hated him. He was so aloof. He was always picking on somebody or charging people with trivial offences. He even threatened to have me jailed when I got off *Tristram* for having a five-minute rest.

'Go on then, stick me in fucking jail,' I said. 'Where's the jail sir,' I continued.

He was lost for words, but I knew that the first time he could get me, he would.

We were all in our trenches waiting for the rumble of the planes when we noticed somebody with a flashlight walking around with the rations. It was Langham.

Now imagine what that flashlight would look like in a dark area looking down from a plane.

'Get that torch out.'

'Get that fucking light out.'

'Hey, fucking switch that off you wanker.' Voices from all around our location shouted.

'Shoot the cunt.'

And all you could hear around the location was the sound of lots of weapons being cocked, mine included. Besides, who would know that I hated him so much.

'No. No. No. I'm only joking.' A voice shouted in panic. The light suddenly went out and the noise of a man scrambling away was heard.

After that incident WO2 Langham was one of the nicest people you could ever have met and would do anything for you. Funny that, no air raid happened.

The following day, rumour control was at it again. The big push would be happening, but nobody knew when. One thing I knew was that we would have to do it quickly, as supplies were getting short.

The other worrying thing was the reports of dead American mercenaries that were creeping through to us. I thought that they were supposed to be on our side, but I never heard another thing about it until years later, when I read Vince Bramley's book *Excursion to Hell*, which was about the Paras' assault on Mount Longden.

It was just after dark, when the sky was suddenly lit up with explosions. The night sky flashed red, then white, then black, then red, then white and so on. The push was well under way. Thank fuck I'm here a few miles behind rather than on the front line. Whatever happens, it's going to be shit or bust.

3 Para had mounted an assault on the heavily defended position of Mount Longden. 45 Commando attacked the Two Sisters Hills and 42 Commando took on Mount Harriet, supported by the guns of 29 Commando and the naval gunfire of some of the navy frigates. The Scots Guards had a bloody battle as they seized Mount Tumbledown. But it wasn't all going our way, as *HMS Glamorgan* had been hit by an Exocet as it was bombing Argentinean locations.

The battle raged all night. It was always going to start at dusk or dawn. The Army recognises the vulnerability of forces at those times.

The constant fire, the explosions and the lighting up of the sky carried on all night. The next day all was quiet again.

We were all wondering what had happened. Had we taken the positions, because if we hadn't, the general opinion was that we were fucked. All we heard was that it had gone quite well.

Quite well?

'But how many men died last night?' I thought. 'How many are lying injured now at this moment? Fuck the Argentineans,' I thought.

At that point I couldn't give a fuck about them. Seeing active service is an intense and frightening experience, especially for someone who'd chosen to join the Army as a means of getting an HGV licence. It is very difficult for people who haven't lived through the horrific scenes I have witnessed to understand how, in the heat of the moment, I thought: 'Why take prisoners? Shoot the Spick bastards.'

Over the next few years, when my temper got up and I'd explode, Carole, who was to become my wife, would say that it was because of what I'd seen in the Falklands. Nowadays it's called post-traumatic stress disorder and counselling is available. When I saw the *Galahad* explode, knowing that some of our guys were on it, I didn't understand what my rage meant.

Another thing that pissed me off was that we'd been issued tinned corn beef. I looked at the bottom of the tin as I was opening it and it said: 'Made in Argentina.' I threw it away: 'Fuck that, I'm not eating that shit.'

Fuck Argentina. I hated them, even though most of them were conscripts and were told that they were just going to the Falklands on exercise. Fuck Ardiles and fuck Maradona.

We waited and waited. Two days later, a white flag was spotted flying over Port Stanley. It was relayed over the radio: Menendez had agreed to surrender.

When we heard the news, there was no cheering. We were pleased of course, but we were exhausted and rapidly running out of food, water and ammunition.

The infantry had done a great job, but at what cost?

Our unit hadn't lost a single man, but I wondered about the Marines and the Paras.

Jock shouted: 'Does that mean we're going home today?'

We just looked at him, but he was serious.

'No I don't think we'll be going home just yet,' I said.

Back in Argentina, Galtieri had ordered his troops and Menendez to carry on fighting after all. Even though Port Stanley was now surrounded, the Argentinean troops were still well stocked with food and ammo, even if there was nothing left of their artillery. But General Menendez decided to negotiate a surrender.

After the surrender there were about 8,000 prisoners who were taken to the airfield and placed in a makeshift POW Camp. Some of them were transferred to Fitzroy. Again we listened over the radio for news. A curfew had been imposed in Port Stanley.

Over the next few days, we just hung around keeping warm and waiting for orders. Every morning the twenty or so Argie POWs were marched down from Fitzroy to our location to pick up daily rations.

I said to a sergeant: 'Fuck me, do we have to feed them now as well?'

They looked frightened to death. They walked down the hill with their hands in their coat pockets trying to keep warm. We guarded them as they were handed a box each and took great delight in teasing them.

'Maradona's a wanker,' I growled in one ear.

'Qué?' he replied.

'You fucking know what I'm saying.' I kicked him up the arse.

I hated these fuckers now. Invading our islands. (They were ours even though I'd never heard of them before.) They had killed our troops, and they were the reason that I was now stinking, filthy and tired. They'd even given us fucking corned beef to eat and if these bastards won the World Cup... I just wanted them to suffer.

Reports were now coming through that some of the Argie conscripts had been shot in the knees so they wouldn't run away in battle. I looked at their faces. Were these conscripts or regulars? I didn't know at that point and I didn't care. We tried to keep busy during the days as we waited for news.

We were ordered to keep at ready state just in case pockets of the enemy decided that they didn't want to surrender.

I lit a fire to keep warm. I looked at *Galahad* and *Tristram* looming like ghosts in the water. The Sergeant Major, Kevin Townsend, came over. 'I need five or six guys to go on *Sir Galahad*,' he said. This was to get as much kit off as we could. By that he meant personal kit. After all, the survivors had got off in a hurry and they needed clothing. Our task was to go back onto the ship, which was by now deemed safe, even if it was still smouldering, and to collect as many Bergans as possible, which we would then empty out to make emergency clothing packs and distribute them to the survivors.

Sailing over on the lifeboats was an eerie sensation. We climbed aboard. The deck was still warm and what hit me was the sickening smell. I just wanted to get off as quickly as I could.

We searched the deserted quarters, which hadn't been touched, and grabbed as many bags and Bergans as we could.

Back on shore, we made big piles of combat jackets, combat trousers, jumpers, boots, towels, washing kits etc. and then put them into Bergans, ready to move them out for distribution.

A day later, we were still hanging around, so we decided to have some shooting practice.

Over the water, about 1,000 metres away, a farmer had some cows grazing. Possible targets? The other thing we had noticed were the ducks. So we used them for target practice, instead. One of the lads got a duck straight through the neck. We stuck a fag in its mouth and took a photo, which was going to be mounted in our unit club with the caption: 'Smoking is bad for your health.'

'Who's that running towards us?' Jock said.

'Dunno. But he looks pissed off,' I replied.

This guy, wearing civvies' clothing, was running towards us screaming, shouting and waving his hands. We were still lying down with our weapons pointing towards the water, which separated two stretches of land. He reached us out of breath. He was an islander. The first one I'd seen close up. He spoke with a funny accent, much like a South African or an Australian.

'Which one of you bastards shot my cow,' he screamed.

I pretended that I was asleep, but I must have been moving as I was laughing to myself.

All the other lads just turned away and left Jock to waffle his way out of it.

'It wasn't us, we've just been firing into the water,' Jock grovelled.

'I bet it was those fucking Paras over the ridge,' one of the other lads piped in. 'Yeah, they are fucking nutcases,' another chipped in.

The farmer calmed down, even to the stage of apologising to us. I was still lying down and biting my lip so that I wouldn't burst out laughing. I bet the last thing on his mind this morning when he woke up was that somebody was going to top his cow.

Later on that afternoon, the farmer came back to apologise to us again for blaming us for shooting his cow. He brought with him ten of the biggest steaks I'd ever seen, which we quickly got cooking over the fire. We all sat around the fire and got stuck into these steaks.

Geordie piped up: 'What shall we shoot tomorrow?'

Everybody fell about laughing.

81 Ordnance Company was split into platoons all over the islands, and most of them had now made their way to Port

Stanley, which by now was becoming more ordered, with supply ships coming and going.

The airfield was also being repaired after having been subjected to continuous bombing and it would soon be ready to receive the first Hercules transporter plane from Ascension.

Our location was moved a bit at a time, but we would sometimes jump on a chopper and get a ride to Port Stanley where we could join up with the rest of our company. However, it appeared as though some of us would have to stay here for the foreseeable future.

It was near the end of June when, one morning, I noticed that a lot of people had boarded the *Sir Galahad*. It was to be towed away and sunk as a war grave.

We soon realised that there was a service underway on board, so we went up to the top of the cliffs to observe. The remnants of the ship were towed out of Port Pleasant as a bugler played the 'Last Post'. I knelt down and cried, like most of the lads. It was the most moving experience of my life.

I took one last look at our location as we lifted off the ground in the Wessex helicopter. I was sad to leave some of my mates behind after what we'd been through, but I knew that it wouldn't be long before I saw them again. I was also looking forward to seeing Port Stanley, the place I'd heard so much about.

I was alone. More of the lads would join me the following day, but first I had to find the rest of my unit. The other problem was finding somewhere to kip.

We landed on the racecourse just outside town. The racecourse had been cleared of mines, which the Argies had so kindly left behind. I jumped out of the chopper and made my way to the road, which led all the way into Stanley.

I started to walk down the road. I noticed Moodybrook Barracks to my left, where the Argies had humiliated our marines in April by making them surrender due to lack of numbers.

The roads and pavements were still littered with discarded weapons and ammunition, mostly small arms. The Argentineans had been using FN or FAL 7.62 rifles, which were similar to our standard SLRs.

I was wearing my SMG strapped over my head and dangling at chest height. I noticed an Argie FN rifle, which I picked up, inspected and hung over my shoulder.

I carried on and absorbed the aftermath of battle: bombed-out buildings, craters and empty trenches lined the side of the road.

I carried on walking past a group of Paras, who had found a dead Argie in a garage. It appeared as though he had fled his position and that he had frozen to death. The two Paras grabbed him, one by the arms and one by the legs, before sticking a lighted fag in the deceased man's mouth and, after a shout of one, two, three, they threw him in the back of a truck, much to their amusement. I heard the body hit the floor of the truck like a piece of furniture.

'What a waste of a fag!' I thought as I walked past.

Fifty yards on I found another rifle, this time it was an FAL. I picked it up and put it over my other shoulder. Now I had a weapon over each shoulder along with my SMG.

I walked round the corner looking like Rambo when I was attacked by an Alsatian. It had me pinned up against the wall. All this hardware and I was screaming for someone to get this dog away from me. A guy whistled and the dog left me alone and ran off.

I brushed myself off and tried to look tough again, but I'd been noticed by a couple of the islanders who were laughing and shaking their heads at me. I got on my way quickly. I headed to the Falkland Islands office near the jetty, where I was reunited with most of my unit, including Yatesy. We'd been split up since San Carlos.

They had been clearing out a booby-trapped shed round the back. I went over to help. The Argies had wedged grenades between crates and had pulled the pins out so that when they were moved the lever would release and the grenade would detonate.

I was looking round for wedged grenades, when I saw a brand-new 9mm pistol still wrapped in it's greaseproof paper.

'Fucking having that,' I said as I put it in my ammo pouch. 'Where are you kipping?' I asked Yatesy.

'In a derelict house,' he said. And that was my new home for a couple of days.

Our unit had started to regroup and we had to report to the shed every morning for tasks or jobs.

Yatesy and I managed to nick an Argie truck, which we claimed for our unit.

Stores were coming frequently now, even beer and fags. Our staff sergeant had found a derelict shop just round the corner from the bombed-out church. We all got stuck in cleaning it out and commandeered it as our new unit bar. We bought beer from the NAAFI that had just opened and provided us with somewhere to go at night.

We also pinched a few tables and chairs from here and there. All our new bar lacked was a jukebox and pole dancers, but at least we could go there and talk about all of our experiences.

Every morning we had something different to do and every morning we had to pass the Argie prisoners who had been made to stay behind to help clear the minefields.

After a couple of days of kipping in the derelict house, one of the lads had found a family who was willing to take him in. A lot of troops had been doing this and most of them had been welcomed with open arms.

So I decided I was going to spend the morning knocking on doors, only to be told by most of them that they already had troops there.

I knocked on one and a lady aged about sixty opened the door.

'Come back at five when my husband is here,' she said. So I did. Bill and Evelyn Poole treated me like a long-lost son and welcomed me into their home. It wasn't far from our newfound bar as well. She showed me to a bedroom. I was in heaven. Clean sheets and a bed at last. But first I would need to take a bath.

They found me some clothes out of Bill's wardrobe to put on while Evelyn would take all my clothes to wash. I couldn't wait to get into the bath.

As I undressed in the bathroom it suddenly dawned on me that I hadn't had a wash or a hot shower since leaving the QE2 nearly five weeks earlier. I also hadn't changed my socks or underwear in all that time.

I was covered in dirt. Although I'd tried to shave in the field, I had fluff all over my chin and I also had long sideburns. I was also aware that I couldn't feel any of my toes: it was to be about six months before I got all of the feeling back.

Evelyn washed all my Army kit and threw away my underpants and socks.

I inched myself into the hot tub. I was going to enjoy this. I was in heaven as I lay there and soaked myself, but the water soon turned black and I had to empty the bath and fill it up again three times before I was eventually clean. When I'd finished, it took me ages to clean the ring-mark off the side of the bath.

Evelyn had cooked me a meal of potatoes and mutton, a typical Falklands dinner.

Afterwards, we sat in front of the fire with a drink swapping stories, and for the first time I realised what I'd been fighting for. Sitting with a couple of English-speakers in an English-style home with furniture and decorations just like my mum's house, I felt that we were justified in defending this small patch of home from the Argentineans.

It was very interesting to hear their side of the stories and how they had coped during the Argentinean occupation.

All I wanted now was to go to bed in my nice clean sheets in my own room with my own thoughts.

'Take that truck. Get some jerry cans of fuel and take them to Moodybrook,' said our staff sergeant to Yatesy and I the next day.

We got the fuel, which included kerosene, and dropped it off to some troops dossing down at what was left of Moodybrook Barracks. We then decided to have a look around.

A hundred yards past the barracks were a set of trenches left by the Argies. The location had obviously taken a bit of a pounding. The trenches looked as though they'd been abandoned in a hurry. Clothing, boots and helmets were strewn all over the area. I stepped on what looked like a big black sponge and my boot sunk in. The more it sunk in, the more the colour began to change to red.

'Aargh, what the fuck's this,' I shouted.

Yatesy had gone ahead and came back, looked down at my boot, which had parted the charcoal surface to reveal bones.

'Let's have a barbecue,' Yatesy laughed. It was obviously a body part of some sort. I wiped my boot on some grass and carried on.

We found an Army ration pack: it was similar to ours, but they had been issued with whisky and fags. I hated them even more now!

I collected some items, including a steel helmet and a cloth cap, which had blood on it. After I'd washed it, however, it looked like new. Yatesy picked up a pair of boots.

It was snowing the next day and I worked it out that I would miss nearly a complete summer. It was boiling back in the UK, but down here we were freezing.

The advance party troops had gone home and the good news was that because we'd been involved in the war we would not be garrisoning the islands.

The only trouble was, we could not start departing until the 1st Battalion of the Queen's Own Highlanders had arrived to relieve us.

Hercules aircraft had now started to arrive and depart,

bringing men and stores in and taking men out. Most of the troops had sailed home, but the quickest way was to get on that once-daily aircraft back to Ascension and then catch a VC10 to Brize Norton.

A couple of us managed to get on a flight out a few days before the majority of our unit. I wasn't sad to leave I must admit, but I would miss Bill and Evelyn.

We climbed aboard the Hercules and grabbed what space we could, which was restricted because it had been fitted with two big extra fuel tanks and we had to sit around them.

I noticed three stretchers on the side of the plane, which could be used as bunks.

I quickly claimed one, as it had a window near it and there were only two or three windows in the aircraft. I quickly fell asleep after watching the islands disappear over the horizon.

The flight would be about fourteen hours, but I wanted to get into the cockpit to watch the mid-flight refuelling operation. It was a great sight.

After landing at Ascension we were informed that we would be catching the next VC10 the following day back to Brize Norton.

There was no accommodation, so yet again it was a case of dossing down where you could. This time, however, it was boiling hot. We'd gone from one extreme to the other.

We landed at Brize Norton late at night. It was raining. I could see the terminal building where lots of families were waiting. I knew that nobody would be waiting for me, apart from, I hoped, a Land Rover to take me back to Aldershot. I came down the steps and walked across the tarmac. I saw all the families hugging each other, including the couple of lads that I was with.

I noticed Jock McFarlane, a lad from our unit who had stayed behind in Aldershot. I shook hands with him and jumped into the Land Rover and off we went. We got back in the early hours of the morning.

Chapter Nine

I walked round the empty barrack block. I went to my room, but it felt so funny to be back here. Nothing had changed. There was just a load of dust everywhere.

The next morning I reported to Captain Turrell, who had also been part of the small party to have stayed behind.

'How was it?' he asked.

'Not to good,' I replied.

He then informed me that the unit would be going on a few weeks' leave when they got back, which would be two days after me.

He also said that it would take a while before we could replace all of our stores and vehicles and that the unit would be quiet for a month or two. After all, most of it had gone down on the Atlantic conveyor. Millions of tons worth of equipment, from clothing and food to vehicles of all types, had been lost.

He said that I could go on leave the next day for two weeks and that he would also ring Stuart Henderson to say that I was back and that I could go to pre-season training when I got returned from leave. Stuart was delighted to hear that I was okay and it was arranged that I would go home for two weeks and then go into full-time training for a while on my return.

The next morning I set off for Aldershot railway station with what little clothing I had left. I walked down to the station, walking through the town centre, where I went to a shop that printed slogans on T-shirts. Five minutes later, I walked out wearing a white T-shirt bearing the slogan: 'Last Stop Before Goose Green.'

It felt funny walking through the streets full of people laughing and just carrying on enjoying their lives. I wondered if they knew whether there had even been a war.

I had already rung my mum to tell her when I would be home.

I caught the train to Waterloo to get the connection to Manchester and then on to Bolton. By the time I arrived in Bolton, I pretty much fell off the train. I'd hit the bar on the London to Manchester leg of the journey and was as pissed as a fart. I went straight to a nearby pub and had a few more drinks before arriving at one of my mates' houses, where I stayed for an hour before deciding to walk the last part of the journey home.

I walked round the side of our house and heard lots of noise. I saw bunting hanging from the houses. I recognised some of my mates and my Auntie Mary. They were all looking down the street at the bus stop. I wondered why they were all here and why they were all looking down the street. Nobody saw me as I clung to the pebbledash walls of our council flat before falling flat on my face.

Suddenly I heard: 'He's here!'

I'd been spotted. I realised that they were having a street party for me, but they hadn't reckoned on my coming in the back way.

Then there were lots of cheers as I was helped to my feet with bits of pebbledash sticking to my face. It was good to be home.

Because I had been away for more than two months I had saved all my wages, all of which had been paid into the bank. However, I blew it all in two weeks as I went on a non-stop bender – afternoons and evenings. I don't know why, but all I wanted to do was to get pissed. I also wanted to fight people. For some reason I was angry all the time. I was losing it. There was only one thing to do. Play football.

I made my way back to Aldershot and decided that I was going to report for training at Reading the following day.

I turned up at Elm Park where all the lads welcomed me back. They were well into pre-season training. Now I had something to focus on.

All of our unit had arrived back and were on leave, so it was great to use the time to get into full-time training. I was full of enthusiasm and did well to keep up with the running.

Training consisted of both morning and afternoon sessions. I loved it. All the lads wanted to hear about my experiences, but all I was interested in was how had they been playing since I had left at the end of April.

Neil Webb had left for Portsmouth and his dad Dougie was now in charge of the reserves. I worked so hard that week before going home for the weekend.

On Saturday night in Bolton we went back into the local on Blackburn Road called the Borough.

They had hired a new barmaid since I'd left.

'Who's the girl?' I asked Dave.

'That's Carole,' he said.

I walked up to the bar and said to Carole, in my best chat-up-line voice:

'Wanna hear some war stories?'

I told her that I was a footballer, hoping to impress, and I also added that I was in the Army. We soon started to see each other, but it was a pain being in Aldershot. She would come down to see me on the train and we would stay at Scouse Weedon's house, because females were not allowed in the barracks.

Things were going well playing for Reading reserves and the goals kept on going in. I was still playing for the unit side in the afternoon before making my way to Reading for the evening kick-offs. I didn't know it, but Reading manager Maurice Evans was already considering me for the first team. I had already been on the bench for a pre-season friendly, but I didn't get on and never expected to, as I knew that I was only there to make up the numbers, but one Thursday, Captain Turrell pulled me into his office. I walked in and saluted as normal.

'Private Stant,' he said: 'I have just had a call from Maurice Evans and he wants you to report to Elm Park tomorrow for training as he wants you to play for the first team on Saturday against Newport County.'

I couldn't believe it, me making my first-team debut! I was so excited I told all my mates at the barracks. That night, I rang Carole from the phone box and told her. We arranged for her to come down for the game, but she would have to come down on the train and it would arrive at London Euston at three on Saturday morning. Shit, this was a dilemma, how was I going to pick her up? It also worried me that I wouldn't be getting my much-needed sleep for the biggest game of my life so far. That night I went to sleep as usual in my squeaky Army bed, tossing and turning. I couldn't get the game out of my head, even though I had to be at training in the morning.

Vic Day picked me up at nine o'clock and took me to Reading in the duty Land Rover. It was great to train with the first team. It became clear that the team was struggling with injuries and that I was to partner Kerry Dixon up front. Later that day when I got back to Aldershot, I still couldn't get over the fact that I was going to be playing the following day. I rang Carole just to check that she would be on her way and to confirm what time I would be picking her up. After that it was just a case of waiting and hopefully not falling asleep.

I borrowed Scouse's Skoda and went and picked her up. I couldn't sleep anyway.

We arrived back in Aldershot at about 6.15 on Saturday morning, nine hours before kick-off. We managed to get some sleep in the barrack room and we woke up at about 10.30am. I went over to the cookhouse to bring back some breakfast while Carole had a shower.

I came back and Carole asked:

'Does this place have a hairdryer?'

'A fucking hairdryer? Are you sure?' I said.

About one o'clock we set off for the game, once again in Scouse's Skoda. Two mates from the base, Ginge Lane and Jock Laing, wanted to come to the game as well, which pleased me, as Carole wouldn't be sat on her own.

I made my way to the player's entrance. A few of the players were outside signing autographs, but nobody asked for mine. I looked at the match program ... Phil Stant, No. 8 – I felt so proud.

I looked at their team. John Aldridge, Tommy Tynan ... never heard of them. In goal for Newport was Mark Kendall.

'Didn't he used to play for Spurs?' I asked.

'Yeah,' Dixie replied.

The kit man put out a short-sleeved No. 8 shirt for me:

'Can I change this?' I asked.

I wanted the long-sleeved shirt that I normally wore for Reading reserves as I was embarrassed about all of the tattoos up my arm.

'Who the fuck are you?' 'League debut is it?' 'Big-time Charlie demanding another shirt.' All the lads were ribbing me, but I was conscious of my tattoos.

After the warm-up we went back to the changing room for Maurice's team talk.

I was oblivious to his words. I now felt tired through the lack of sleep and nerves. I just hoped that I wouldn't fall over the ball or mess up in front of this big crowd. I kept telling myself to enjoy it because I'd been dreaming of this ever since I was a kid.

A thought kept nagging me. Will Maurice change the team before kick-off? Would he say he'd made a mistake by picking me and say sorry?

The now-familiar buzzer went round the changing room. All the lads came up to me to shake my hand, even the apprentices. I went out eighth in line, the same number as my shirt.

Maurice was at the dressing-room door. He stopped me and grabbed my hand. 'Good luck, son,' he said. No he hadn't made a mistake, I was definitely playing.

Newport were already on the pitch when we ran out. What a feeling running out onto the pitch to the cheering crowds. I started to kick a ball about as our skipper, Martin Hicks, tossed the coin. A photographer then ran onto the pitch and I had to pose for a photograph in front of all these people. I just wanted the game to start.

We had to change ends. We were defending the goal where all the Newport fans were. We kicked off. Within a minute, their big centre-half Keith Oakes had caught me with his elbow as I beat him to the header. I could taste blood.

'Welcome to the real game,' I thought.

Ten minutes had gone and I had only touched the ball twice, albeit simply and effectively.

Stuart Beavon played the ball through; Dixie was onto it like a flash. 1–0. The crowd went mad. I started to get into the game with nice passes and control, slowly putting to bed all those years of self-doubt.

Seventeen minutes had gone. Lawrie Sanchez played a long ball forward. The Newport defender Vaughan Jones was trying to clear, but I beat him to it. He was off balance, the ball bobbled into the box, I stuck out my left leg and lifted it over Mark Kendall and into the goal. 2–0.

I'd watched *Match of the Day* often enough to know what I was going to do next.

I ran to the crowd shaking my fist behind the goal. I looked at the joy on the fans' faces.

Dixie was the first to congratulate me, followed by all the other lads. What a feeling to score on my league debut. I waved over to Carole and my mates Jock and Ginge.

Keith Oakes kept using his elbows and I quickly learned that I had to protect myself. I was now in a man's game.

Newport pulled one back from the penalty spot just before half-time, but we were playing well and I knew that we could score more in the second half; so it proved with Dixie making it 3–1 with his second.

Soon after, Dixie went for with a challenge with Oakes. I saw his elbow catch him on the cheek. Oakes was pole-axed. There was blood everywhere. Dixie just walked away. Oakes was taken to the side of the pitch. The Newport manager, Colin Addison, was going berserk on the touchline, but the referee hadn't seen it. Oakes was walking down the track aided by the physio. Blood was spurting everywhere.

'I'll fucking get you, Dixie, you bastard,' he screamed as he walked past.

Seventy-five minutes had gone and there was another long ball over the top. Dixie got to it first. Two of us were one on one with Kendall. I was screaming for him to pass so that I could run onto it and stick it in the net.

'Dixie, Dixie.' I thought he was going to pass, but he didn't. He slid it past Kendall and into the net. 4–1. Dixie had completed his hat-trick. Newport pulled one back, but we ended up winning 4–2. At the end we clapped the crowd. I didn't want to leave the pitch.

The atmosphere in the dressing room was fantastic. We were

all cheering. Maurice grabbed me again. 'Well done, son,' he said, before he went on to the other players. We jumped into the bath singing. I couldn't wait to get into the players' bar where I had organised tickets for Carole, Jock and Ginge.

I was dried myself off and sat down near my peg to reflect on the game. Another victory and I'd played a small part in it.

'I'm going to get pissed tonight, big style,' I thought to myself.

'The BBC want to speak to you,' Stuart said.

'Fuck off. The BBC. Why?' I said. I thought he was joking, but it was true. They wanted me to give an interview on the radio via a telephone link.

I got changed and went into the secretary's office.

'Er ... hello,' I said tentatively into the receiver and then proceeded to give an interview. When it was all over, I made my way to the players' bar and, this time, signed loads of autographs. I eventually went into the bar and saw Carole, Ginge and Jock. She kissed me.

'Well done,' she said.

'I've just given an interview to the BBC,' I said.

'Fucking no way,' said Jock in his thick Scottish accent.

We were surrounded by all the other players and families in the bar and I now felt that I truly belonged there. About six o'clock we set off back to Aldershot.

After getting well and truly pissed that night, we were going to stay at Scouse and Sue Shearin's married quarters. We got into the car and put on the radio to listen to my interview.

In all my excitement I couldn't even remember what I had said. I cringed as I heard myself:

'Er ... well, er ... yeah, not bad, er ... yer know, that's right, well er...' etc.

Fucking hell! I sounded like Fred Dibnah.

After that they interviewed Bryan Robson and he sounded much more professional, but who cares.

As we drove back to Aldershot I didn't know it then, but I was to cause a real stir.

Unknown to us, while we were in the unit bar getting pissed, I was headline news on the *Nine O'Clock News* and *News at Ten*. The story was about the Falklands soldier who had scored on his league debut. They used a black and white picture of my goal.

In the bar I kept going over the goal in my mind, we had a real celebration. We eventually got to bed in the early hours of the morning.

Early on Sunday morning, we were woken up by a banging on the door of Scouse and Sue's married quarter.

'Who the fuck are you?' I heard Scouse say.

The next minute, Scouse walked into our bedroom wearing just his boxer shorts and scratching his balls.

'It's for you,' he said and went back to bed. I went to the door. It was a photographer. Fuck knows how he had tracked me down.

'Any chance of some photos?' he said.

'Do you know what fucking time it is?' I said.

'Yeah, it's 10am,' he said.

'Is it?' I replied.

He wanted me to put on my uniform and march up and down outside.

'OK,' I said. It took about half an hour. After that we went back up to the bar for a few more drinks.

On Monday morning, as I reported for duty as normal at MT Platoon, the picture of me marching up and down in my uniform was splashed over the back pages of the newspapers.

After about an hour I was summoned to the OC's office. I marched in, saluted and stood at ease.

'Morning Stant,' the OC said. 'Well done at the weekend.'

'Thank you, sir,' I said.

Captain Turrell had now joined us. I saluted him. He looked

anxious as he saluted back. I suddenly became worried. What had I done wrong, I asked. Nothing, they both replied. Apparently, most of the top brass in the British Army had watched the news on Saturday night. They wanted to know who I was and why I wasn't playing for the Army side. It was considered an honour to play for them.

The Army side was picked from the best players throughout the whole of the British Army. It was headed by Major Dobson, a now-retired major. Over the weekend he had also received a lot of calls from the Army's top brass.

Of course, he had no idea who I was and it must have made him look stupid. It must have pissed him off big time. Imagine, a soldier who was good enough to play league football but who was not good enough to play for the Army. The truth was that they hadn't even heard of me.

I was told to report as soon as possible to the military stadium on Queens Road, where I would join up with the Army squad to play the RAF on Wednesday night.

'I'm sorry sir, but I don't want to play for the Army,' I said.

Captain Turrell put his head in his hands.

'What do you mean, Stant? To represent the Army is one of the greatest honours a soldier could have,' Major McDougald, the OC, spluttered.

I took a deep breath:

'With due respect sir, if the Army team didn't want me before, why should they want me now?' I continued. 'I'm sorry sir, I only want to play for my unit if needed and Reading.' I marched out.

McDougald relayed our conversation to Dobson who must have had a bollocking from the top brass. I was called back to the OC's office. He was pleading with me to join up with the Army squad. After all, it would reflect well on both him and the unit if I played in the team. Then he dropped a bombshell. If you don't join up with the Army squad, you will be stopped from playing for Reading.

The bastards were now blackmailing me. I had no choice, so I reluctantly went to join up with the squad.

When I arrived, the lads were already training. WO2 Alf Coulton was the coach. He was also the manager of Walton and Hersham, a non-league side.

I introduced myself halfway through his session. All the rest of the team looked at me. I could feel their jealousy. Those lads were well-established, good Army players. And here I was after being on the TV over the weekend.

'Where's your boots then?' Alf barked at me.

'At Reading in the boot room,' I said.

'Well you'd better fuck off and get them,' he said and carried on with the session.

I could hear some of the lads laughing as I turned and walked away. I made my way to Reading, collected my boots and returned to join the Army squad.

We played the RAF that Wednesday night and I scored two as we won 3–1. Now I had to play for the Army as well.

I couldn't understand all the fuss, after all Dixie had scored a hat-trick and I'd only scored one but was getting most of the attention.

Carole was now staying down in Aldershot. We stayed at the Shearin's married quarter and she started to prepare for our wedding, which was three weeks away.

I rejoined my unit on the Thursday morning after the RAF game, which had been watched by Maurice Evans and Stuart Henderson.

On Saturday, Reading were due to play Walsall away and once again I made my way to training on the Friday morning for the game on Saturday. Carole and I drove to Elm Park to meet the team bus. Carole was to drive the car and follow the coach all the way to Walsall to watch the game, but Maurice suggested that I stay in the car with her and that we follow the bus together. We stopped at West Bromwich Moat House at about 10pm, a couple of minutes behind the coach.

As we pulled into the car park, I jumped out of the car and shouted to Carole.

'I'll see you inside.' I didn't want to be late.

I got inside the hotel as the lads were just starting on some toast. I sat down near to Laurie Sanchez and Kerry Dixon and started to unwrap some butter to spread on a slice of toast when, suddenly, the doors burst open and an irate Carole shouted at me:

'Don't you ever leave me in a car park again.'

I was so embarrassed as all the team and officials looked at me. I ushered her back outside.

'I'm hungry as well,' she said.

So I quickly took her to a café near West Brom's ground and ordered pie and chips for her. We then went back to the hotel, where I finished off my pre-match meal of beans on toast.

Reading and Walsall were both in the lower reaches of the Third Division, so it was an important game for both sides. I was up against a young lad like myself. Lee Sinnott was making his league debut. We didn't play very well that day and were 2–0 down with fifteen minutes to go. I received the ball on the edge of the box, sidestepped Sinnott and crashed the ball past the diving Ron Green. The ball hit the post and flew into the back of the net. We pushed and pushed trying to get an equaliser, but it never came.

We finished the game on top, but lost 2–1. However, I'd scored again. Two goals in two games: I was happy that I'd done enough to keep my place for the following week's FA Cup first-round tie against non-league Bishops Stortford.

I knew the other lads were not far away from full fitness, including striker Pat Earles. I'd never played in the FA Cup and that would be another milestone.

After the game, Maurice pulled me to one side and said that he wanted me to sign non-contract forms. He would offer me £60 per match plus £18 for playing for the reserves. Brilliant I thought, it would supplement my wages.

The following Monday, I was summoned once again to the OC's office and once again Captain Turrell was there. This time they were both smiling.

'Another goal then,' Captain Turrell said.

'Yes sir,' I replied and then went on to tell him of Reading's offer. He was delighted for me. The OC stood up.

'Stant. We've had a call from London Weekend Television. They want to send a guy called Jim Rosenthal to do an interview with you.'

'You're joking sir!' I stuttered.

'No I'm not,' the OC replied.

Every Saturday there was a programme called *World of Sport* and they had a feature called 'On the Ball' that used to be fronted by Brian Moore but which had been taken over by Ian St John. I had watched it regularly ever since I was a kid.

They wanted to do a piece about how army lads kept fit and suggested that we took Jim over the assault course.

The OC was delighted. It was great publicity for both his unit and the Army in general. Jim was coming on Friday, the day before the FA Cup match and the feature was to be screened the following week, on the morning of our wedding.

Ten weeks had passed since I had met Carole and I couldn't wait to marry her. We had decided on that particular day, because Reading's game was on the Sunday at Millwall.

I did a few interviews for the tabloids during the course of the week. Apparently this Falklands soldier had captured the public's imagination. I couldn't wait for Friday to come around. Some of the lads had been handpicked and we were to tackle the Para assault course wearing Bergans on our backs: Jim Rosenthal was to join us.

Before the TV crew and Jim arrived, we all got our Bergans and packed them with just rubber foam. They looked full. We got a Bergan for Jim and we put a 10-ton vehicle jack and other bits in it. It weighed well over 60 pounds.

The crew turned up and Jim introduced himself. He was a great guy. The camera crew were then taken to the assault course to set up for filming. One of the cameras was set up near the water jump.

Jim struggled to get the Bergan on and we had to help him with it. He looked the part with his Army-issue combat jacket and trousers. It was a great laugh with the sergeant major screaming at Jim Rosenthal to 'move himself, move himself'. At the water jump, Jim fell in; it was great TV.

Afterwards, we had lunch in the cookhouse, but we didn't tell Jim what was in his Bergan. In fact, I didn't tell him until I met him some years later at the PFA awards in London and we had a good laugh about it.

Jock Laing was going to be my best man with Yatesy, Scouse Shearin and Tony 'Killer' Wild as my ushers. He was called Killer not because he'd killed somebody in the war, but because he'd run over and killed a Turkish civilian worker in Germany and had been transferred to our unit.

I had been friends with Jock since he joined the unit just before the war. He survived the Falklands, Ireland, Bosnia, The Gulf War and the Zeebrugge ferry disaster. Talk about a cat with nine lives.

Friday afternoon we started my stag do early at about 3pm. Most of the lads were due to join us later on. After a few pints of lager, Carole appeared in the club, looking shaken. She had been arranging flowers at the church.

'What's up?' I said. She was out of breath having run the half-mile to the unit bar all the way from the church.

'Did you remember the licence?' she asked, which I should have picked up from the register office.

'Oh fuck,' I said, looking at my watch. It was ten minutes to five.

I quickly got up and ran into town. I reached the office dead on five. The clerk was locking the door.

'I thought you'd forgotten,' she said and reopened the door to get me the paperwork.

I was so relieved. What would we have done? Everything had been arranged, including the coach party from Bolton. How would I have been able to cancel everything and tell everybody that the wedding was off just because I hadn't picked up the licence. These thoughts all passed through my mind as I walked back up Salamanca Park hill.

Carole was relieved when I got back. At least she could relax now. So could I ... I proceeded to get well and truly pissed.

The next morning, Tony Bushnell picked me up nursing a hangover. We'd arranged to hold a kids' coaching session the morning of my wedding, much to Carole's annoyance.

'I've got to be back for 11.30,' I said.

I finished the session and got back just in time to greet the coach from Bolton. I jumped on, said hello, covered in mud and went off to get changed.

The wedding went without a hitch and we all made our way to the reception, where we watched a recording of the Jim Rosenthal interview on 'On The Ball', which had been on TV while we were getting married.

What I didn't know was that after all this publicity, my dad would start to take notice of me. He watched the interview while he supped a pint in his social club.

He spat his beer out at the end of the interview when Ian St John said: 'Oh and by the way congratulations to Phil and Carole who get married today.'

That was how he found out that I was getting married.

Chapter Ten

A proposed posting to Antwerp never materialised and I carried on playing for Reading reserves. I was still hoping that I would get picked for the first team again. And I did.

Stuart had been on to Captain Turrell and asked if I could be available on Tuesday night to play away against Millwall in a cup competition. I was delighted: the only problem was that on that Tuesday morning I was unloading a lorry. I knew it would take ages and I needed to get ready to meet up with the Reading lads. We had just had a new sergeant posted in who was supervising me unloading the truck.

'I've got to go in a minute sarge,' I said.

'You're not going anywhere until this truck's unloaded,' he said.

'But sarge, I've got to go.' I started to get uptight. Sergeant Cooke didn't like football and he didn't like me. I was falling into a trap without realising it.

'I don't care how long it takes you. You're not going until this truck is unloaded,' he said.

I jumped down, put my face in his and shouted: 'Unload it yourself you fat fucking waste of space.'

The next minute I was being marched in front of the OC on an insubordination charge. The OC had no choice. Captain Turrell couldn't help me now.

The OC sentenced me to seven days in the glasshouse.

We didn't have a unit jail; if any of our lads got sentenced, they had to do their time in 2 Para nick – it was a feared place.

As I was marched away to start my sentence, I couldn't believe what was happening to me. I had a mental picture of the Reading team coach waiting for me at the pick-up point with Stuart looking at his watch and wondering where I was. But Captain Turrell had informed him of developments.

At the time, Carole was having a wives' coffee morning in the club when Captain Turrell walked in to tell her the bad news.

'I'm sorry to tell you Mrs Stant, but Phil has been suspended for seven days.'

'Oh that's good,' she said. 'At least he can spend some time with me now,' she carried on. We'd moved into our married quarter the Monday after the wedding.

'No. You don't understand. He's been taken into custody,' he went on.

I was marched into the 2 Para nick, only to be met by a sergeant.

'Look here, if it ain't that poser footballer. I hate football. It's a puff's game, wrong shaped ball,' he said, spitting in my face as I stood to attention. Perhaps I had got too big for my boots.

I was locked in a tiny cell, when the duty officer came in. He was a young Lieutenant, not much older than me.

'Now then you fucking Crap Hat, clean this cell up,' he barked. I wanted to hit him, but it would have only made things worse.

Carole was allowed to visit and she would sneak cigarettes into me. Being locked up was a horrible feeling. I had to stay in solitary, as they thought that the other sentenced Paras, who were also doing time, might want to beat the shit out of a Crap Hat.

I was let out on Wednesday morning after serving nearly four days. Why was I being let our early? I reported to Captain Turrell's office.

'Make your way to Reading. You're in the squad for tonight's game at Plymouth.'

I was chuffed to bits. I went to see Carole and off I went. I don't know what strings had been pulled, but on the way down I was reading about myself in the *Daily Mirror*, which went on about me being released early from the glasshouse to play for Reading at Plymouth Argyle.

'How the fuck did they know about that?' I thought.

I started and played the whole game at Plymouth, but we went down 3–0. On the Saturday we were to play a local derby against Oxford United at home and I was to be on the bench. This time Carole and I caught the train and got off at Reading station to look for a taxi.

This guy came up and said: 'It is, isn't it. It's you, isn't it?'

'Who?' I said looking round.

'It's you, Phil Stant,' he said.

'Yeah, it's me,' and Carole and I jumped into a taxi laughing our heads off: the price of fame!

Oxford were 3–0 up and the two centre-halves, Gary Briggs and Malcolm Shotton, looked frightening. I replaced Lawrie Sanchez with ten minutes to go, but the game was already over.

The ball dropped on the edge of the area and I hit it first time, but it thundered off the crossbar. That was our last chance. It was not going to be our day. We sat in silence in the dressing room. Gary Donellan, one of our wide players, made a remark that Stuart Beavon's white shorts were never dirty. Fists were soon flying and both had bloody noses as we tried to keep them apart.

Beavon's suit was ripped. It was the first of many dressing-room fights I was either to see or be involved in.

I also had a heavy heart as I knew that that was probably my last first-team chance. Soon I was going to be posted.

Maurice had mentioned a one-year contract, but I was now married with a baby on the way and there was no way that I'd buy myself out of the security of the Army for a one-year contract. I ended up playing the last few games for the reserves.

My posting came through. We were going to move to Germany for three years to a place called 3 Base Ammunition Depot in Braacht near Moenchengladbach. 3 BAD was renowned for having a good football team and I was pleased, so was Carole, even though she was not allowed to travel as our first baby was due shortly.

I tried to get compassionate leave so that I could stay at home with her until the baby was born.

Carole had moved up to Bolton to stay with her parents, Mavis and Harold, and our furniture had been put in storage ready for the move to our married quarter in Braacht.

The Army refused me leave, ordering me to report to my new unit, which pissed us off a bit. However, they did say that when the baby was imminent they would get me back to the UK straightaway.

I reported to 3 BAD, was shown to my barrack room and was told to report to see my new OC in the morning. I marched in the next morning and introduced myself.

'Welcome to 3 BAD,' said Colonel Hopkinson.

'Thank you sir,' I replied.

'Right, get your kit ready to fly back to the UK,' he said.

'Sir?' I looked at him with a bemused look on my face. I was thinking that Carole must have gone into early labour and that she had been in touch with my new unit.

'You're going back to join up with the Army football squad to play against West Bromwich Albion at Aldershot,' he said.

'But sir, I only flew in last night,' I said.

'I know, but this has just come through this morning,' he went on.

This pissed Carole and I off even more. They wouldn't let me stay with her on compassionate grounds, but they were prepared to spend a lot of money flying me back just to play in a football match for the Army.

I flew back, played in the game, which we lost 4–0, and then flew back to Germany. A week later, I was on the plane once again, this time making my way to Carole's parents in Bolton.

She was to be induced. I took her to the hospital and was able to see her later on that night.

She asked me to bring her some food in the morning when I returned, as she didn't like the food at the hospital.

I woke up on Saturday morning and went to Bolton General Hospital, which was about ten minutes away by foot. On my way, I remembered what she'd said about bringing some food and, as I was walking, I passed a pie shop. I was hungry myself. So I popped in and bought two pasties and two meat and potato pies.

I arrived at the hospital to be told that Carole was in the early stages of labour, lying on a bed. The nurse came in to check on her every ten minutes. I started to read the paper as I sat on a chair.

'Oh, by the way, do you want a meat and potato pie?' I said, showing her what I'd bought as the caring husband. She just looked at me, then the pie, and was sick all over the side of the bed.

'Well, do you mind if I have it eh? I'm starving,' I said.

After a few hours' labour, Hayley Louise May was born at 3pm on Saturday, 18 June 1983.

I looked at the clock.

'Kick-off time,' I shouted as everybody looked at me wondering what planet I was from.

We arrived in Germany, thanks to Harold's packed Ford Cortina, via Zeebrugge and moved into our married quarter, which was a two-bedroomed flat. No. 6 OP de haag.

I knew that I would enjoy this posting as it was an ammunition depot and field exercises were very rare, all of which would give me plenty of time for football.

I soon started to play for civilian teams. One was a team called Willich FC Moenchengladbach and played in a non-league called the Landesliga. The only problem was, I kept getting sent off.

One time it was for hitting a 'boxhead' (squaddie slang for a German) on the nose for a debatable tackle from behind. Our German coach was screaming at me from the touchline: 'Phil, *nichts mehr bitte.*' (No more please).

Fourteen months later, Carole gave birth to Craig Philip Arthur on 3 September 1984. Hayley spent most of her formative years sleeping, but Craig was a little so-and-so and only slept during the day.

We enjoyed life in Germany and, shortly after passing my HGV1, I was promoted to Lance Corporal.

Carole had started to work full time as a receptionist at the Army medical centre in Rheindahlen.

Money was still tight and, like most families at the base, we ordered our furniture from a guy called Hans Peter, who had a shop in town that ran a hire-purchase scheme.

The only problem was, when he delivered it, it aroused the attention of the other squaddie families and you could see them hiding behind the net curtains and having a nosey at what you were having delivered. Everyone was at it, though.

Two-and-a-half years into the posting, I unexpectedly received another order. I was to be sent to the Royal Army Ordnance Corps EOD (Explosive Ordnance Disposal) bomb disposal unit in Hereford, working alongside 22 SAS.

It came out of the blue, but once again we packed our

belongings in the big MFO boxes, the standard Army-issue boxes used to pack up your belongings when it's time to move on. I borrowed some money from my bank in England and settled the bill with Hans Peter.

A few weeks later, we were moving into our married quarter at Stirling Lines in Hereford. The bomb disposal units covered all the UK, including Northern Ireland. Hereford's task was to cover all of Wales and the West Midlands. I had to do a course at Central Ordnance Depot Kineton before they would let me loose in the white transit van, which was home to the 'wheelbarrow' – a robot designed for defusing devices.

Carole and I were unpacking the boxes and she wasn't happy because the house was a mess. The garden hadn't been touched for ages.

'Give it a month and I'll see if we can get another quarter,' I said.

Then there was a knock on the door.

'Who's that banging on the door?' I said. After all, we didn't know anybody.

We both looked down the hallway and saw a big shadow covering the whole of the pane of glass in the door.

'Who's this monster?' I thought as I opened the door.

'Are you Lance Corporal Stant?' he said.

'Yeah, that's right,' I replied, somewhat bemused.

'I'm Sergeant Ned Kelly and I run the squadron football team. I hear you play.'

'Yeah, I do,' I said, getting more interested by the second. And that was it...

Ned, a veteran of the Iranian embassy siege was sat in the lounge with a cup of tea. I'd told Carole that the unit didn't have a football team, but I was wrong. Twenty-two SAS played in a local civilian league called Army Hereford.

On the Saturday I was picked to play against Pegasus – a good side in the league.

As I walked into our changing room, Ned introduced me to the rest of the team. It became very clear, very quickly, that I was an outsider.

They may have distanced themselves from me, but I was sure that I could win them over with my performances on the pitch. Most of them had big black moustaches and were very tanned.

I had been informed in advance that the fixture against Pegasus was always a grudge match. I soon found out that most of the games were grudge matches. Anyway, we won 4–3 and I scored all four of the goals. In the bar afterwards, I was suddenly part of the family and soon became a regular.

I was also enjoying the new job. It took me a while before I was competent with the wheelbarrow. I used to practice on old cars that we had acquired for training purposes.

The wheelbarrow was a fantastic invention and had saved lots of lives, especially in Northern Ireland. It was a small-tracked vehicle with a hydraulic boom attached to it. On the end of the boom were two shotguns for taking out windows – mostly on cars – and two tubes called 'pigsticks'.

The pigsticks were filled with water and you would attach a small charge, which would activate the pigsticks and render the device safe.

Most terrorists' improvised explosive devices (IEDs) had some kind of timer unit on them which would detonate the explosives, most of which were usually handmade. The pigsticks were ideal for disrupting the timer unit, thus making the IED harmless.

The water came out so quickly that it could take your hand clean off if you put it in front it. All the gadgets were remote controlled by myself, as the No. 2, from the back of the Transit via a monitor, which was supplied by a video camera, perched on the top of the boom. The No. 1, usually a sergeant or above, would then put the bomb suit on and go and make safe the devices.

The No. 1 would only suit up and go if you couldn't get to a device by remote means, i.e. the wheelbarrow; that would be the case if the device was situated upstairs. It was exciting stuff, especially if you actually got a shout.

In the 1980s, Birmingham was an IRA target and, on one or two occasions, the Rackhams store was the scene of false alarms.

The false alarms would piss me off. I wanted a device to be found so that I could get to work. The adrenalin would be pumping as we chased our police escorts with our blue lights flashing. Usually on an IED shout, you would call up the Royal Signals who had Electronic Counter Measures (ECM) as back-up, just in case it was a radio-controlled device – ECM jammed any rogue radio signals.

One week, we were on location acting as back-up for Special Branch at a Conservative Party conference, when we had a shout about a car with Irish plates that was illegally parked.

Alarm bells starting ringing with Special Branch, especially after the Brighton bombing. The streets were blocked off and the main road was cordoned off. A big crowd was watching about 1,000 metres away behind a police line.

I sent the wheelbarrow down the road towards the now-isolated car. My No. 1 and the police were glued to my monitor in the back of the van. One of the signals lads popped his head in the back of the van and confirmed that there were no rogue signals.

That meant that it was either a timer or a mercury tilt, like the one that killed Airey Neave, the Conservative Shadow Northern Ireland Secretary. Whichever it was, we'd soon find out.

I swung the wheelbarrow round and looked into the back of the car. Nothing.

'Get inside the fucker,' said Nobby Clarke, who was my No. 1.

'Glad to,' I said.

I lined up the shotgun and blasted out the rear passenger window. I then extended the boom inside the car and moved the camera left and right.

'Shit, nothing,' I said.

'Get in the boot,' said Nobby.

I reversed out and swung her round. I was going to have to use the pigsticks to open the boot with a controlled explosion. I lined her up and was just about to pull the switch, when one of the police said:

'Who's that fucking idiot?'

With that we both looked out of the back of the van and saw a guy in a suit waving a briefcase and shouting. He looked the worse for wear and had a blue and white rosette pinned to his suit. He was trying to run towards the car.

'What's he saying?' I said impatiently.

'Something about, what have you done to my fucking car,' said Nobby.

'What. Oh shit.'

We jumped out of the van. The guy was a delegate at the conference, but he was still arrested.

Early one Sunday morning we were told, via the radio, that there was an incendiary device, with a five-gallon petrol tank attached to a timer unit.

'Wow. Fifty-metre fireball at least if that goes off,' said my No. 1, who this time was a captain.

We got to the building, which was the headquarters for a national company. I got the wheelbarrow out. Connected her up and got her armed.

The only problem was that the barrow was going to have to climb up a couple of steps to get to the main entrance. However, I managed to get her there without having to send down the No.

1. The device was placed right next to a big plate-glass entrance.
I got her as close as I could and we examined the device through
the camera.

It didn't look like the work of professionals but, nevertheless,
it was still a threat.

I spotted the timer unit and aimed a pigstick right in the
centre. I was sweating. I didn't want to detonate it myself by
doing something stupid and my other concern was the glass
entrance. With a small controlled explosion using my left
pigstick, I disrupted the timer unit. Spot on and I never even
touched the glass windows. I was quite pleased with myself as we
drove home after the clear-up operation.

It was a really interesting job and you could get some really
good shouts.

Another one came at Highgrove House, the home of Charles
and Diana.

Two men had been seen in the grounds and we were called in
just in case anything had been planted.

After an all-night search nothing had been found, and I was
dozing away in Charles' armchair when a captain walked in and
shouted at me:

'Get out of that chair. Who do you think you are?'

'Sorry sir,' I replied as I pulled myself up.

Charles and Diana were not in residence, so I didn't think he
would have minded if I'd sat down for a rest.

We also travelled to Gatcombe Park, the home of Princess
Anne, to X-ray a suspect package. Some nutter had sent a
package through the post, which contained just books
of matches.

It wasn't always the terrorist threat that made the job
interesting, but also unexploded ordnance that was always being
dug up in people's gardens, such as grenades used by the Home
Guard during the Second World War who would bury them and

then forget all about them. The Midlands was also hit hard during the Blitz and incendiary devices dropped by the Luftwaffe were regularly dug up.

One day I'd just finished my lunch when we got a shout. This time it wasn't an IED but an old lady who had dug up a Second World War bomb while tidying her garden in Coventry. The police were in touch by radio as we made our way with blue lights flashing and sirens wailing.

Word had got through to us that the street had been cordoned off and that the situation was dodgy. Sure enough as we arrived at the scene, the street was full of people watching from behind a police line.

We made our way into the garden after speaking to the old lady and a policeman who gave us a good description. By then I had my doubts as to whether or not this could be a goer. We looked at the bomb, which we both knew straightaway was dead.

'Shit.' I would have loved to have stuck a pound of plastic explosive to it and blown it up in situ enabling us to put on a bit of a show.

'Leave it to me, Nobby,' I said. 'I'll have some fun with this.'

I picked up the piece of ordnance and carried it gently round the side of the house. There were gasps from the watchers as I made my way into the street.

I could see the little old lady looking worried. I pretended by my actions that it was live. As I turned round gently, much to everyone's horror, including the old lady, I dropped it in front of me with it landing at my feet.

Nobby was pissing himself laughing. The old lady nearly had a heart attack. I just picked it up and threw it in the back of the van.

I think we both saw it as a wasted journey, but the police were only following procedure. We worked well with the police most of the time and we would often visit police training headquarters to give lectures about our role and to give them advice on what to do if they found something naughty.

But the wasted trips, as I would call them, pissed me off, especially the time when I was on call one Saturday.

As I was preparing to go onto the field with the lads for our warm-up, my bleeper, that Ned was holding, went off.

'Sorry lads, gotta go,' I said.

Once again it was an old piece of ordnance...

Regardless of the distractions, the soccer team was flying. We won trophy after trophy. The big problem with being in an Army team was the availability of players and the difficulty in establishing a regular team, especially when you were based in Hereford, where you were only ever two minutes away from being sent to anywhere around the world.

The team would change weekly, but I managed to forge good partnerships up front with Eddy Edwards, Billy Frear and Johnny 'Two' Combes. Johnny acquired his nickname because of his love of combing his hair; it was always immaculate.

It was a good squad, nevertheless. Ned was a born organiser and we had a great captain in Billy Smith. We also had support from comedian Jim Davidson, who would come down from time to time to watch us play and then have a piss-up with us afterwards.

Near the end of the season, Ned decided that it was time for us to have a team photo with all the silverware that we had won. It was difficult getting everyone together at the same time, but Ned managed it.

I made my way to the pavilion through the back gate past the Paludrin Club where we always celebrated our wins. Most of the lads were already changed. I quickly put my strip on and noticed all the lads milling around.

'What we waiting for?' I said to Ned.

'Three of the lads, but they're on their way,' Ned replied.

'Fuck. I'm on duty in half an hour, Ned. I hope they're not going to be long,' I said anxiously.

'Don't worry son, they're here,' he replied.

'Where?' I said looking round.

'Up there,' he said, looking skywards.

I looked up and saw a chopper with three lads, Bill, Eddy Stone and Rusty parachuting in wearing the all-familiar black suit uniform of the SAS.

Eddie landed ten yards away from me and quickly ripped off his black uniform to reveal his football strip, which all of them had on underneath.

'Sorry we're late, lads,' they said in unison, much to the groans of the rest of the lads. I just stood there in amazement.

Carole and I had been unhappy with our married quarter and had asked to change. We were granted another married quarter about half a mile away on Hoarwithy Road. The only problem was, our garden backed right onto the squadron helicopter-landing pad. It didn't bother us, though, because the garden was much nicer and so was the house, and the Paludrin Club was more accessible via the back gate.

We had reached the League Cup final against our local rivals Fownhope, which was to be played on Tuesday night.

After our game on Saturday, Ned told everybody not to be late for the Cup final. I had a problem: a requirement of my job was that I had to be licensed every six months. You had to pass certain practical tests and procedures, all of which involved aspects of bomb disposal.

If you failed, you then had to wait for another six months before you could have second crack at it and, besides, I didn't fancy being stuck in an office for six months as I liked being in the field. I was due to go to the southern location on Sunday night and was expected to return on Thursday night. Ned blew his top.

'This is fucking important,' he said in his Cockney accent.

'Yeah, so is my fucking job,' I replied.

Ned went into deep thought.

'Leave it with me, son,' he said.

What that meant I had no idea, but I suspected that he had a cunning plan.

First thing Monday I was first on. I was involved in a simulated terrorist attack in which I had to dispose of a bomb that had been left inside a house. I passed with flying colours, but I still had to stay until Thursday. The Army was my career and my family now, and any football I played was just an added bonus.

At lunchtime on Tuesday, a major, who was running the licensing exercise that also involved the police, came over to me as a few of us ate lunch.

'Lance Corporal Stant, who the fuck do you think you are?' he bawled at me.

'Sorry sir, I don't follow,' I said as I stood up.

'A fucking helicopter from Hereford is on its way to pick you up and take you back to Hereford to play in the Cup final tonight. Be on the parade ground at two o'clock with all your kit,' he carried on.

I couldn't believe it: not a taxi or the duty driver in a Land Rover, but a fucking helicopter. I didn't know how Ned had pulled this off, but I didn't care.

I made my way to the parade ground and, right on time, a chopper landed at two o'clock. The pilot was a guy called Andy, who also lived in the married quarters. He flew a civilian chopper as, for obvious reasons, the SAS don't use Army choppers.

I jumped in the front seat after dumping my kit in the back and put the headsets on so that I could talk to Andy. We took off and I pointed to our location where the lads were now back on exercise.

Andy hovered for a moment over the location at about 100

feet. I couldn't resist giving everybody a wave, especially the major, who was pissed off.

Off we went, it would be about an hour to get to Hereford, which would give me plenty of time to grab something to eat and to have a little rest before meeting up with the team for a 6.30 kick-off.

We'd been in the air for ten minutes when a call came through from Stirling Lines. We would have to turn around and make our way to London to pick up a captain.

'Sorry Phil, but we've got to do it,' said Andy.

It didn't bother me: I fancied a chopper flight around London anyway.

It was great. Andy flew us all around the city before landing at the pick-up point near to the Thames. Andy shut off the engines while we waited, and he also took the opportunity to refuel.

We waited for half an hour, but there was no sign of the captain. Forty-five minutes passed and there was still no sign. At this rate I was going to miss the match. He turned up after just under an hour's wait.

Now I knew that I would be late. Andy radioed through back to Hereford and told them the situation. He also sent a message to Carole to meet me at the ground with my boots. As we were coming into Hereford, it was dark and raining. We flew over our house and I realised that they would just have kicked off. I looked at our garden and was horrified when I saw that all of Carole's washing had fallen off the line.

A staff car was waiting. The captain got out of the back of the chopper and made his way towards it.

'Sorry sir, this is for Lance Corporal Stant,' said the young Tom.

The captain looked flabbergasted. I turned round and waved at Andy who was laughing his head off. I jumped into the car, leaving the captain standing there in the rain holding his briefcase.

The young Tom got me to the ground just round the corner from Hereford United's Edgar Street ground. I ran from the car to the changing rooms. I saw Carole holding a bag, which contained my boots.

'Thanks,' I said out of breath. 'Oh, and by the way, your washing is all over the garden,' I carried on as I ran off into the changing rooms.

I quickly got changed and made my way to the touchline.

We had started off with ten men as they had expected me to arrive shortly. We were 1–0 down and it was a free-kick to us. The referee waved me on. I ran onto the pitch and made my way into the box to await Rusty's free-kick. The whistle blew, Rusty took the free-kick and I headed it straight into the net.

From the kick-off, I went steaming for the ball and took out one of their players. A scuffle evolved, with me right in the middle of it. I'd been on the pitch for about sixty seconds and was now walking away after being sent off.

Ned was glaring at me. I knew that he would be fuming, especially after all the trouble that he'd gone through just to get me there.

We lost the game 5–1. Afterwards Ned gave me both barrels and threatened to bill me for the aviation fuel. I was gutted that I'd let the lads down.

We'd won the league for the second year running as well as a couple of cup competitions. We also played a Manchester City XI in Manchester, which included one or two first-team players. At half-time we were sat there and in walked Bobby Charlton, who was a friend of Ned's and who gave us a half-time team talk.

Carole and I liked Hereford. It was a small market town and we redecorated our quarter.

We even tidied up our garden, which included a patio that I had made with loose chippings I had acquired after several trips to the A49 where the council had a big pile of the chippings.

I was watching the TV. Brazil were playing Italy in the 1986 World Cup finals when there was a knock on the door. Carole went to answer it.

'Phil, there's a policeman at the door he says that you've stolen some chickens.'

'Chickens?' I said dumbfounded. 'I haven't stolen any fucking chickens.'

The policeman came into the lounge.

'What's this about chickens?' I said.

'Nothing,' he said. 'It's about stolen chippings,' he carried on.

I looked at Carole who said: 'Sorry, I thought you said chickens.'

I was still none the wiser until he looked out of the window, which looked onto the back garden and pointed outside.

'Those are what I mean,' he said.

It then clicked: the council chippings that I'd used from the side of the A49. Somebody had seen me shoveling them into the bags and putting them into the boot of my car.

I wasn't charged, but I had to return them to the pile. Not before the policeman had reminded me that during one of my lectures at the police training centre at Ryton near Coventry I had booby-trapped his chair.

Ned knew a few people, I could see that. I'd already met Bobby Charlton and I also met him again, along with Manchester United's chairman Martin Edwards, when they came to our Player of the Year presentation at Stirling Lines. He also knew John Newman, the ex-Exeter, Grimsby and Derby County manager, who was now in charge at Hereford United.

I didn't know it, but Ned had already mentioned my name to John and he was keeping an eye on my performances in the local league. We played Hereford United at the beginning of the season at Edgar Street in a friendly.

I managed to score, but we still lost. John invited me to play for the reserves.

Once again it was great to play at this level, even though it was only for the reserves. I had also recently been recalled to the Army squad. Playing local football was okay, because apart from the odd occasions it didn't interfere with my work commitments. However, if I played for the Army again, it would mean travelling all over the place and I didn't fancy that. Besides, it would definitely interfere with work.

I wasn't at a depot anymore. I was at an active unit and I enjoyed it. I travelled down to Aldershot, where I had been summoned once again against my wishes, to play for the Army.

We won 2–1 against the RAF and I decided that I would seek out Major Dobson, who was still in charge of the Army team.

I explained my predicament, telling him that I just wanted to play for Army Hereford and Hereford United reserves. He was having none of it. It was the same old story. If you don't play for the Army, which after all was a great honour, you can't play for Hereford United reserves.

I drove home that night pissed off, which was unfortunate for a fox just crossing the road as I hit it at 70mph.

The next day I decided I would go and see John Newman at Hereford United to see what the chances were of me being a pro. If he said no chance, which was what I was expecting, then I would have no choice but to carry on playing for the Army side.

I pulled up outside Edgar Street and saw John walking towards the dressing room entrance. 'John,' I shouted as I jumped out of the inconspicuous Transit van with RAOC Bomb Disposal written all over it.

'Hey, I want a word with you,' he said.

I followed him into his office. We both sat down. John spoke first.

'I would like you to go full-time here at Hereford United,' he said.

It didn't register, what did he say?

'What did you say?' I said, wanting him to repeat it.

'I want to offer you a two-year contract as a pro here.'

'Fucking hell, me a pro,' I thought. I had three years left in the Army, but John was offering me a two-year contract to be a pro. However, it would have cost £600 to buy myself out of the Army and there was no way that I had that sort of money.

John offered to pay the £600 and would pay me £180 per week.

'I'll leave it with you,' John said.

I drove straight home to tell Carole. We were both chuffed to bits. It would take at least a month to buy myself out I thought, so I'd better not waste any time.

I went to see my commanding officer straightaway and filled in the forms for my pre-voluntary release (PVR). I then went to find Ned, but he already knew. All the lads were pleased for me, especially Rusty, who had had a similar offer from Southampton years earlier before he'd joined the SAS and who still wondered what might have happened had he gone for it.

'Where are we going to live?' said Carole, pointing out that we'd have to move out of the married quarter. She carried on:

'We'll have to get a mortgage.'

'What's a mortgage?' I said.

After all, when you're in the Army everything is provided for you and, to a certain extent, you are wrapped in cotton wool.

We were soon house hunting and the date was coming closer. I delivered a cheque for £600 to the paymaster at Stirling Lines, courtesy of Hereford United.

We managed to find a new house. It was going to be on the new Bobblestock Estate, but it wouldn't be ready until about six weeks after we had to move out of the quarter. We asked the Army if we could stay in the quarter, but they refused. We pleaded with them, just for six weeks, but they were having none of it.

Fortunately, one of Carole's friends put us up for a few weeks before we got a holiday cottage until the house was ready. It was rather sad handing all my kit back in. We put our furniture into storage. I had had some good times as well as some bad, but on the whole I'd enjoyed it.

Carole was pleased. She had hated Army life because of the insecurity of never knowing where I might be heading. Little did she know of the financial insecurities associated with playing professional football in the 1980s. I signed my first-ever pro contract at the beginning of November 1986. We had moved in with Carole's friend on the Saturday and I reported for training on Monday.

Chapter Eleven

I arrived at the ground at about 9.30am and walked into the dressing room.

It was my first day as a professional footballer. The dressing room was empty. I walked back out and onto the pitch, half expecting John Newman, and perhaps a photographer or even a TV crew, to greet Hereford's new signing. There was nobody. The place was deserted. I knew that I had arrived early, but the place was like a ghost town.

I looked around at the empty terraces. Where was everybody? I then made my way to the boot room and heard a noise. I knew the sound well. It was a brush bashing up and down on a boot. This time it was a soccer boot and not an Army-issue DMS boot.

I popped my head in and saw a young apprentice called Danny Corner.

'Morning Dan, where is everybody?' I said.

'They are all down in London,' he replied.

Hereford had been drawn against Fulham in the FA Cup and had drawn 3–3 at home. The replay was tomorrow night at Craven Cottage and the players had gone down early on Monday morning.

John Newman had obviously forgotten to tell me. Danny found me some training kit. A red sweatshirt, black shorts and some red-and-white hooped socks. I looked like Ronald McDonald with my now-longer hair.

It was all a bit of an anti-climax as I ran around the pitch a few times before showering and making my way back to the house where we were staying.

I did the same the following day and on Wednesday. Hereford lost 4–0 in the replay and it was Thursday before I would meet up with the squad for training.

Hereford was a smashing little club. The year before, they had just missed out on promotion to the old Third Division. This year they were struggling and were in the bottom half of the table, which was very significant as, for the first time in history, the bottom club would be relegated to the Vauxhall Conference. No more re-elections by clubs being looked after by their mates on Football League committees. Also long gone were the days when Hereford United were feared FA Cup underdogs.

Everybody remembers their finest hour: beating Newcastle United, Malcolm Macdonald et al, 2–1 after extra-time and a replay, with that fantastic Ronnie Radford goal which he celebrated with a guy wearing a Parka jacket. Everybody remembers that goal. Now it was different at Edgar Street. Crowds were down to 2,000 and everybody was shit scared about finishing bottom.

Fucking hell. I'd just got out of the Army. What would happen if we finished bottom? What would I do then?

The following Tuesday the reserves played at Bristol City and lost 2–1. I scored and, in doing so, I became the reserves' leading scorer, having played a few games before I'd got out of the Army.

The next day in training, the first-team squad were preparing for that night's Welsh Cup-tie at home to Wrexham. John invited me to train with them. After they had finished the set pieces, John gave his speech about how he wanted to beat Wrexham, who were managed by ex-Hereford player Dixie McNeil.

'And you,' he pointed at me, 'will be sub tonight. You've earned it after your performance last night,' he continued.

Crikey, I was in the first team already, only a sub I know, but I was still chuffed to bits. I told Carole when I got home.

I persuaded her not to go to the game because I didn't think that I'd get on. Jim Steele had scored early on and, with five minutes to go, John put me on. It didn't make any difference. We still lost the game, but at least I'd had a taste of first-team action.

There were a lot of experienced players at Hereford, including Jim Harvey, John Delve, who was ex-QPR, Ollie Kearns ex-Reading, who was injured at that moment after an incident in the Cup replay at Fulham. Stewart Phillips was the main striker along with Ollie, whose dad, Archie, was a director on the board.

Ian Wells and I were the other strikers who were there to put pressure on Ollie when fit and Stewart.

We didn't have a training ground, but any piece of parkland would do. Sometimes we would train round the corner on the pitch where, the last time I played on it, I had nearly been billed for aviation fuel.

We didn't have a game on the Saturday because we'd been knocked out of the FA Cup, but the following Wednesday we were due to play Newport County, who were still in the Third Division, in the Freight Rover Trophy – a competition for lower league clubs, which gave them a chance to play in a final at Wembley. It's had so many names since, including the LDV Vans Trophy.

Ollie was injured which meant that Wellsy would partner

Stewart up front. In the days of naming only one sub, surely that meant a place on the bench.

On Monday in training Stewart pulled his hamstring and John announced that I would make my full debut in the tie.

All the same thoughts returned. Would I make a fool of myself? Would I last the pace? After all, I'd only been training full time for a couple of weeks.

When I was at Reading a few years earlier, I was a very fit nineteen-year-old, now I was a pro at twenty-four, which was late to come in...

I arranged tickets for Carole. Some of the Army lads were coming down. One of them, Kev Williamson, gave me some serious pre-match advice.

'Have a Mars bar and a wank, it's always worked for me. That'll sort you out.'

I didn't take up his advice, but I did try to get some sleep on the afternoon of the game, but I was so nervous and the kids downstairs were making a lot of noise.

I turned up at the ground. Fans were milling around again. The floodlights were already on. John gave his usual good luck speech and we got changed.

I looked at the match programme and in it was an action shot of me from the previous week's game against Wrexham.

I looked at the Newport team. No. 1 Mark Kendall. Fucking hell is he still there? The same Mark Kendall who I had scored against on my league debut for Reading? Here we go again. The buzzer went in the dressing room. All the backslaps and handshakes and good lucks from everybody didn't stop me from feeling nervous.

Once the game started, however, any nerves disappeared. I found that I had gone back to my non-league habits, like sliding in all the time. Peter Issacs, our physio, kept shouting at me to 'stay on your feet'.

The first half ended 0–0 and was very scrappy. My only thoughts were: 'Please don't sub me, John.' He didn't and the second half was better.

An hour had gone. It was still 0–0. Then I was put through. As I chased the ball, I could see Mark Kendall running out and I knew that he would get to the ball just before me. We both challenged for the ball, we were thirty-five yards out with Mark well outside his area. The ball broke loose and I got up first, I saw the ball and just thought about hitting it as hard as I could towards the direction of the goal before the oncoming defender got to it.

I swung my right boot and lofted it as hard and as high as I could. I saw another defender running back trying to cover the empty goal. It was like slow motion.

'Fucking hell,' I thought. 'It's going in.'

The ball dropped just under the bar and rippled the net. I went mad, waving my arms to the crowd, all 1,700 of them. Once again I'd beaten Mark Kendall.

I was ecstatic. Two minutes later, my good friend, right-back Ian Rodgerson, beat a defender, took the ball to the byline, pulled it back and I rammed it home from six yards. 2–0. Thinking that things couldn't get any better, with five minutes to go, Ian Wells slipped me in for a one on one with Kendall. I ran with the ball, this time Kendall stayed on the edge of his box.

By now I was absolutely knackered and didn't have the energy to take it round him, so I decided to shoot when I was a couple of yards in front of him. It wouldn't matter if I missed, after all I'd scored two. I got my head down and just swung my right boot, it beat Kendall and whistled into the top right-hand corner of the net. A hat-trick on my debut for Hereford.

The crowd was cheering, but I was breathing out of my arse. I had no energy to celebrate and I just sunk to my knees. All the lads were jumping on me; I couldn't move, my legs had gone. My brain wanted a rest.

'How long left ref?' I said.

'Two minutes,' he said.

I got up and thought: 'I'll just walk for two minutes.'

There was a big cheer when it was announced that I had been named Man of the Match, which would include a trophy, a video of the game and a meal for two at a local restaurant.

One last attack, Ian, or 'Dodge' as we called him, put me in again. This time it was a tight angle, but I just shot across the goal aiming for the far corner: it hit a defender and went in: 4–0.

I tried to claim this goal as well, but it was given as an own goal. The final whistle went, we applauded the crowd and I wearily made my way off to the cheers. Everybody was shaking my hand. After a shower, I made my way to the players' bar. En route I saw the club secretary, Joan Fenessesy, who was talking to Archie Phillips, Stewart's dad.

'Well done,' she said.

'Thanks Joan,' I said.

Archie looked at me, pulled his cigar out of his mouth and said:

'It's okay scoring a hat-trick on your debut, but the test will come if you can do it week in week out.'

I was pissed off with him for saying that.

'Is it because I'd taken Stewart's place in the team?' I thought to myself. But Archie was right. I would have to do it week in week out.

I made my way into the players' bar, which was upstairs in the Starlight Rooms at the HUFC Supporters' Club. Everybody wanted to buy me a drink. Ned was there with some of the other Army lads sat with Carole. I was very tired and after a few celebratory beers we made our way back to Sue's, Carole's friend who was putting us up.

The next day we had a day off, so I decided to take Carole out for lunch with the vouchers that I'd been given as Man of the Match.

We made our way to the restaurant and ordered our meal. We were sat there talking about the game when the waitress came out of the kitchen with two meals on a tray.

I looked at Carole and said: 'Our meals are here'.

We both looked towards the waitress who shouted out: 'Two complimentaries.'

We slid down in our seats and gave a little wave to the waitress. She brought the meals over, but I could feel everybody's eyes on us. We quickly ate our meals and left.

On the Saturday we were due to play Cambridge United at home in the league. I didn't think that John would have thought about leaving me out after the other night's game, so I was penciled in to make another league debut at home.

Bruce Haliday put us one up before John Beck, later to become one of my managers, equalised from twenty-five yards.

In the second half, I put us 2–1 in front after rounding keeper Keith Branagan from a Wellsy through ball and sliding it into an empty net. It wasn't enough, we lost 3–2 and in the bar afterwards we all nervously looked at the league. We were getting sucked into the relegation zone.

Stockport were at the bottom and were well adrift, but they had recently appointed a new manager, Colin Murphy, so things were far from certain. Personally things were going okay. I'd scored four goals in two games and I had managed to rent a cottage outside Hereford on a short-term lease until our house in Bobblestock was ready.

The only reason that I got it on a short-term lease was because it was a summer cottage. There was no heating at all and now, in December, it was freezing.

The kids had to sleep with their coats on. There was a small open fire, which we could light, but we would need some coal or logs. There was no way it would warm the house up, though. We managed to borrow a couple of portable gas heaters, one of which we positioned at the top of the stairs in the hope that it would transmit some warmth into the bedrooms.

It made no difference whatsoever. It was still freezing and when we all woke up in the morning, you could not see out of the windows because of the ice that had formed from our breath during the night.

One day I suggested that we try to light a fire in the small open hearth. The trouble was we had no fuel to burn.

'Fuck this,' I thought and picked up an axe that I'd seen in the small garage.

I climbed into our old battered silver Datsun Sunny hatchback – which I'd purchased second hand in Germany from a squaddie called Winker Watson, courtesy of a bank loan, which I still hadn't paid off two years down the line – and drove off. I soon found a small wooded area and started hacking some small trees.

It took ages to cut some of them into logs so I thought 'fuck it' and chopped down nine or ten branches, put the seats down in the back of the car and loaded the car with tree branches. I drove home slowly, as the branches were hanging out of the back of the car and I couldn't shut the boot.

When I got back I put them in the garage and started chopping like a mad axeman. At least we now had a bit of fuel. Every day after training I would pop into the woods and chop down some more.

After the Cambridge game we were due to play at Halifax Town on the Friday night. A photographer had been sent by the *Sunday People* to take some shots of me for a piece in that week's paper.

During my warm-up he had me standing and pointing in the centre circle. It was so embarrassing.

'I thought you wanted some action shots,' I said.

'I'm getting some now,' he said. 'Besides, I've got to get home.'

'Cheers mate,' I said, freezing as I looked round at the desolate Shay ground with a few spectators making their way in.

It was open-ended behind each goal and the wind was whistling through. We lost 2–1 to a struggling Halifax side. In years to come, The Shay would become a happy hunting ground for me.

'Stant blows 'em up,' was the caption in the *Sunday People*.

Stewart and Ollie were now fully fit and I was to spend the next couple of months in the reserves.

I'd made my mark and I knew that I'd be ready when the chance came again. After all, I was still learning my trade, even at twenty-four years of age.

Off the pitch we would soon be moving into our new house: a two-up, two-down terrace. At least it would be our own, even though I wondered how we would find the money for our 100 per cent mortgage.

Carole's mum provided us with a carpet for the lounge, which she had in her garage at home, and we managed to buy a fridge advertised in the *Hereford Times* for £20.

Carole made some wardrobes for the kids' bedroom. They slept in bunk beds and had to share their room with the tumble dryer as there was no room anywhere else.

Dodge and his mum and dad, Mary and Alan, who were to become good friends, lived round the corner, as did another United player, Mike Carter.

Another of my friends, SAS man Kev Williamson, also moved onto the estate, so we had plenty of friends nearby.

Christmas 1986 and John Newman had arranged a Christmas bash for the players and their wives at our chairman's bar and restaurant in the centre of Hereford called Saxtys.

Peter Hill, the chairman, was also a well-known estate agent. We had the meal upstairs and we were having a great time. The beer and wine was flowing and everybody was enjoying themselves. The only problem was that every time somebody went downstairs to the toilet or to the bar a guy there would start to give us some stick. He was going on about how shit we were and that sort of thing, but we just ignored him.

Later on that night, as the bar was closing and John had left along with most of the other wives and players, a few of us stragglers went downstairs to the bar, as we had the following day off the next day.

Ian Dalziel, our left-back, got the drinks in and we all hung around the area. Steve Spooner and Dodge were in conversation.

The guy walked up to Daz and carried on about how shit we were. Daz said: 'Leave it alone, we're on a night out.'

The guy wouldn't stop and I was pissed off with him. I just walked up and smacked him right on the nose. I heard the girls' screams as his nose exploded and he fell over the tables.

Daz turned to me: 'What the fuck did you do that for?'

I looked at the guy being consoled by the manager of our chairman's bar.

'Don't talk, just hit him for abusing us,' I said to Daz.

'You're not in the Army now, you're a pro,' said Daz.

I knew he was right, but it didn't stop Daz and I from squaring up to each other.

The restaurant manager quickly got us out before the police came. We heard afterwards that he had told the police that it was the guy's fault and I never heard another thing.

Carole was furious with me. I knew I was in the wrong. Lesson No. 1: don't hit your own fans.

In the morning, Carole pointed out that if John Newman found out I would be in serious trouble and that could mean a fine. She was right. It would be better if I went to see him straightaway and explain before somebody beat me to it, even though I was nursing both a hangover and a sore wrist.

By now I was also feeling guilty. Daz was right: I'd let myself down. I knocked on John's door.

'Come in,' he shouted.

'Fucking hell, don't shout gaffer,' I thought.

'How ya doin' kid?' was John's usual greeting.

I began to tell him the story. I felt good, I was getting it off my chest. I went through the whole story and then finished it with 'and then I thumped him one'. I sat there wondering how much of a fine I would get or, even worse, a suspension from the club, as John sat there with hands on chin staring at the ceiling.

'Do you mean that big lad who'd been abusing us all night?' he said.

'Yeah,' I said sheepishly.

'Fucking good job, because I'd nearly hit him earlier,' he said.

What! I couldn't believe my ears. I was getting away with it, even my manager was supporting me.

'Now get out and don't be late for training in the morning. Oh and how's the kids?' he finished off.

'Fine thanks gaffer,' I said as I made my way out and home.

Now I felt a lot better. I also knew that John was pleased because I'd told him first and he hadn't heard it from someone else.

He was a players' manager and, rightly or wrongly, he would support you. In private, though, he would give you both barrels.

In March, Stewart was injured again and I got another chance. It was against Torquay United at home. We drew 2–2 and even though I didn't score I thought I'd done enough to keep my place. Stewart was fit the following Friday as we prepared for our visit to Burnley at Turf Moor. Burnley was a big club, but at that time they were struggling for their lives. How they ended up at the foot of the Fourth Division was anybody's guess.

Colin Murphy had performed miracles at Stockport and, after being so far adrift, they were now off the bottom of the league table. They had beaten us a couple of weeks earlier at Edgar Street where I had been an unused sub.

Colin walked past our dugout at the restart and said to the gaffer:

'Hi John. How are you?'

'Not bad Colin, thanks,' replied the gaffer and with that turned to me and said: 'I hate that twat.' I was in stitches in the back of the dugout.

The gaffer named the team for Burnley and I was not included. For the first time in my short football career I thought I was hard done by. John wouldn't name the subs until the day, so I didn't even know if I was on the bench.

After training I knocked on his door and explained that I thought it was shit that he was leaving me out after my performance the week before against Torquay and that it was out of order. John made his excuses about how he was the manager and that it was he who picked the side and that nobody, not even me, should argue the fact. On that note I walked out, slamming his door behind me as I went.

I thought I was right. After all, I felt, as a pro, if you are left out of the team you have a right to ask the manager why. The papers would have you believe that players do it all the time.

I went home in a sulk and told Carole the story.

'Get back and apologise,' she said.

'What?' I said.

'Get back down there now,' she said.

She was right; I'd made a big mistake: who the fuck was I, a novice, telling an experienced manager how to pick his team.

I drove straight back to the ground. I knocked on his door again.

'Come in,' he said.

I explained how sorry I was and how I was out of order. John looked at me:

'Fuck off,' he said.

With that I knew that the conversation was over and that the chances of me making the bench were now minimal. I was right. I sat in the Bob Lord stand watching the game thinking how stupid I had been. To make matters worse, we won 6–0, with

Ollie grabbing a fantastic hat-trick and Stewart also getting on the score sheet.

Lesson No. 2: don't question the judgment of your manager, especially if he's on your side.

We saw the season out safely after some good home wins. Burnley survived on the last day, as did Torquay, who were playing at home. Their game had to be delayed after a police dog bit a defender, Jim McNichol, and a goal in injury time kept them up.

The unfortunate victims of the first-ever relegation into non-league were Lincoln City, who for months had held a comfortable, mid-table position, but who had gone into freefall in the latter part of the season.

In the last week of training we went up to Haulgh Woods, outside Hereford, where we would do our midweek cross-country running. This particular session was being taken by our physio, Pete Issacs. I was at the back struggling when Pete shouted at me.

'Trouble with you Stanty is that you're not fit.'

'What me, not fit, I'm fucking knackered,' I shouted back. I carried on at him because there's nothing worse than when someone's having a go at you when you're knackered. But what he was about to say rang true in my head.

'It's alright for you, you old twat, you don't have to do this,' I shouted at him as I went past.

'No I can't, but I wish I could,' he replied.

Those words registered. He was right. I bet he wished that he could swap places. After all, his favourite phrase was 'life's not a rehearsal'. I swore to myself that I wouldn't have a summer off and that I would train every day to get myself as fit as I could.

The season had finished. After the last day, we all went to a pub in town and commiserated with Chris Leadbitter, the Hereford player who had been released from his contract. Talking to him really brought home how much I had given up to play professional football. I had given up the only career I knew and all of the financial security that my wife and children deserved for the simple thrill of scoring goals. I sat there thinking about the following year and what it would be like if I had been in Chris's position. I didn't even want to think about it. I'd only played a bit-part in our survival that year, but I was determined to try harder. I was determined that by the time we played Coventry City in a pre-season testimonial game for our captain Mel Pejic, I was going to play a part.

The next day and every day until the start of pre-season, I would run six miles wearing a black bin liner underneath my T-shirt. I also needed a job to earn some extra money, so I got one taxi driving and also took on some truck-driving work for a local firm throughout the summer: regardless, I still fitted in my running at whatever time of day I finished. I used my HGV1 licence, which I had acquired while I was a squaddie in Germany, and it came in handy for delivering steel for a local company to South Wales.

It was okay but I hated roping and sheeting the steel, especially when it was windy or raining, but I worked hard all summer with driving and my fitness training. The pounds dropped off and by the time pre-season came round I was flying.

John had brought in a couple of signings, but the real coup came when he brought in Ian Bowyer, who had been released by Nottingham Forest, as player-coach.

This time I felt fitter and stronger and was determined that when my chance came I would take it. I played in some of the pre-season games including the fixture against Coventry, but I still didn't make the squad for the first three games.

We had made a bad start to the season and we were bottom of the league with just a point.

On the fourth game, we were playing Colchester United at

home and we were desperate for the three points. John started me up front with Stewart. It was 0–0 with three minutes to go and a draw was on the cards, but Steve Spooner miscued a shot from the edge of the box and I dived forward and directed the ball past the keeper to win us the game and three valuable points.

The next game I was on the bench against Wolves, who had been in freefall and had found themselves in the Fourth Division, which, like Burnley, was criminal for a club of that stature.

But Wolves were rebuilding under Graham Turner and had a lethal strike partnership in Steve Bull and Andy Mutch. Halfway through the first half, Bully hit a volley from all of forty-five yards and it flew over keeper Kevin Rose and into the net. It was a fantastic goal and he got another before half-time.

'Stanty get ready,' said John. I had about twenty minutes left.

I came on and promptly got on the end of a Steve Spooner cross and scored with a header past, yes you've guessed it, Mark Kendall, who had recently been signed by Wolves. We huffed and we puffed, but couldn't equalise: I still thought that I'd done enough again to stay in the side.

In the bar afterwards, I felt a hand on my shoulder; it was Mark Kendall.

'I'm fucking sick of you,' he joked. 'You always score against me.'

'Well you shouldn't be such a shit keeper,' I replied having a laugh.

I wasn't laughing soon after, because once again I was back on the bench and playing no part. We had been drawn against Cloughie's Nottingham Forest in the League Cup with the first leg to be played at the City Ground.

Forest had a good side with Lee Chapman leading the line, a young Des Walker and Franz Carr wide on the right. They also had a good left-back called Stuart Pearce.

We got battered 5–0 and I didn't get on, but I still enjoyed the experience of going to a club like that, as well as travelling on the first-team coach. After Army life when I was one on a base of thousands, it was nice to feel a little bit more like an individual.

Ian 'Bomber' Bowyer, as he was known, got a fantastic reception from the home fans and I sat in the dugout wondering how he must have felt going back to a club where he had been a legend and team captain.

The pressure was growing on our manager John Newman. We were struggling in the league and the crowd was starting to get restless. In our home game against Peterborough, I was once again on the bench and was just walking towards the players' entrance after signing some autographs when I heard:

'Ey, what the fookes up wi' thee?'

I recognised the voice immediately. It was my dad with his head hanging out of the passenger side window of his articulated lorry wearing the same flat cap and a Captain full strength between his lips.

He parked his lorry up and I took him into the supporters' club where the club steward John Powell promised to look after him.

I was chuffed to bits. I couldn't recall the last time that my dad had actually seen me play any football, let alone professionally.

We were losing 1–0, the crowd was on John's back. I felt sorry for him as he had to endure all the chants in addition to one or two 'Newman out' banners. He put me on shortly into the second half. I worked my socks off, not just to get an equaliser, but to try to impress my dad. It made no difference. We lost 1–0. Again I made my way to the bar. Carole was sat with my dad:

'What did you think then?' I asked dad.

'Fucking crap first half,' he said.

'Yeah, maybe, but what about the second half when I came on?' I said.

'Oh, I'd had enough by half-time. I came into the bar and had a pint,' he said.

Even Dad had recognised that it was a poor game, but I was a bit pissed off that he'd rather have a pint than watch me. Cheers.

He came back to our house after I'd managed to persuade him that our settee would be more comfortable than sleeping in his cab. I also told him that I would drop him off in the morning at 5am so that he could be on his way.

'But I've got a TV and a kettle in my cab,' he protested.

'Get in the fucking car,' I said.

I woke him up 5am as I'd promised. As I shook him, I noticed he went to sleep with his flat cap on.

'You're going to need a fucking transplant to remove that cap,' I said.

I dropped him off and watched him drive away, wondering when the next time I would see him might be.

After another defeat away at Halifax, John's time was up. Bomber had a team meeting and informed us that John had been sacked and that he was to take over. I immediately felt sorry for John. He had bought me out of the Army and had given me the chance to play professional football. He had been like a father figure, not just to me but to all the other players, their wives and their families. I had the utmost respect for him and I immediately wrote him a letter thanking him for what he'd done for me.

The other dilemma was that my contract only took me to the end of the season. Bomber might not want me and where would that leave us? John had already indicated that there was another contract ready for me in May, but he was gone now. Perhaps I would end up working at the local chicken factory.

The next day I turned up at the ground wearing a travelling tracksuit to catch the coach with the reserves to Bournemouth. As I parked the car, I noticed that Ollie Kearns was sitting on the coach. I didn't think that Ollie had been selected for the reserves. As I locked my car, Bomber came out and informed me to go home and prepare myself for tomorrow night's second leg against Forest, as I would be starting.

This was my chance to impress the new manager. Once again I had the feeling that I wasn't good enough to play against these guys. I also felt sorry for Ollie, as he'd been dragged in to join the reserves for the trip to Bournemouth. But then I thought, would he feel sorry for me if I'd taken his place?

Nevertheless, I was keen to impress and once again I worked hard. We'd already lost the first leg 5–0 and had absolutely no chance of pulling it back. We all knew that, but the game presented other opportunities, such as playing against internationals and impressing our new manager.

It was still 0–0 halfway through the second half. Kev Rose kicked it long, Stewart Phillips flicked it on and I knocked it past Des Walker, went past Steve Sutton in the goal and hammered it in from a tight angle.

I went to celebrate. I ran past Stuart Pearce who was mouthing 'For fucks sake'. I couldn't believe it. I had scored against a side like Nottingham Forest. It was all going so well, but then Nigel Clough scored from a header in the last minute and the game finished 1–1.

I had made my mark once again. I couldn't believe it: I was in the team for the next league game at Cardiff, which we won 1–0, thanks to a goal from Steve Spooner.

The following week I was in the team yet again, but we lost at home to Scunthorpe. I remember the game well, because I ended up with five stitches in the back of my head following a collision with a defender.

Every week I seemed to be on the team sheet. I really started to look after myself by having early nights and sticking to a healthy diet. I still liked to have the odd drink, but I was no stranger to discipline and there was no way that I was going to ruin my chances by drinking every night. I had even packed in the taxi driving and lorry driving. The biggest thing was that the goals were also going in. I'd scored against Stockport in a 2–0 away win as well as against Exeter in a 1–1 draw.

We'd knocked out Barry Fry's Barnet in the FA Cup, 1–0 away, thanks to my second-half goal and I scored my first brace since my debut in a 4–2 home win against Hartlepool.

I was still embarrassed by my tattoos. This was long before the likes of David Beckham and Freddie Ljunberg and their elaborate tattoos. I'd had a few since my Army days and one or two on my forearm when I'd experimented with Indian ink in my maths lesson at Sharples High School. I'd always worn a long-sleeve shirt when playing pro football, so Carole and I went to Boots in Hereford to look for some make-up that would cover up my tattoos if I had to wear a short-sleeved shirt, which was sometimes the case when we played away, as the away strip only had short sleeves.

We explained to the shop assistant what I was after and I tried various colours on my arms. After picking up one of them, I made sure that I always placed it in Pete Issacs' physio bag so I knew where it was.

Before each game I would disappear and apply this women's make-up to my arms. After a while Ian Dalziel said to me:

'Why do you do that?'

'Because I'm embarrassed about my tattoos, professional footballers don't have tattoos,' I replied.

Daz pointed out that a lot of players have tattoos and that it would be more beneficial if the defenders saw the tattoos because they might think that I was some kind of nutcase and that I'd be ready for battle. I thought it was a good idea and I quickly forgot about the make-up.

'Fuck them, let them see all my tattoos,' I thought.

Carole had also cut my hair and by mistake had taken a big

lump out of the back of my head when she had been practicing with the clippers. There was only one thing for it. Skinhead. The next game, at Orient away, we got stuffed 3–0 and I suddenly became the target of abuse, with my skinhead and my tattoos. It was a reputation I liked: the ex-Army boy with a skinhead and tattoos. I don't take any prisoners.

The only problem was that I was starting to attract the attention of the referees and would sometimes get booked for trivial things, simply because of this new reputation.

One fixture that I couldn't wait for, as a now-regular first-team member, was Bolton Wanderers away. Bolton, like Wolves and Burnley, had also fallen on hard times and had found themselves in the basement division. We had lost at home to them in early September and I was determined that this time it would be different. I would be going up there as a first-team regular and as Hereford United's top goalscorer. I couldn't wait. I knew all of my family and Carole's family – who were Bolton fans – would be going. Even my mum and sister Shirley would be there. Bomber helped me to arrange tickets for everybody.

As I came out for the warm-up, I stepped up on the bank and onto the pitch. I remember looking around the ground. This was my ultimate dream. If only I could have been playing for the Wanderers. I remembered all the games I'd seen here, all of my heroes who had worn the white shirt. I looked towards the embankment end where I'd stood years and years ago as a kid with my dad and noticed that half of it was gone due to the building of a supermarket. I then realised that I'd only been on this hallowed turf – graced by legends such as Nat Lofthouse, Frank Worthington and Peter Reid to name but a few – twice: once when I scored my goal with the paper cup and the other time when I had been chased across it at half-time by some Wolves fans in 1978. We lost 1–0 and Bolton went on to gain promotion via the play-offs with Phil Neal in charge.

Afterwards in the players' bar I saw Carole and her family as well as Mum and Shirley. Shirley quickly came over to me and said:

'Sort him out will you,' pointing to my dad.

I didn't know that he was coming and how he had got into the players' bar I'll never know.

I suddenly realised that I had a major situation on my hands. Mum and Dad hadn't seen each other for eighteen years. Dad was pissed. My mum was in one corner and he was in the other.

It was embarrassing as I picked up Dad in front of lots of other families and guests and took him down the tunnel. Suddenly Phil Neal walked past us. Dad looked up.

'What you fucking looking at Neal?' he shouted as Phil just carried on walking past us.

It was definitely a serious situation. He'd lost his flat cap and was cursing anyone in sight. I got him to go home with his mate Geoff with the help of a taxi and then had to go back in and speak to my mum who was upset because he'd ruined her day. He'd ruined *her* day!

By April, we were safe in the league, mainly thanks to Newport County who were destined for relegation – shortly after that they folded because of mounting debt problems. I was sorry about that because I always seemed to score against Newport.

At the end of the month, I, along with others, had not been offered terms for the following season and I feared the worst.

I thought: 'Fuck it, I'll ring other clubs and see how the land lies.'

For the first time I started to feel like a professional footballer. I looked like a pro and I also felt part of this exclusive club – it was a sensation that I'd never had before. I was at home in the dressing room now. Not as an outsider, but as someone who belonged there.

I rang Dario Gradi, the Crewe manager, and explained my situation, that I was out of contract and asked whether he would be interested.

'I'd always be interested in someone like you who chases lost causes,' was his reply.

His team was also in the lower reaches of the Fourth Division, but they always played good football and, in David Platt, they had a player who scored goals for fun. I was pleased with his answer and felt a little relieved in the knowledge that if I didn't get a contract at Hereford, I might get one somewhere else.

One week to go before the end of the season and we were travelling to Orient away. I was on my way to the front of the coach to change the radio station when Bomber grabbed me and said:

'Oh, and by the way, I'll be offering you a new contract.'

'Cheers,' I said as I made my way back to my seat at the rear of the coach. I sat down relieved. It was a huge weight off my mind.

Tuesday night saw our last home game, against Burnley. Before the kick-off, I was presented with the Player of the Year trophy.

Our last game of the season was a nightmare journey to Hartlepool, where we won 2–1 with yours truly on the score sheet: the goals confirmed me as the club's top scorer. By the end of the season, I was really pleased with my achievements.

I signed a new one-year contract and could now enjoy the summer with my £10-a-week rise.

I was grateful for the one year, even though I had asked for two, but I knew after signing my contract that I would have to work harder and that that included doing all the running again during the summer.

Chapter Twelve

Once again I ran every day during the summer. By the time pre-season came around, I was raring to go. We had one or two interesting fixtures in pre-season, including a game against Norwich City, who were managed by Mel Machin, at home.

It was our first home pre-season match and it was one of those days when everything went right. My touch and passing seemed to be spot on. In the second half, I chased for a ball with defender Andy Linnighan. I reached it first before cutting inside and firing a left-footed shot past keeper Bryan Gunn and into the net. We won 1–0.

I played quite well during pre-season and it was brought to my attention that Norwich were now monitoring my progress. Crikey, other clubs were now watching me!

Another thing I wanted to be part of was to be the division's top scorer. I'd established myself in the first team and now I wanted to finish as I high as I could in the goalscoring charts.

I really thought that this could be the season when I could make my mark in pro football. I knew that I'd had a good pre-season and I couldn't wait for the season proper to start.

Our first game was at Scunthorpe United away, which was a special occasion as it was the first league game to be played at the new Glanford Park. I'd heard rumours that Norwich were still watching me. During the warm-up I was just jogging along on my own. It was a typical opening-day fixture, with the sun shining. Bomber had picked himself today and, as I stretched off, he came up to give me some instructions. Before he ran off to carry on with his own warm-up he said:

'If you have a good game today, I'll offer you another contract.'

I just stood there as he ran off. Twenty minutes before the kick-off and he'd just dropped a hint that he was about to offer me another contract when I'd just signed a new one five or six weeks ago. I'd asked for two years in the summer, but had only got one. Why would he do that now? However, I also knew that I'd get a bit more money.

I walked off the pitch to get myself ready, with my head spinning. My first thoughts were what a nice guy to do that for me: it wouldn't take me long to work out why.

We lost the opener 3–1, but our first home game against Cambridge went well with me getting my first goal of the season in a 4–2 win.

On the Tuesday, we played Second Division Plymouth, who were now managed by Ken Brown, in the League Cup. We were eventually knocked out over the two legs, but at least we gave a good performance away from home.

In the meantime, I was negotiating this new contract. For some reason, Bomber now wanted me to sign a two-year contract, which I would have done earlier in the summer. Hereford wanted to extend the deal, which would give me an extra tenner a week. The money wasn't an issue; it was the offer of another year's security which was the attraction.

I asked for a signing-on fee of a couple of thousand pounds hoping that I could pay off some debts. But no chance: I signed the contract, but there was no announcement in the local paper that I'd extended it.

Shortly after, rumours were going round that Plymouth, as well as Norwich, were now watching most of our games. Things were starting to add up. It was naivety on my part that I didn't realise that I was now a club asset as a result of my performances and also the fact that I was still learning about pro football both on and off the field.

But then again at least I had two years' security to fall back on. At least I wouldn't be working at the chicken factory just yet.

Our last game in September was away at Lincoln City and, by this time, I was now top of the goalscoring charts of the Fourth Division. I used to love picking up the tabloids to look at the list and seeing my name on top.

Lincoln had recovered from their relegation from the Fourth Division, had won the Conference and had regained their league status after one year's absence thanks to Colin Murphy, who had taken over after they had gone down.

Shortly into the second half, we were 2–0 down when one of their defenders caught me from behind. Referee Graham Pooley waved play on, but as we both got up we ended up in a tangle, with the defender falling on the floor as though I'd pole-axed him. I'd made no contact with him, but the crowd was going mad and had influenced the ref before he brandished my first pro red card. I was gutted. I slowly made my way off. The ref had been conned and so had I.

'If I had really touched him, he wouldn't be fucking getting up,' I barked at Pooley.

Sure enough, by the time I was halfway across the pitch, the defender was up again and jogging about with a smile on his face.

The red mist was building and I was struggling to keep calm. A supporter got out of his seat as I neared the changing rooms. He was shouting obscenities at me. I just stopped and stared at him and for one second I thought about going towards him and punching his fucking lights out.

Is this the way it was, to cheat and then to take the piss out of me? A steward must have been reading my mind and he quickly ushered me to the away dressing room, where I could unleash my fury by kicking the fuck out of the dressing-room door and pretending that it was that supporter's head.

The lads came in after the final whistle. It had finished 2–0. There was silence. Bomber looked at me and I pleaded my innocence. I had calmed down now and was glad that I'd taken it out on the door rather than on the supporter.

I didn't go into the bar afterwards because I knew that I would have tried to have got my own back on the defender and that it would be the wrong time. I made sure that he knew that I would be waiting for him when they came to our place, but I would have to wait until February. I scored more goals before the start of my three-match ban.

I was now on eleven goals in eleven games and I wondered how my three-match ban would affect my position as the league's top scorer. Bobby Williamson of Rotherham was scoring freely and was now catching me up. I missed the games at Carlisle, Stockport and Peterborough.

Gary Stevens had taken my place up front and had scored two goals in three games. I started to wonder if I would get my place back.

My return came against Rochdale at home on Tuesday night. Gary Stevens had been left on the bench. I felt sorry for him, as he'd done well in my absence.

After Bomber had put me straight back in the side, the pressure was now on me to perform. I duly obliged, netting my first-ever league hat-trick in a remarkable 4–4 draw.

At the beginning of December, I was still top of the goal-scoring charts with fourteen goals. The rumours started again. I knew that a lot of top-flight clubs had been to Edgar Street in the previous few weeks. Speculation was rife. It was rumoured that a club had offered £100,000 for my services: big money for the Fourth Division and big money for Hereford United. I wondered who it was and if the rumours were true.

The week after losing 4–1 at York, Bomber called me. We didn't have a game the following Saturday as we'd been knocked out of the FA Cup by Cardiff.

'We've had a bid for you,' he said.

'Who from?' I asked.

'Scarborough.'

'Fucking Scarborough,' I said. I was taken by surprise; I was expecting a team like Norwich or Plymouth.

Neil Warnock was the manager of Scarborough and they had won league status at the expense of Lincoln the season before last.

'He wants you to go up and talk to them,' Bomber went on.

So I made my way home to break the news to Carole.

At the time Scarborough were second in the league and looked a good bet for promotion. We, on the other hand, were stuck in mid-table obscurity as usual. I must have made an impression on Neil Warnock a couple of months earlier when I scored in a 3–1 defeat!

I set off the next morning and arrived at Scarborough's McCain Stadium. It was a typical non-league set-up with only one little stand. I had my reservations.

At least we would be living by the sea which would be nice for the kids I thought as I looked at the ground and noticed a new patch on the stand roof where a Wolves fan had fallen through it the previous season.

I found Neil's office and he made me feel welcome from the moment we met. I quickly decided that he was the sort of guy that I could work with. We discussed his ambitions and how I was the last piece of his jigsaw. I was really impressed.

That afternoon I was to meet the chairman, Geoffrey Richmond, to discuss terms. Neil also wanted me to stay and watch a first-team game against Darlington that night and to stay over. I spoke to Carole on the phone and suggested that she came up with the kids for a look round.

'Oh, the chairman will send his Rolls for her. I'll arrange it so that she gets picked up tomorrow,' said Neil.

It sounded good to both Carole and I. Great, in fact. Carole getting picked up by a Roller and me being put up in a hotel and Scarborough were paying for it.

I met Geoffrey and we quickly agreed terms. An extra £50 a week plus an £8,000 signing-on fee to be paid in four installments of £2,000, with the first installment to be paid when I signed. Great stuff, we could now pay off some debts and pay the mortgage arrears. I also negotiated removal fees as well as estate agent's and solicitor's fees.

The plan was to meet the Scarborough team at a pre-match meal they were having locally, watch the game, go back to the hotel and then wait for Carole in the morning. It was great to meet my new team-mates to be. Everybody introduced themselves, including captain Steve Richards.

'The last time I saw you, you had your hands around my throat,' he joked as we shook hands.

I watched them beat Darlington before returning to the St Nicholas Hotel in Central Scarborough. The next day I waited ages for Carole.

'What's keeping them?' I thought.

Around lunchtime, I saw an old battered Ford Orion pull up with Carole getting out looking stressed and the kids were crying.

'Some Rolls Royce,' I thought, but after a five-hour journey of numerous wrong turns, she finally arrived.

After a bit of lunch, we made our way back to the ground for our final meeting with Neil and Geoffrey Richmond.

We waited in the boardroom. I saw the previous night's local paper and splashed on the back page was a picture of me with '£100,000' as the headline. I realised that it was also a massive fee for Scarborough. Neil and Geoffrey both walked in looking solemn.

'Hereford have pulled the plug,' said Geoffrey.

'Sorry. I didn't catch that,' I said, bemused.

'The deal's dead,' said Neil.

I couldn't understand it. Neither could Carole. 'Why?' we both said.

'Hereford are saying that they only gave us permission to talk to you and that they hadn't agreed a deal with us,' said Geoffrey.

Then why the fuck am I up here talking terms with you, dragging Carole and the kids all the way to Scarborough. We couldn't believe it. Hereford were now pulling out of the deal at the last minute.

I wondered if they couldn't get a replacement. How could they turn down that sort of money? All of these thoughts were spinning around in my head as we began our long journey back to Hereford.

After stopping at former Hereford player Steve Spooner's house, who now lived in York after having joined them in the summer, we arrived back late on the Thursday night. Nobody had contacted me or left any messages for me from Hereford United.

We were due to play Burnley at home on Saturday, but on Friday morning I stayed away from the ground and didn't go training. At midday the phone rang. It was the club secretary Joan, asking where I was.

'I want to see the manager and board of directors this afternoon,' I said.

I suddenly realised that I was in a strong position to ask for an extraordinary board meeting. Joan got back to me.

'Be at the club at two,' she said.

We got a babysitter and made our way down to the club.

In the boardroom were the chairman Peter Hill and director David Vaughan as well as Stewart's dad, Archie Phillips. I wanted to know why they had pulled the plug.

The chairman, Peter Hill, said that they had not agreed anything, but that they had felt that it would be okay for me to talk to them. Then why send me all the way up there, we protested.

We both had a feeling that there was more to this. Bomber backed up the chairman's story. We were also sure that the board had accepted the bid, but that they had changed their minds while I was up there and were using the excuse that they'd only agreed that I could talk to Scarborough.

It started to get heated. I started to raise my voice and argued that we'd been messed around from start to finish.

David Vaughan, one of the directors, started to get up out of his chair.

'And you can fucking sit down,' I shouted, which he did.

I made the point to Hill and I wanted an answer.

'Did you agree a financial deal with Scarborough?' I asked.

'No we did not,' said Archie. The room went silent.

'That's right, Archie, no we didn't,' said Hill.

'Yes we did,' said Archie, changing his mind.

Archie had come clean. Carole and I both got on quite well with him and he made a point of not messing us about.

Carole asked for the minutes of the board meeting when they had agreed the deal with Scarborough, but they declined. Thanks to Archie, however, we walked out knowing the truth. However, I'd lost all respect for Bomber, Hill and Vaughan.

I agreed to play the next day against Burnley, but my head wasn't in it. We drew 0–0. I decided to forget everything and resolved to concentrate on doing well for myself. I wanted that Golden Boot award at the end of the season.

Off the field, however, the relationship between Bomber and I had deteriorated further. We hardly spoke. As I walked past his car on the way to the training ground, I would spit on it, only to come back and find a big splash of phlegm on my windscreen.

It seemed that he was trying to wind me up. The goals were still going in, though, and I scored my twenty-fifth goal of the season at home to Lincoln in a 3–2 win. I was looking around for the defender Davis who I thought had conned the referee into getting me sent off in our previous meeting, but he'd got injured in training on the Friday morning. Surprise surprise.

We'd also reached the semi-finals of the now-named LDV Vans Trophy. We played Wolves in front of a 10,000-strong crowd at Edgar Street. Steve Bull scored both goals in a 2–0 win for Wolves, but shortly before the end Bomber substituted me. I was fuming. I was convinced that he was trying to make a fool out of me. I got showered and, as the whistle went for the end of the game, I made my way to the players' bar.

The game had finished about five minutes before and there I was ordering a pint of lager at the bar. I felt a prod on my shoulder. I looked around. It was Bomber.

'Get back to the dressing room, now,' he shouted.

Everybody in the bar was looking at me.

I made my way back to the dressing room where I found the lads with heads in hands still in kit. The dressing room was in silence. I walked in. I looked at Bomber who was holding a cup of tea. I sat down next to captain Mel Pejic. Bomber started having a go at me. Once again the red mist was building up and Mel could sense it. I launched after Bomber who'd accused me of not trying.

The lads quickly separated us. Mel was holding me back. Bomber was threatening to throw his tea at me.

'Don't accuse me again of not trying, you wanker,' I shouted at him with a final volley as I walked out of the changing room and slammed the door behind me.

Our relationship was really strained now and, in a training session after more abuse, I threw a corner flag at him, javelin-style. I couldn't understand him. After I'd stormed out of the dressing room after the Wolves game he said to the lads:

'If some of you had his passion we wouldn't be a bad side.'

Yet I always felt as though he was trying to belittle me.

One day, he found out that Carole's mother was ill, but that we couldn't drive up to Bolton because we had no tax on the car. So he lent us his sponsored car. I couldn't weigh him up.

After doing something like that he would then put me in the reserves. Was he after a reaction?

I was playing against Bournemouth reserves away on a Wednesday afternoon. I scored in a 1–1 draw. We were walking off at full-time. Harry Redknapp, Bournemouth's manager, pulled me to one side and asked:

'Phil, are you out of contract in the summer?

'No,' I said.

I now realised that I'd made a mistake in signing that contract but, then again, I hear that Hindsight United are the best team in the land. At least I was aware of Harry's interest, though.

My first real injury came against Burnley away. On the way

there, the team bus got stuck in traffic and we had to get changed onto the coach. We arrived at the ground at 2.45pm and ran straight onto the pitch with no warm-up.

Just before half-time, I collided with a defender and got a dead leg on the front of my thigh. I was in agony. Peter, the physio, tried to patch me up at half-time, but I knew that I would play no further part in the game.

My thigh looked like a balloon and I could hardly walk. I hated being injured. I'd worked hard to become a regular. Suspension had been bad enough, but to miss a game through injury was torture.

I missed Tuesday night's game at Colchester and it was touch and go for the following Saturday's home game against Darlington.

I had a fitness test on the Saturday morning and passed myself fit, even though I was still in agony. Still, I managed to score a goal in a 1–1 draw before coming off after an hour. It had taken my tally, including cup games, to thirty goals, which had included another hat-trick against Peterborough.

I was still chasing that Golden Boot. The Golden Boot only includes league goals. Bobby Williamson was still chasing me.

Usually, around March time, the PFA send you a form so that you can fill in the nominees for your Player of the Year and Young Player of the Year. You also fill in eleven players from your division. I filled my form in and sent it back. I'd voted for John Barnes as my Player of the Year and I'd forgotten all about it when Mick Maguire of the PFA rang me up to congratulate me on being selected the Divisional Team Player of the Season. It felt fantastic that my fellow professionals had voted me as the best No. 9 in the division.

Mick was also checking that I would be attending the PFA dinner at the London Hilton Park Lane. I confirmed that I would be. Defender Gary Stevens and our goalkeeper Kevin

Rose also confirmed that they would be going, so we decided to travel down to London together on the Sunday.

Before that we had an away fixture at Grimsby Town on Saturday. The date of the game was 15 April 1989. We were soon a goal down at Blundell Park. It was typical April weather: a sunny afternoon with a slight breeze. The pitch was hard and bobbly as we entered the final month of the season.

I was having one of those games where nothing was going right: a 'real stinker' as they are usually described.

We were 1–0 down at half-time. We made our way into the changing room and sat down. I was still feeling frustrated. Bomber launched into me, accusing me of loitering on the half-way line without intent. It pissed me off and only added to the frustration that I was already feeling.

'Stanty, you're coming off. Ben you're coming on,' Bomber said, as he pointed to young Ian Benbow who had already started to get out of his subs' suit.

Oh no, here comes the red mist. As I took my boots off I just lost it and threw them in the general direction of Bomber. My New Balance right boot hit the wall and bounced upwards smashing the fluorescent light on the ceiling. Bits of shattered glass went everywhere, as did piles of dust, which descended all over the players.

Some of the players started to cough because of the dust. Bomber just looked at me with that 'fuck-off' look.

'Everybody over in the corner,' he ordered.

All the players made their way and huddled up in a corner with me at the opposite end of the changing room, sat on my own. It was a ridiculous situation as Bomber carried on with his half-time team talk.

I got in the shower. Afterwards, I made my way to sit in the dug out, half expecting Bomber to tell me to fuck off.

He didn't and I sat there as the game went on. Benbow

equalised for us. 1–1. After a couple more minutes, I looked up at the electronic scoreboard situated above the bottom goal. Now and again they would flash up other scores, but a message came up: 'FA Cup semi-final ... Liverpool v. Nottingham Forest ... match abandoned due to crowd overspill.'

My immediate thoughts were what a big crowd they must have had at Hillsborough today if the match has had to be abandoned. I never thought any more about it. The game finished 1–1 and I had calmed down. When the lads were in the shower I went to seek out Bomber to apologise for the half-time incident and I was truly sorry.

I couldn't find him, so I asked one of the press guys where he was. It was pointed out that his son Gary had gone to Hillsborough and that he was trying to find out if he was okay. Bomber had also discovered that this was more serious than crowd overspill. I left it. I would go and see him on Monday as he would have already left in his car.

By the time we got onto our coach with our fish and chips waiting for us, the whole horror of Hillsborough was filtering through to us via the radio on the coach. As we left Blundell Park, we all sat in silence as we made the long trip back to Hereford listening to the constant updates from the home of Sheffield Wednesday.

By the time I got home a lot had happened and I turned on the TV so that I could see the day's events. The earlier argument had paled into insignificance.

The next day, Gary Stevens picked me up and along with Rosey we drove off to London. We had decided that we weren't going to stay overnight, but that Gary would drive back late Sunday night. I'd hired a black suit and tie for the evening and we travelled down in jeans and T-shirts. We managed to find somewhere to get changed and made our way to the London Hilton.

We made a beeline for the bar. Straightaway I noticed players who I'd only seen on TV. I felt great to be part of this family. I had twenty quid to spend.

'I'll get them in,' I said to the lads as I joined the queue at the bar.

Chris Waddle and John Barnes were in front of me and I heard Chris Waddle say in his Geordie accent:

'Haway Barnsey, get the beers in.'

I managed to get to the bar.

'Three pints of lager mate, please,' I said to the barman.

The barman brought the drinks and I gave him a £10 note. He returned with a few coppers' change for me.

'Wow, hang on mate, I gave you a tenner,' I said, as some of the other players at the bar started to look at me.

'This is the Hilton, mate,' the barman replied.

Fucking hell, a tenner blown on one round, which was only three pints. I decided when we'd all bought a round that I would go on my own.

The dinner was a very subdued affair after the events of the previous day in Sheffield and the comedian was cancelled. But I felt real pride as my name was read out as a member of the PFA Fourth Division side. I looked behind Brendon Batson and there was a big board with all the names of the players who had been honoured by their fellow professionals. When all the names had been read out, we had to go on stage to collect our medals.

On the final day of the season we were at Halifax Town away. I was now on twenty-seven league goals, which along with cup goals took my tally to thirty-two. Bobby Williamson was also on twenty-seven, so I was desperate to score.

Five minutes before half-time, I volleyed home a Paul McLoughlin cross. We won 2–1 in the end. My tally had ended at up twenty-eight league and five cup goals – thirty-three in all.

As we made our way off the pitch, I asked the press lads how Rotherham had done away at Cambridge. They had drawn 0–0. I was chuffed to bits: I had won the Adidas Golden Boot award.

I sat there in the dressing room with the lads congratulating me. I reflected on my season: thirty-three goals, the Golden Boot winner and selection for the PFA Divisional award. Not bad for a season's work. Now I knew what I wanted to do.

Chapter Thirteen

A few weeks after the Scarborough affair, Neil Warnock had left and taken over at Notts County, who had just sacked John Barnwell. Ironically John Newman was the assistant at Notts. I watched on the local TV sports section as Neil was interviewed.

'I wonder if he would sign me for Notts?' I thought.

A few minutes later the phone rang. It was Neil.

'I've just seen you on TV,' I said.

Neil confirmed that he would love to have me at Notts. He wouldn't be able to do anything until the summer, but he promised to keep in regular contact.

The Monday after the Halifax game, all the lads met at the club for the traditional manager's meeting about who was being retained. I knew that I would not be released as I was still under contract.

That morning, when I went to see Bomber, I handed in my first and only transfer request. I knew that if I wanted to play at a higher level then I would have to leave Edgar Street. Besides, my relationship with Bomber was at an all-time low since the Scarborough affair. I also knew that by finishing as the league's top scorer there would be interest from other clubs.

Harry Redknapp still wanted me, but as I was under contract it could be a problem for Bournemouth. However, Carole and I still contacted estate agents down there to send us details of house prices. Ken Brown also wanted me at Plymouth, but I was staggered when he told me that Hereford had slapped a £200,000 price tag on me, which, at the time, was a fortune for clubs in the lower divisions.

I decided to take on an agent: a guy called Alaister, who worked for Mel Stein and who had Paul Gascoigne as well as the actors from *Dempsey and Makepeace* on his books.

'I don't want a fucking acting job,' I told him.

Neil Warnock was in constant touch, but the summer was dragging on. Notts County, along with other clubs, were frightened off by the transfer fee. I felt that Hereford were pricing me out of a move.

We went up to visit Carole's parents and I decided to pop in and see Phil Neal, who was manager of my hometown club, Bolton Wanderers.

How I would have loved to have signed for them. Wimbledon had now joined the chase for my signature as well as Swindon Town. Phil invited me into his office.

'Yeah, I want to sign you, but have a look at this,' he said.

He pulled my details out of his tray, which had been circulated by Hereford and in red biro he circled £200,000.

'I asked about you yesterday,' he said. 'But there's no way that Bolton can afford that kind of money.'

We shook hands and I made my way out of Burnden Park.

A couple of days later, Neil rang me to say that his chairman had put in a bid of £150,000 and that they were waiting for a response. That was it. Notts had put in a bid. Neil was in regular contact and I had decided that Notts County were the only club I wanted to sign for. Neil suggested that I came up for talks and to meet the chairman, Derek Pavis.

I made my way to Nottingham, where John Newman showed me around Meadow Lane. I was really impressed. It was the world's oldest Football League club. John showed me the executive boxes, something they didn't have at Hereford. I wanted to sign for them there and then, but Hereford didn't even know that I was up here.

Neil drove me across Nottingham for a meeting with the chairman. I had respect for him straightaway. Derek was a strong character who used to be on the board at Forest during Cloughie's reign. I quickly agreed terms, but I knew that the stumbling block would be the fee. We shook hands on a deal with Derek saying as we left his office:

'We've shook hands on a deal, you know.'

'Yes, we have,' I reassured him and off I went for the drive back to Hereford.

The transfer fee frightened me a little as well. I knew I would be leaving in a record transfer deal for that division. Crikey, imagine the level of expectation of the fans of my new club, even though this it was still the lower reaches of the league.

I kept on training by running down the country lanes. I waited by the phone, but no call came. I wanted the move sorted out straightaway, so that we could move up there and settle in before pre-season. I kept in touch with Neil, but the clubs were still haggling over the final fee.

Every few days I would pop into the offices at Edgar Street to see if there was anything going on. Finally, I got a call from Ian Bowyer.

'We've done a deal,' he said.

'Thank you,' I thought. After all, nobody knew about my talks with Notts.

'Oh right,' I answered, sounding surprised.

'Yeah, with Plymouth,' he said.

'Plymouth?' I asked.

'Yeah, give Ken Brown a ring,' Bomber said.

I didn't ask him about Notts County, otherwise that would have given the game away and he would have known that I'd been talking to them.

I didn't ring Ken Brown straightaway. I rang Neil Warnock instead and told him of Bomber's telephone call.

'I'll get back to you,' he said.

I then rang Ken Brown out of curiosity, who confirmed Bomber's call. But I was only interested in Notts. An hour later, Neil rang me to tell me that a deal had been done at £175,000. I took a deep breath: £175,000 in 1989 – that was a big fee at our level.

I'd already agreed terms, so the signing was a formality.

I signed a couple of days into pre-season, on the same day as Craig Short, who had joined from Scarborough for £100,000. Nicky Platnauer had signed from Cardiff City the week before. I'd joined a club who had a blend of experience, with the likes of keeper Steve Cherry, defender Nicky Law, Phil Turner, and with also a nice blend of youth, which included youngsters like Tommy Johnson and Mark Draper.

We also had a good team spirit. Straightaway I looked for some rented accommodation, so that Carole and the kids could move up.

We had sold our house quite quickly, but we wanted to move into rented accommodation in the short term so that we could find a home that we liked.

In the meantime, I stayed in a local hotel with Shorty and Plats. Pre-season was as hard as usual, but I managed to score a couple of goals.

Our first league game was away at Orient, a place where Notts hadn't won for years.

Two days before, we had signed midfielder Phil Robinson from Wolves. It was a typical first game of the season, played in hot sunshine.

The first thing I noticed was the amount of away support that we had. The last time I'd played here was the season before, when I'd scored two.

Halfway though the first half, Phil Turner crossed and I scored with a diving header. I couldn't wait to celebrate in front of my new club's fans. We won 1–0, which was a great start to the new league campaign. At least I had started to justify the price tag.

However, things would go disastrously wrong over the next few games. On the Tuesday we lost 3–1 at Shrewsbury in the League Cup, with Wayne Fairclough getting sent off early doors for snapping John McGinlay in half. The following Saturday we lost 1–0 at home to Blackpool to a freak goal. We then redeemed ourselves by beating Shrewsbury 3–2, with myself getting on the scoresheet, but we still went out of the competition.

We lost 3–2 at Bristol Rovers the following Saturday just after I had been hauled in to see the chairman who gave me a bollocking for sticking my tongue out on a team photo. And the following Saturday we drew 0–0 at home to Reading with me hitting the executive boxes from the penalty spot.

At the time Carole and I were still in rented accommodation, but were soon to move into a new house.

Neil brought in a new striker, Gary Chapman from Bradford City. Chapy started scoring goals straight from the off, while I watched from the bench. We won a few games 1–0 and started to climb the table.

We beat Swansea away and there was a good feeling in the camp. Notts County always travelled in style. We had a double-decker executive coach with the players up top and the directors and staff downstairs. It was a very comfortable arrangement, with tables and leather seats.

I would start my tricks after a few beers, and my party trick was to slide open the ceiling hatches, which in those days could be slid right back allowing you to stick your head out of the top of the coach.

There were two, one at the back and one at the front and the trick was to climb out of one, crawl along the top of the coach whilst travelling at 60mph and then to get back in through the other hatch at the front of the coach. Of course, I was the only one stupid enough to do it.

It was a silly trick to do, but it took me back to my Army days when you would do daft things like that as part of the norm.

Once, back in my Army days, we had to travel to Scotland from Aldershot for a military exercise. There were five of us who had to travel in the back of the Army truck for the expected eight-hour trip up the M6 and, by the time we reached Birmingham, panic had set in as we had run out of beer.

'Fuck,' said Yatesy. 'What will we do now?'

'I know,' said Killer, as he dropped his pants and pissed into an empty can before drinking it.

We all stood there amazed. We all looked at each other before doing the same, at least we would have a good supply, plus it was free – beat that.

We then started to dare each other to run one at a time and launch ourselves onto the rope that was hanging at the back of the truck before surging out like Tarzan into the slow lane and back into the truck.

As I was crawling halfway down the roof of the coach, I looked up and saw Tommy Johnson pop his head out shouting in his Geordie accent:

'Come on Stanty, you can do it,' before disappearing and closing both hatches, leaving me stranded at 60 mph.

'Bastard,' I shouted, before Tommy reappeared, laughing his head off.

I couldn't wait to get back in safely. I sat next to Shorty. The beer was flowing. Steve Cherry came walking past. Steve was our goalkeeper and had played in the FA Cup semi-finals for Plymouth. Shorty had his feet up on the table with his training shoes off and Chez took off one of his socks and threw it out of the window.

'What did you do that for?' said Shorty as Chez walked back to the card school laughing.

'Fuck this,' said Shorty after a couple of minutes.

'Where are you going?' I said.

'Back in a minute,' he said, as he made his way to Chez's seat, where his new trainers were smartly placed at the side of his seat.

Shorty picked one of them up and threw it out of the window. I watched as it bounced on the hard shoulder and into the grass.

Shorty returned to his seat. It took the lads and I by surprise, as Shorty is a gentle giant. (I found this out when I once called round to his house and he opened the door wearing a gigantic pair of Tigger slippers.)

Chez started to walk to our seats. He was pissed off.

'You fucking told him to do that,' he said, pointing to me.

'You what?' I said getting to my feet. Next minute we had each other in a headlock and were swinging punches at each other. All the others joined in. Punches were flying everywhere. It was madness. Meanwhile, downstairs, the directors and staff were enjoying a quiet drink listening to soft music, unaware of the bedlam on the top deck.

The end result was Swansea 0 Notts County 0, with Shorty minus one sock and Chez minus one Adidas trainer, which he reliably informed us was 'brand fucking new'.

As we got off the coach on our return to Meadow Lane, Chez was walking off wearing only one trainer. He was behind us. We heard him shout: 'You might as fucking well have this one then,' as he threw the trainer at us, but he missed and it whacked our chief executive, Neil Hook, on the back of the head. Hooky went down like a sack of potatoes – it mushave hurt.

Typical footballers that we were, we just pissed ourselves laughing while our physio, Dave Wilson, tried to help the dazed chief exec to his feet.

It was a memorable trip and, typical of our team spirit, we all had a good laugh about it come Monday morning.

I was getting a bit pissed off. I was always on the bench and was now an expensive reserve-team player. It was frustrating, but at least the reserves had got promoted to the Pontins First Division the year before, which meant that we were playing against all the big clubs.

We played Nottingham Forest in front of 5,000 people at the City Ground. Waiting to go up the tunnel, I felt a big slap on my back – the sort that fucking hurts. I turned round ready to lamp somebody when I saw Cloughie smiling at me with his thumb sticking up.

'How are you?' he said.

'I'd be better if you hadn't slapped me so fucking hard, Mr Clough,' I replied.

I had a lot of respect for him.

After we had played Forest in the County Cup in a pre-season match, he had said in the paper that I could be the bargain buy of the season.

We lost that particular game 3–1, but I managed to score at the Trent End before Neil Warnock hauled me off, fearing that I would get sent off.

We drew the reserve game 4–4 in a classic match; it was a pleasure to play in.

After another bollocking from the chairman Derek Pavis, this time for mooning over the balcony at the people dancing below at the Commodore Hotel, including the chairman and his wife during an official club function, we travelled to play Liverpool at

Anfield. Before the game we had a tour of the ground. I couldn't wait to play. Even in the reserves we were playing in front of bigger crowds than the first team. Eight thousand saw Liverpool beat us 3–1, with Jan Molby scoring two. In the last minute, I got onto the end of a Mark Draper cross and fired it past Mike Hooper in the Liverpool goal.

'Fucking hell, I've scored at Anfield,' I thought.

After the game I was full of myself. We had lost, but I'd scored at Anfield. It was only a reserve game, but so what. I was first out after getting showered and I stood outside the away dressing-room door turning round to see the legendary sign above the tunnel. 'This is Anfield.'

I looked down the corridor; there was nobody else in sight. I was leaning against the wall just savouring the occasion. I looked round, I couldn't believe it. Kenny Dalglish, the Liverpool manager, was walking down the corridor towards me.

'Shit,' I thought to myself.

In the space of one second I had many thoughts. What shall I say? Should I say 'Hello Mr Dalglish' or 'Hello Kenny' or even 'How are you doing?'

I was just about to say 'Hello Mr Dalglish' when he said to me in his Scottish accent. 'Alright Phil, how's it going?'

'Not bad thanks, Mr Dalglish,' I stuttered as he disappeared around the corner.

Fucking hell. Kenny Dalglish had just called me Phil. I couldn't believe it. Now I really was on a high. I rushed back into the dressing room where the rest of the lads were still getting showered. I slammed the door and shouted:

'Lads, lads, you'll never believe this, but Kenny Dalglish just called me Phil.'

There was silence before they all shouted in unison:

'Fuck off you lying bastard.'

'It's true, it's true,' I carried on, but then realised that I had no witnesses. I wasn't bothered that nobody could confirm my story as I looked out of the window of the coach as we pulled out of Anfield.

The first team was still winning and we were near the top of the league and, by the beginning of December, I got back into the side. We beat Fulham at home and I scored two at Cardiff in another win.

Our next game would be against Shrewsbury at home on Boxing Day. We were now settled into our new house and, three days before Christmas, our dog Lizzie was going berserk at three in the morning.

'What's wrong with her? She's not normally like that,' said Carole as I got up to check things out. The dog was still barking. I went downstairs and looked around. The TV and video were still there. I looked out of the front window. Nothing.

'Fuck this.' I crawled back to bed after I had given the dog what for.

In the morning I was about to set off for training. I noticed that the garage door was slightly open, but never thought anything about it.

I opened it. The garage housed my sponsored car with 'Phil Stant Drives With Village Motors' emblazoned on it. Every door was open. So I just went round and closed them all. I was still half asleep. I then started to realise that something wasn't right when I noticed all these wires hanging from where the stereo should have been. The clincher, though, was when I looked through the windscreen and saw an empty space where all my Christmas booze should have been, apart from one bottle of Lemonade.

I started to shout: 'Bastards, bastards, bastards.' Carole came running out.

'What's up, what's up?' she said, alarmed.

'Bastards have nicked all the Christmas booze,' I shouted.

I was fuming: anything but the booze.

'Well the dog was telling you,' she said.

'How can a fucking dog tell me,' I shouted back.

I now wished that I had checked the garage. I felt so guilty that I started to stroke the dog, but she just stared at me with an I-told-you-so look.

Carole looked around. A few tools had also gone.

'It could have been worse,' she said, standing in her dressing gown.

'Could it?' I replied sarcastically.

We learned from the police that the thieves had done four or five houses in the area that night.

'Some consolation,' I thought, as I pictured the thieves drinking my beer on Christmas Day.

Christmas is traditionally a busy period for footballers and you have to watch what you eat and drink. Christmas Day training is used for preparing for the Boxing Day game.

On Christmas Eve, our friends Craig and Joanne Short came round for a quiet drink. It was about ten o'clock when the phone rang. It was Dad's wife Christine, who he had married years earlier. We were in touch every now and then, and I knew that he hadn't been well, but I wasn't prepared for her news.

He had died a short while ago. It was devastating news, as I'd only just started to get to know him properly again.

I felt cheated. There were lots of questions I still needed the answers to, but now I knew that I would never get the chance.

Shorty and Jo left as I gathered my thoughts. I decided to give Carole her present there and then. I'd bought her a brand new microwave oven and had hidden it in the loft.

The next day, which was Christmas Day, I decided not to say anything in training and asked Shorty to stay quiet. I'd just got myself back into the side. We beat Shrewsbury 4–2 on Boxing

Day, with me getting two of the goals. It gave me a lift, especially after the events of the last couple of days. Three days later, we beat Birmingham 3–2 to go top of the league, but things were to turn again as I was left out of the side again.

I soon realised that there would be no Golden Boot presented to me this season. I would often go and have a word with Neil Warnock, but he would never see me on his own, he would always call in his assistant Mick Jones. I think he thought that I might hit him.

The team was still winning, though, and that was the main thing. We had also reached the Southern Final of the Freight Rover, which had been renamed once again: it was now called the Leyland Daf Cup. We were to play Bristol Rovers and lost the first leg at Bristol 1–0.

Notts County were one of the few clubs who had never played at Wembley. This season we had two chances, either in the play-offs or with this competition.

That the oldest league club had never played at Wembley didn't seem right, but perhaps this would be the year. Once again I was on the bench. It was still 0–0 halfway into the second half of the second leg. Warnock told me to warm up.

It was a cold night, but I didn't need to warm up. I was ready.

Meadow Lane was packed and full of anticipation. We were on the attack. Phil Turner crossed from the right and I beat Shorty to power it into the net. I ran screaming to the fans, but I soon sensed that something was wrong. Looking around, I saw all the lads surrounding the ref, Brian Hill. He'd seen an infringement with Shorty pushing a defender. I couldn't believe it.

'Fucking hell, it had to be me who'd scored the goal only for it to be disallowed,' I thought.

The game ended 0–0, meaning that Bristol went to the final at Wembley.

When the final whistle went, the crowd were baying for Brian

Hill's blood. There was a pitch invasion and all hell broke loose with loads of mounted policemen trying to restore order.

In the dressing room we just sat in silence as we heard the cheers coming from the Bristol dressing room. Mick Jones patted me on the head.

'Unlucky son,' he said.

'Unlucky? That just about sums up my whole season,' I said.

He nodded and walked out.

We had qualified for the play-offs. Automatic promotion was out, but we'd had a fantastic run. I'd even got back into the side, scoring against Northampton, before losing my place through suspension as a result of the bookings I'd accumulated in the reserves.

We were due to play Bolton, my hometown club, in the play-offs. I was desperate to be involved.

But I was unable to regain a place in the squad for the last five games of the season; a place on the bench was the most I could hope for.

As we prepared for the first leg of the play-off, which was to be played at Bolton, Neil took the starting eleven while the rest of us went for a small-sided game with Mick Jones.

Things were going okay until our goalkeeper, Kevin Blackwell, who the club had brought in as cover for Steve Cherry, accused me of not trying. I saw red and we were soon squaring up with Nicky Law trying to separate us.

I'd always got on well with Blacky, but he tried to headbutt me, so I responded with a right hook, which caught him a peach on the nose. He went down with blood spewing everywhere.

All the lads stopped, including the first team who had been alerted by Mick's screams of: 'Fucking hell, fucking hell.'

I looked at Blacky, who was in a right state as the physio Dave Wilson tried to stem the flow of claret while helping him to his car.

I was still fuming as Neil shouted: 'Stanty, get back to the ground.'

I made my way back to Meadow Lane, a fifteen-minute drive, which gave me time to think.

'Why did you do that?' I said to myself.

I felt sorry for Blacky. I looked at my hand and I had a small cut between the fingers where I had caught him with the punch.

By the time I arrived back at the Lane, Blacky was sprawled on the treatment table. The white sheets were now covered in blood. I walked in and tried to apologise to him but, not surprisingly, he told me to fuck off. Dave Wilson gave me a disgusted look.

'Oh fuck him, Willow, have a look at my finger please, its bleeding,' I responded, as Dave pushed me out of the treatment room. I got changed and went home.

I couldn't turn back the clock. It had happened. Carole was furious when I told her.

A couple of hours later, I went round to Kevin Blackwell's house to try and apologise again, but to no avail. Years later, at a Notts County reunion when he was managing Leeds United, we were able to laugh about the bloody nose I'd given him.

'Funny thing is,' he said, 'was that I suffered from terrible nosebleeds from the age of five. But after our altercation, I never had another one.'

Neil rang me and asked me to come to the ground first thing in the morning.

The result of the meeting was a suspension from the club until pre-season; I was also fined two weeks' wages and was further punished by being transfer listed and missing our fixture at Wembley. I was informed by Neil that if the press found out about it, it was just a training ground incident.

Notts then went on to beat Bolton over two legs and then beat Tranmere in the final on Notts County's first-ever appearance at

Wembley. The team was given a civi reception, which I was ordered to go to.

All the lads were made to go on the balcony and wave to all the Notts fans, who had made their way to Nottingham's market square.

As they cheered our names, all I could think was: 'If only they knew.'

Once again I worked hard during the summer on my fitness. There had been one or two enquiries, but nothing concrete. Notts were looking to recoup the whole £175,000 they had paid for me.

When the pre-season friendlies arrived, I wasn't included in any first-team squads, just the reserves, mainly made up of youngsters. In fact, in one game we played Leicester United and I even played in goal.

Graham Carr had recently taken over at Blackpool and, after three league games, they were bottom of the Fourth Division and wanted to take me on loan.

It was a breath of fresh air to get away from County.

Chapter Fourteen

I was now at a club that wanted me and also with a manager who had tried to sign me before. I knew Blackpool well from family holidays when we'd stay at my auntie's hotel.

The ground was now very shoddy, but the playing surface was excellent.

On my first day there, we trained on the pitch and I looked around the old stadium that had witnessed some of the greats like Matthews and Mortensen.

I looked over and remembered the day years ago when a Blackpool fan had been stabbed during a game against Bolton. It was eerie, as the place was on its knees: the stadium was rundown and the team was bottom of the league.

I would spend one night a week in a bed and breakfast and would then move to a hotel in Lytham at the weekends, when Carole and the kids would come up.

The rest of the time, I would stay at Carole's mum and dad's house in Bolton with Harold driving me to the M61, where the

Manchester lads, Alan Wright and Trevor Sinclair, would pick me up. I was just glad to get back to playing first-team football again.

My first game was against Northampton away and we lost 1–0. We had played well, though, and I had hit the post.

After the game, Graham's assistant, Billy Ayres, came into the dressing room and delivered some shocking news. York City's striker, Dave Longhurst, had collapsed during the game against Lincoln and had later died.

Billy was visibly upset, as Dave had been one of his players when he was manager of Halifax Town, as was Graham, who had had him as a player when he was manager of Northampton. The dressing room went quiet. The result didn't seem so important now.

After scoring five goals in twelve games during a three-month loan period, where we had moved up the league after some fine wins, including one against local rivals Burnley, it was time to go back to Notts.

I had really enjoyed it at Blackpool, but the club had no money for a fee and I was informed by Billy that the chairman, estate agent Owyn Oyston, preferred to have a new electronic scoreboard than a new striker.

Back at Notts County I was now training permanently with the reserves or the youth team and had no sniff of a first-team squad place.

Lincoln City had replaced Blackpool at the bottom of the league and, after recently having regained their league status after being the first club to fall through the trapdoor, I am sure that the alarm bells were ringing.

'Do you want a month on loan?' Neil asked.

'Yeah, I don't mind,' I replied.

Lincoln were now managed by the former Leeds and England striker Allan Clarke.

After lunch, Neil called me into his office. 'They have got a game tonight against Grimsby Town in the Lincs Senior Cup and they want you to go and have a chat.'

Carole got a babysitter and we set off to Lincoln, but just outside Nottingham the fog came down. It was a real pea souper. It took us ages to get to Lincoln, but we finally made it.

Carole stopped the car and I pushed down the window. I still hoped that the game would be on, but the fog was really thick and we couldn't even see any floodlights. We had been driving round for ages.

'Excuse me love, do you know where the football ground is?' I asked a lady at a garage.

'Yes, it's just down there on the right, you can't miss it,' she said, pointing in the direction we had just come from.

I burst out laughing. Can't miss it! We could hardly see in front of our noses.

'Thanks love,' I said.

Eventually we found it. The game had been cancelled thirty minutes before kick-off. We made our way up to the executives' lounge where all the players were having a drink. Geoff Davey, the chief executive, introduced himself and introduced me to Allan Clarke, a player I had admired as part of the great Leeds side of the 1970s.

Alan took me to one side and said: 'Tell me about yourself. What are your strengths and weaknesses?'

I began to describe myself – as a cross between Pelé and Johan Cruyff.

'Okay. I'll see you at training tomorrow and we'll sign the loan forms,' he said as we left the ground.

On my way home I started to think:

'Why would he ask me that? Surely as a manager you should know everything about the player you are going to sign.' I had got the impression that he hadn't got a clue who I was and didn't know anything about my background.

One thing was certain. If I went there, it was going to be a battle. I didn't mind that, though, and at least I'd be playing first-team football.

The next day I met the lads, including the old warhorse Steve Thompson and the ex-Leicester and Charlton defender and goalkeeper Mark Wallington, who had also starred for Leicester.

Our first game was at home to Gillingham on the Saturday and we got stuffed 3–0.

As I came out of the changing rooms, I had to pass a mob of supporters chanting for Clarke's head. I looked at Carole as I walked into the bar with a what-the-fuck-have-I-done look on my face. I saw Steve Thompson and Geoff Davey talking at the bar and got the feeling that something was up. This was going to be a long month.

On Monday morning, the lads were told to wait in the dressing room as the chairman John Reames wanted to talk to the players. We were all sat down when John came in and quickly said:

'Allan Clarke has been sacked and I'd like to introduce you to your new manager.'

With that Steve Thompson stood up and John Reames walked out. It was all over in less than twenty seconds.

During the training, the lads were having a laugh with me, blaming me for Clarke's departure. Afterwards, I went to see Thompson to see if I could go back to Notts, but I had to stay for the month.

I played four games for them and calculated that during those four games I only had one shot on target, which came off the underside of the bar, during a defeat against Darlington. The month really dragged on and when it had finished I compared it to my release from the glasshouse when I was in the Army.

I was actually glad to be back at Notts, even though I knew it would only be reserve-team football, but I was still hopeful that I could get a permanent move away.

It was good to have a laugh with the lads again, but Blacky and I kept our distance and often totally blanked each other, even when we played together in the reserves.

After Christmas, Neil called me into the office again.

'Huddersfield Town want you on loan with a view to a permanent move.'

This was more like it. Another big club, although I would have to travel most days, but the news gave me back my appetite.

Their manager was Eoin Hand, the ex-Republic of Ireland manager, and he knew all about me: strengths *and* weaknesses.

He also knew that my fitness was lacking and, straightaway, he had me running before and after training with his coach Peter Withe, whose fitness, even at his age, was unbelievable.

The month flew past and I firmly believed that I was back to my best. The only problem was that I'd only scored one goal in a draw with Swansea. My last game was against Fulham in a 0–0 draw. Eoin pulled me to one side after the game: he was really pleased with my partnership with Iwan Roberts and, although he had no money until he'd offloaded Keith Edwards, he wanted me to stay for another month. I was really happy about that.

What I didn't know was that Fulham had also been watching me. When I got home that night, Neil rang me to inform me of Fulham's interest.

'Where will you be tomorrow?' he asked.

'At the ski slopes in Swadlingcote with Carole, but you can leave a message at our friend's house if you need me,' I said.

Carole loved skiing and while she did her bit on the plastic slopes, I would sit in the bar with the kids throwing glühwein down my neck.

Afterwards we made our way to our friend's house, where my mate said: 'Notts County have been on the phone.'

'What did they want?' I slurred.

'They want you to ring them,' replied my mate.

I picked up the phone and rang the club. Neil Hook, our chief executive answered.

'Hookey, you fooker,' I shouted down the phone when he answered. By now the glühwein was taking serious effect.

'Stanty, where are you? We've been trying to get hold of you all afternoon. The Fulham manager and his wife are in my office and they are here to sign you,' he said.

'Fucking hell,' I said.

'Yeah, fucking hell,' replied Hookey.

'Better let him know that I've had a couple. We are on our way now,' I said as I put down the receiver.

Shit that was fast. My mind was racing. What about Huddersfield? But Fulham wanted to sign me permanently.

'I'll wait and see what they say first,' I said to Carole.

As we drove to the ground I started to warm to the idea of playing in London. After all, Fulham was another big club with a great history, a club who had boasted great players over many years. They were now managed by Alan Dicks, who had previously taken Bristol City to the First Division.

After a short meeting, we shook hands and I went off with Alan to discuss terms. Fulham had agreed to pay £80,000 and Notts had decided to cut their losses, which was fine by me.

We quickly agreed terms, but I needed a couple of days to think about it. Alan was pushing for me to debut at home against Preston on Tuesday night. I had a few moments with Carole and decided that I should go for it.

Meanwhile, there was another problem. Hookey couldn't get hold of a secretary to type out the forms. There was only one thing for it. Carole typed out the contracts and that was it, I was now a Fulham player and I had to report for training first thing in the morning.

Chapter Fifteen

I would have to make my way to the ground by train. I had negotiated the use of a club car, which I could collect when I got down there.

It was decided that I would stay in the Ramada Inn in Earls Court and that the club would foot the bill for the first few months!

I got up early on Monday morning and caught the train to Kings Cross. I then had to make my way to the training ground at Banstead in Surrey.

Once again, there a new set of lads to meet and Alan introduced me to his assistant Ray Lewington.

I was aware of a sense of coldness between them straightaway. It turned out that Lew had been the manager and the chairman, TV pundit Jimmy Hill, had brought in Alan while Lew was on holiday. I'm glad to say that I would get on with both of them, but I wouldn't take sides.

My first training session with the lads was a five-a-side game, which was just a light session I thought before the following night's game.

The Fulham keeper at the time was Jim Stannard, who had been a stalwart at the club for years either side of short spells with Southend and Gillingham.

Whenever players go to a new club, other players always test out their reactions. During the kickabout I had a chance to score past Jim, but completely miskicked the ball.

'Fucking how much?' screamed Jim, indicating that I had been a waste of money.

I bit my lip and ignored him as we carried on with the game. A couple of minutes later, I volleyed one right past his ear and into the net.

'More than you, you fat cunt,' I said as I jogged away, inwardly congratulating myself. I turned around and the lads were pissing themselves laughing, including Jim. From that moment on, I knew that the lads had accepted me.

After the game, we went into the gym where Alan had us doing a leg circuit, which I thought was a bit strange the day before a game.

After training I picked up the car and made my way to the Ramada where I would have to hang around until our report time the following night at 6.30pm.

I checked in and they put me in a room on the eighth floor. It had a great view and I could see Fulham's ground to my right and Stamford Bridge to my left.

It was a long night, just sitting in front of the TV; there was a bar downstairs, but it took you ten minutes to get down there.

At Notts I was only five minutes away from Carole and the kids. Now I was miles away from home and stuck in a hotel room. I decided to go for a walk. Past Earls Court I went and carried on walking for about a mile. I saw two guys wearing leather trousers, holding hands as they walked into a nearby pub. I started laughing. I don't think I'd ever seen a gay couple before.

I decided to walk back and, as I passed the pub, another guy wearing leathers came out and said:

'What time is it please?'

'It's ... er ... fucking seven thirty pal,' I said in my deepest, gruffest Lancashire accent and walked on without looking back with my hands clasped over my arse.

I walked past the hotel and turned left past Fulham Tap pub and down the road towards Fulham Broadway. It was a much nicer walk and one I would do from now on if I wanted a stroll.

The next day I couldn't wait for the game and I got to the ground early. It was early February and it was a cold night. I sat in the dressing room reading the programme when the rest of the lads started to turn up.

I could hear them as they walked to the changing rooms, which were situated in the cottage at the corner of the ground.

'Awight my son,' was the general greeting from most of them as I soon realised I was the only northerner in the team.

Jimmy Hill came in to introduce himself and wished me well. As he was talking to me all I could think of was: 'What the fuck are you wearing?' as I looked at his trousers. I was sure that he had borrowed them from Rupert the Bear.

Fulham needed a win, as they were hovering just above the relegation zone.

Just before kick-off, I noticed that the groundsman Steve was painting the penalty spots and the centre circle.

'He's leaving it a bit late,' I said to Gary Brazil.

'Oh that's his pre-match ritual,' he replied.

I had a little chuckle at the groundsman who looked as though he had just come out of a Vietnam War film with his long hair and headband. I was to find out later on that he took his job very seriously and that he didn't have a footballer's sense of humour.

The game started and I felt at home straightaway. The lads were brilliant with me and, to cap it off, I scored the winner with a header to mark another goalscoring debut.

A week later, I also scored in a 1–1 draw at promotion-chasing Tranmere. I picked the ball up, beat two players and chipped the keeper, Eric Nixon, from forty yards; it was one of my better goals and one that I still have on video. I ran to our supporters behind the goal who were celebrating and shouted: 'Does he want some fish with that chip?' pointing to Nixon.

After a home defeat by Southend, I scored again in the 1–1 draw with Reading before the game I had been waiting for, Bolton Wanderers away.

Again all the family were there, but we lost 3–0 and, to add salt to the wounds, I was booked for trying to put defender Phil Brown into the embankment.

It was a frustrating time for the team. We would have a good result, followed by a bad one and we couldn't put a consistent run together to move away from the relegation zone. Mansfield Town were also in the relegation fold, so it was going to be a six-pointer when we met them on 1 April at The Cottage.

They had already beaten us in the Leyland Daf Trophy a few weeks earlier and a healthy Midlands rivalry ensured I received a bit of stick from their fans because of my time at Notts County.

I was having some lunch in the hotel before the game when in came the entire Mansfield squad looking smart in blazers. Their manager was George Foster and guess who was with him? Yes John Newman, who had left Notts to join George at Mansfield.

I had a chat with them before leaving for the ground.

It was a typical relegation battle, with tackles flying in all over the place. The game changed when Mansfield defender Kevin Gray was sent off for a tackle on Justin Skinner.

Suddenly there were chances. Before Gray's dismissal they had been few and far between for both sides. Eighty minutes had gone and I got onto Mark Newson's cross and slid it past Andy Beasley into the Mansfield goal.

Five minutes from time, Alan substituted me and, because I was near to the Cottage, I made my way to the changing rooms to the applause of the Fulham fans instead of going to the dugout. This meant that I had to go past the Mansfield fans situated behind the goal at the Putney end.

They were hurling abuse at me as some of them ran to the fence calling me all the names under the sun. As I neared the tunnel, which led into the Cottage, I turned around, stuck a finger up and shouted: 'Fuck you all!' I then disappeared down the tunnel. Shortly afterwards, I heard the cheers as the ref blew the final whistle.

The lads came in cheering and it was a great atmosphere; we all knew how important the result was. After a shower I got changed, only to see a policeman sticking his head through the door talking to Alan Dicks. The policeman was there to arrest me and to give me a caution.

'You're fucking joking,' I said to the copper.

'I'm sorry, but we have had a complaint by a spectator and we have to follow it up,' he replied.

'Well, why don't you go and arrest that lot then? They were swearing at me, so *I'm* making a complaint,' I said.

It was now taking the shine off the result for me and I knew that the FA would be involved. The policeman left after cautioning me. I couldn't work it out. If somebody had reported me for swearing at the crowd, why hadn't they reported the people around them for swearing as well? However, at least I'd scored the winner.

'Fuck 'em,' I thought.

Around this time we had put the house on the market and had decided that we would look for something in London. We soon found out that we would only be able to afford a garage. It was so expensive.

In Nottingham, we lived in a new three-bedroom detached house, but in London we wouldn't be able to pay for the front door. We spotted a house that maybe we could manage at a stretch. So off we went to have a look at it; it was in Worcester Park, south London.

'Oh no,' said Carole as we turned into the street.

We pulled up outside the house and it was one of those moments when you just think 'no'. Outside the house was a car that had no wheels on it and was supported by bricks. Carole looked at me.

'Quick, let's fuck off,' I said as she was driving.

'I can't. He's seen us,' she replied.

'Oh fuck,' I said.

'Get in and get out as quick as we can,' I said, before getting out to meet the guy who owned the house.

'Hello there. I'm Phil and this is Carole,' I said as I shook his hand.

I think that it was the inch-thick layer of nicotine that finally decided it for us.

'I know it needs a lick of paint, mate,' he spluttered, as he took a drag on his roll-up.

'It's not too bad, pal,' I replied, trying to be nice, as Carole stood on my toe.

'Needs a lick of paint?' I thought. 'It needs an assault by the SAS to make it habitable.'

After saying goodbye, we decided at the end of the season that we would find somewhere to rent. At least that would give us time to try and find something we liked.

The next game was another relegation battle. This time we were away at Chester City, who had by now moved from Sealand Road and were playing at non-league Macclesfield Town's ground.

It was pissing with rain and there was a galeforce wind. The game was farcical. Early in the second half, I chased a ball with a defender who pushed me. I slid off the pitch, skidded on the cinder track and crashed into the advertising hoardings. I was fuming again and the red mist descended once again. The only problem was, I was in so much pain that I couldn't get up, which was probably a good thing. All the skin had come off my arm and my thigh and I struggled to get through the rest of the game, which we lost 2–1.

In the showers after the game the water was stinging. In the dressing room, Lew was saying that some of us hadn't tried. He looked at me. I walked over to him.

'Fucking name names, you little shit, Lewie,' I said.

'Well, you could have done better for a start,' he retorted.

The next minute I'd forgotten the pain and we were pushing and shoving each other, before Jim Stannard stepped in. I apologised and Lew accepted it. We were both frustrated, but at least we had a laugh about it later.

We had to bounce back and we did, on Tuesday night against Shrewsbury at The Cottage. During the warm-up I was knocking a ball about with Peter Scott when I noticed the groundsman Steve walking round the pitch with his bucket of whitewash and his large brush.

I was near the centre circle and said to Scotty: 'Watch this.'

I swerved the ball in the direction of Steve and it curled round, skidded off the turf and hit, bullseye, right in the middle of his bucket full of whitewash, which he held in his right hand. The bucket exploded and covered Steve in whitewash. I looked round and Scotty was on the floor. I looked up and Steve was steaming towards me waving his brush screaming his head off, covered from head to toe in whitewash. It was like something out of *Braveheart*.

'Fucking hell,' I shouted as I ran off towards the tunnel,

stepping over Scotty as I made my hasty departure to the sanctuary of the dressing room.

It was weeks before Steve spoke to me again, even after my countless apologies.

The game started and we produced an outstanding display, destroying Shrewsbury 4–0 with Justin Skinner scoring a fantastic volley from the edge of the box. The game set us up nicely for our derby against local rivals Brentford.

Alan Dicks had also signed ex-Spurs keeper Tony Parkes as back up to Jim. Jim was my room-mate on away trips and nobody came near our room in the morning as we used to have farting competitions.

Jim was Premier League in that respect, though, and I could never keep up with him. In the morning, the room smelled like a sewage farm.

When Jim was left out I was paired up with Parksey, probably because we both loved a fag.

I didn't notice it, but I'd also started to pick up the lingo. Making tea in the room one night Parksey looked at me: 'Acker Bilk, son.'

'Yeah, he's a musician,' I replied. 'And a bloody good one at that.'

'No, Acker Bilk,' he said again.

'Fucking talk English, Parksey, will ya,' I said.

'Okay, would you like some milk my son?' he said in a posh voice.

'Oh I get it. Acker Bilk – milk.'

From then on I spoke the same language without realising it.

Against Southend, Scotty informed me that I'd called their midfield player, Dave Martin, 'a fucking cant', which must have sounded funny with a Lancashire accent.

On the Tuesday night it was the local derby game at Brentford. Carole had come down with the kids.

Brentford were flying and it was going to be a difficult game. It turned out to be a typical local derby with not a lot of football played; it was a battle. We also had great support behind the goal from the Fulham faithful and the terraces were packed.

It was a tense game as both teams needed the points for different reasons. It was still 0–0 halfway through the second half as I chased a ball with Brentford player Keith Jones and it ran out for a corner. As it went over the line, Jones kicked it into the crowd only yards away and hit a female spectator in the face.

I ran over to Jones, who stuck his face into mine. I noticed that he had a cut on his lip.

'You little shit,' I shouted in his face. I was convinced that he had done it on purpose.

Suddenly the ref was involved and all the lads were trying to get at Jones. Jones was pleading to the ref and showing him the cut on his lip, indicating that I was responsible, which infuriated me even more.

I couldn't believe that Jones was now trying to get me sent off for something I hadn't done. As all this was going on, the lady in the crowd – who had been hit by the ball – was being attended to by medics as she had cuts on her face. When everything had calmed down we both got booked, which I thought was a little unjust.

The game carried on and, with a minute to go, I ran into the box, side-stepped defender Terry Evans and, via a deflection, put the ball into the back of the net.

The Fulham fans went berserk. It was a great feeling and a great time to score.

After the game, I met Carole and the kids outside and we went back into the ground. We were walking down the exit from the stands when Jones walked past.

'You cheating little twat,' I said as he passed us. I didn't know if I was annoyed because of what he had done to the supporter or for trying to get me sent off.

'What did you say?' he replied, as he turned round.

'You fucking heard,' I said.

The next minute our coats were off. I'd forgotten that Carole and the kids were there. We both came to our senses, put our coats back on and went our separate ways. At least I had scored the winner in a 1–0 defeat of our local rivals.

We had done quite well in the last few games, but we were still not safe. There were three games to go and, if we beat Exeter away at the beginning of May, it would be enough to keep us up and we could enjoy the last two games of the season.

We travelled down to Exeter on the Friday night and I was paired with Jim once again as Parksey had now left because he was fed up with being in and out of the side.

After our evening meal, Jim and I went back to the room and lay on our beds watching the TV. As usual, Jim was farting like a trooper.

Trips away are usually very boring with just the TV to pass the time. About ten o'clock we were both still wide-awake. Jim looked at me and said:

'Fancy a walk my son?'

'Well, there's fuck all on the telly,' I replied.

'Come on, a breath of fresh air might do us both good,' said Jim.

I had a feeling he was right as, just at that moment, he let out a real stinker. We walked out of the hotel and started to walk down a long road as we talked about the impending game. The hotel was situated about five miles outside Exeter and there wasn't a lot about. We walked on until we came to a pub. Outside there was a blackboard and on it, written in chalk, it said: 'Live Music Tonight with Honest John.'

Jim looked at me.

'No way, Jim. If the gaffer finds out we've been in a pub the night before a game we've had it,' I said. And besides, I usually have a good night's sleep before a game. It was always one of my rules.

'Come on, nobody will know. We're miles away from anywhere. We'll just have half and then get off,' said Jim.

'Okay then, just half and we'll leave in ten minutes,' I said.

'Yeah,' said Jim.

We walked in and saw Honest John, who was a short bloke with glasses. He was sat down on a bar stool strumming away with his left leg resting on another stool with a plaster cast on it.

We looked at each other and pissed ourselves laughing as he launched into a Beatles medley.

'Go on my son,' shouted Jim as we waited at the bar with the locals now joining in and clapping.

'Two pints of lager,' said Jim to the barman.

'Oh fuck. Here we go,' I thought.

After about ten minutes, the barman closed the doors for a lock-in.

'Come on Jim, let's go,' I said.

'Let's just have one more,' he replied.

'Oh, go on then,' I said.

Six pints later, we were staggering up the road at two in the morning trying to find our hotel. We eventually found it at three o'clock after negotiating some difficult obstacles, such as curbs, hedges and lampposts.

We hid behind a bush at the front of the hotel to see if the coast was clear. It was decided that I would creep to our room on the bottom floor and let Jim in through the window. The only way in was through the front doors. We could have left the window open for our return, but we experienced footballers knew that this was not the done thing, as it was all too easy for one of the other lads to find out and trash your room, cut up your clothes, or worse.

The Army training came in useful as I did a recce of the

immediate area, entered the building and crept in before sneaking back to the room.

I put my hand in my pockets: 'Fuck, Jim's got the key.'

I crept all the way back outside. I found Jim asleep under the bush with his hands on his balls as usual.

'Jim, Jim, wake up you fat cunt!' I said as I shook him.

'What? What?' Jim replied.

'You've got the fucking key,' I said.

Jim then let fly with the loudest fart that I'd ever heard and we both just sat there pissing ourselves laughing like two little kids.

After that we decided to go for it and we made it back to the room with no further hiccups. I had a sore head in the morning, but by the time kick-off came around, we were both fine.

Twenty minutes had gone. I took the ball round the keeper and, as he slid near me, I made sure that my right foot caught his arm. Penalty. The keeper was sent off and it seemed to take forever before his replacement took his position between the sticks.

Justin Skinner had waited patiently for ages with his hands on his hips and with the ball sitting on the penalty spot. Up stepped Skins and he duly dispatched the ball into the back of the net, much to the relief of us and to the excitement of our travelling fans.

We held out for the win and had saved our divisional status for another year at least.

During the last month of the season, I had moved out of the Ramada and into digs. I had moved in with Graham and Sandy Preston, who were both Fulham fanatics, and they really made me feel welcome.

As I arrived back for pre-season, I needed to find rented accommodation. Carole and I had sold the house and were due to move out soon. I found a place in Slough: it was a bit expensive, but it would have to do until we could find something else to buy.

By now I had really settled in at Fulham and I loved it. I had got used to the 100mph pace of life there and I was now an expert at cutting up other drivers at roundabouts, whereas before I would just sit and wait for ages, hoping upon hope that some polite person would let me in to join the stream of traffic.

Once again the problem with moving into rented accommodation reared its head. We could not move in for two weeks after we had moved out of our house. It was a difficult time, as I was in the middle of pre-season training and Carole was stuck in Nottingham trying to organise the move, pack the boxes and look after the kids.

Most days I was too tired to do anything after having done long cross-country runs around Epsom racecourse, a place I hated.

We had organised for our furniture to go into storage, but Carole and the kids still needed to find a place to stay for two weeks.

'I know, take the kids and your mother, go on holiday for two weeks and when you come back I will have the house sorted out for you,' I said.

Carole was a little disappointed as we both liked the house in Nottingham and moving to London was a daunting prospect for us northerners. In addition, the problem of the kids' schooling would be an issue. The kids were also disappointed that they would be leaving all of their school friends behind.

So Carole took her mother and the kids to Majorca for two weeks after I had promised her that I would arrange for all the furniture to be moved down and be ready in our rented house for when she came back. She had been away for two days when I got a message at the training ground in Banstead. The chairman and the manager wanted to see me.

I made my way to The Cottage, which took me about an hour after getting stuck in traffic. I headed for the chief executive's office, Brian Naysmith, who I got on well with, especially after he had given me a character reference at an FA hearing following the Mansfield incident, for which I received a verbal warning.

'Hi Brian. What's up?' I said as I sat down.

'We're really struggling for money, Phil,' he said.

With that the manager came in with a serious look on his face. Alan Dicks sat down.

'Phil, Mansfield Town have made an offer for you of £50,000 and we've accepted it,' said Alan.

I couldn't believe what I was hearing. It was only two weeks before the start of the new season. We had just moved out of our house and Mansfield was only thirty minutes up the road from Nottingham.

'But I'm happy here,' I said dumbfounded.

Brian looked at Alan before saying to me.

'Phil, if you don't go to Mansfield, the bank is going to stop cashing cheques.'

Fucking hell. I didn't know that it was this serious. Shit. What will I tell Carole? This was still in the time before mobile phones and she was not due to ring me at Sandy and Graham's, as agreed, for another few days.

I made my way out and back to Sandy and Graham's. Not long after the phone rang. It was George Foster, the Mansfield manager. He was ringing from Plymouth as he had taken the Mansfield lads on a pre-season training camp. They were due to come back the next day and I arranged to meet him at Strensham Services on the M5 near Worcester.

We met in the early afternoon and quickly agreed terms in the cafeteria, which was packed with returning holidaymakers.

My main concern was how the Mansfield fans would react to me after my obscene gesture to them during our relegation battle.

George didn't think that it would be a problem and, after we shook hands, we both made our departures. I was to report to Mansfield on Monday to sign and join in with the rest of their pre-season training.

I made my way back to Sandy and Graham's house in Wimbledon, which was a serve away from the All England Tennis Club.

This would be my last night here, as I would make my way up to Nottingham the following day after Fulham's open day at Craven Cottage.

The open day was a huge success, with the fans meeting all the players and with me winning the clay-pigeon shooting contest, which turned out to be the last shots I would have for Fulham.

I left a contact number with Sandy and Graham for Carole when she rang. How could I tell her that I was signing for Mansfield, after moving out of our house, which, as things turned out, we didn't have to do? We would be moving back up again and would have to find another place up there.

Chapter Sixteen

I stayed in a hotel in Mansfield on the Monday night after signing a two-year contract with the Stags and went for my first day's training. Later that night, Carole rang me.

'What's going on?' she said.

'What do you mean?' I said, as I prepared my story in my head.

'Have you signed for Mansfield?' she said.

'How do you know?' I said.

'I read it in the paper this morning,' she replied.

So I told her the whole story.

The other problem I now had was that we needed somewhere to live. I managed to find a house in Sherwood, which would do on a short-term basis until we had found a house to buy. When Carole got back, we went house hunting on the same estate that we had moved out of just two weeks earlier.

They were still building new houses on the estate and we bought an identical house, which would be ready to move into in four weeks' time and which was about 150 yards from our previous home. It was slightly more expensive, but still, at least the kids would be able to go back to their old schools and be with their friends again.

To say that Carole was pissed off about the situation would be an understatement. I was disappointed myself because I had really enjoyed it at Fulham, but I was also excited by the prospect of joining Mansfield, who now had John Newman on the staff as well as Billy Dearden.

I had arrived just in time for the first pre-season game away at non-league Burton Albion in which I was going to make my first start. As we warmed up for the fixture, the teams were read out over the tannoy.

'No. 9 ... Phil Stant.'

'Boo!' came the shout from a small section of the crowd.

'Welcome to the Stags,' said Steve Charles, the captain, as he pointed out that it was the Mansfield fans who had booed me and not the Burton fans as I had initially thought. The boos were an obvious reference to the Fulham incident.

After our 0–0 at Scarborough on the opening day of the season, we were due to play Blackpool, one of my former clubs, in the League Cup. It turned out to be a disaster. We lost 3–0 at home and, to compound the misery, I was sent off for a foul on my former travelling partner, Alan Wright.

On the Saturday, we lost 2–1 at home to Barry Fry's newly promoted Barnet. And then we lost again, 4–2 away at Blackpool in the second leg of the League Cup.

It was a bad start to the season and we were due to play our local rivals, Chesterfield, away on Saturday.

I was also having a bad time. The chances, let alone the goals, were not coming my way. Fortunately, we won at Chesterfield, 2–0, but I was set to miss the next game against Wrexham at home due to my suspension.

The lads picked up another win, this time without me, with a 2–0 win against the Welshmen.

Back after suspension, I was named on the bench for yet another fixture against Blackpool, this time in the league at Field Mill, which meant that we had played them three times in three weeks. The game ended in a 1–1 draw. We were sick of the sight of fucking Blackpool!

I was back in the starting line-up for our next game, a Friday night fixture at Crewe. I was desperate for a goal. I didn't have long to wait before I headed in Chris Withe's cross. Two minutes later, I ran through on my own from the halfway line before being brought down by the keeper as I tried to go round him. Steve Charles dispatched the penalty and we ended up winning the game 2–1. We then went on to win our next five games to go top of the league with me scoring in five consecutive games. Things were looking up. Carole and I had moved into the new house. Mansfield were now top of the league and I had scored in five consecutive games.

In November, we played Burnley at Turf Moor, who were now, along with Blackpool, fighting for the promotion places and who wanted to end our twelve-match unbeaten run. It was probably one of the best games I've played in, even though we lost 3–2.

But things were still looking good. We were now second in the league, three points behind the leaders with a game in hand. Mansfield were also enjoying higher attendances and we were due to be live on Sky TV against Preston in the FA Cup.

Little Craig Stant was the mascot for the Cup game and I led him out and started kicking a ball with him in the goal area where the majority of the home fans were.

I had to feel sorry for him. As he went to kick the heavy training ball, he slipped in the mud and landed on his arse, much to the amusement of our home fans behind the goal.

'Get up,' I said, soothingly, as he looked at me, ready to burst into tears on his big day. 'Don't worry, nobody noticed,' I assured him as I looked at the big muddy patch on the back of his

Mansfield Town shorts. This assurance seemed to satisfy him and he carried on kicking the ball into the net.

It was 1–1 after twenty-five minutes when the fog suddenly descended on to Field Mill and referee John Key from Sheffield had no alternative but to abandon the game, much to the amusement of Martin Tyler and Andy Gray.

We lost the replay, which was also televised live, to a last-minute goal from Preston's John Thomas.

We got through the Christmas period okay and then played Wrexham away on New Year's Day. It was turning out to be one of those games where nothing was going right. We were 2–0 down at half-time. I had been having a good season up to that point, after our dodgy start, but on that particular day I couldn't do anything right. George had had enough.

'Off you come, Phil,' he said at half-time, which frustrated me even more. I got up and kicked the wooden leg of the table.

I suddenly felt this pain in my toe as I realised that the table was made of hardwood. I walked into the shower area so that the other lads couldn't see me and grimaced. The pain was unbelievable and I became even more frustrated: I knew I had broken my toe.

The lads went out for the second half as I sat in the dressing room with ice on my toe. What a way to get injured. Fucking hell. What will I tell people? I'll just have to tell them that it was done during the game.

I played in the next game at York, but my toe affected my performance in a 2–0 defeat.

By March it was still tight at the top of the table with Burnley leading the pack. They were to be our next visitors.

We got off to another bad start and were 2–0 down to two Mike Conroy goals.

Just before half-time, I was chasing a ball on the greasy surface with Burnley's left-back Joe Jacob. We both slid for the ball as it neared the byline and I just saw Jacob's right elbow coming towards my face. I just managed to get out of the way of it as we both crashed into the advertising hoardings in front of the 1,000 or so Burnley fans. Joe got up quickly and ran back to his position. I could feel myself exploding inside. I just wanted to run up and knock his fucking head off.

The cheeky bastard had tried to do me with his elbow and then had the audacity to run off back to his position as though nothing had happened.

I got up and jogged slowly back to the halfway line and, as the keeper took his goal-kick, the referee blew for half-time. As we trudged off the pitch I was still fucking fuming.

Jacob was in front of me as we walked up the tunnel.

'Should I or shouldn't I?' I thought.

However, I was still in such a rage that I just thought: 'Fuck it.'

I made a point of walking past Jacob and caught him with a right hook. I then carried on walking as though nothing had happened as he sunk to the ground.

The policeman who always stayed in the tunnel at home games looked me in the eye, smiled and then turned his back. I looked around, Jacob was still on the floor with all the players – including some of the Burnley lads – stepping over him. I had to smile.

As I reached the top of the tunnel, Burnley's manager, Brian Miller, was shouting at me for smacking one of his players. George jumped in quickly.

'Leave my fucking players alone,' he growled at Miller, who was complaining to the policeman with the policeman responding with a 'Sorry mate, never saw anything'.

At least I had got rid of my frustration, but we still lost the game 2–0.

By April, Aldershot had been kicked out of the Football League and it was ruled that all their results, including goals for and against, were to be made void. This really upset the apple cart: with clubs having points deducted, league positions were affected. For us it meant losing six points and, personally, I lost two goals off my tally. That would affect my chances of winning another Golden Boot for which I was in the running once again along with Blackpool's Dave Bamber.

I made up for it with my first hat-trick for Mansfield against Halifax Town. It all ended up with us needing to beat Rochdale at home on the last day of the season and hoping that Lincoln beat Blackpool at Sincil Bank: that would have enabled us to nick that third and last promotion place. We were desperate to clinch it.

The play-offs were a good idea I thought, but to carry on all the way through to May was a daunting prospect. It had been a long, hard season and most players will agree that they are already looking forward to the break as early as March: it's not only the physical strain during a punishing season, it is also mentally tiring.

We were convinced that if we could beat Rochdale, Lincoln City would do us a favour. It was a carnival atmosphere at Field Mill and the party was really in full swing when Ian Stringfellow put us 1–0 up halfway through the second half. Not long after, I was sent through on my own against the Rochdale keeper, my former Hereford United team-mate, Kevin Rose. I ran into the box and saw a gap where Rosey had got his angles wrong, so I placed it between his left hand and the post. 2–0.

Things were going well, but what was happening at Lincoln?

We didn't have long to wait to find out. There was a massive cheer from the Mansfield fans. They started to shout from the terraces; Lincoln had scored. That meant that if things stayed like this we were up. 'Oh fuck,' I couldn't believe it.

Rochdale pulled one back. Now the nerves had set in and for a minute or two we were all over the place. It came as a huge relief when the ref blew the final whistle, but we got off the pitch as quickly as we could as the fans ran onto the pitch from all four sides.

The Lincoln game had been delayed as a fan had run onto the pitch, which meant that the whole of Field Mill had to wait for the result as they were standing on our pitch.

We were ushered upstairs and into the director's box and waited nervously for the news from Sincil Bank.

The news filtered through. Lincoln had been awarded a penalty in the last minute. I looked at the supporters, it seemed as though everybody had a portable radio glued to their ears.

A massive cheer went up. Lincoln had scored again. Field Mill exploded into noise. That's it – we were up to the Second Division!

After the grueling season we had had, we could now look forward to a well-earned rest. First, though, we had to celebrate. We all ended up in the boardroom with the beer flowing before going down town to celebrate further with the fans.

In one pub I decided to go to the loo. As I stood there nearly falling into the urinal, I noted a Stags fan standing at the urinal next to me.

'Well done, Stanty,' he said.

'Cheers mate,' I replied, with a fag hanging out of the corner of my mouth.

'I've got an apology to make,' he carried on.

I looked at him as I zipped up my flies.

'Oh yeah, what's that?' I said.

'It was me who reported you that day at Fulham,' he said.

I just looked at him and laughed. I walked out thinking: 'You're the sad fucker then.'

OOH AH STANTONA

I knew that when we would have to report for pre-season it was going to be hell after all the work we had done during the season. Once again I took to running the streets. Along with the other players and supporters – who had voted me their Player of the Year – I also waited with anticipation for the fixtures to be published.

In late June it was confirmed that we had a home fixture against Plymouth, who now had Peter Shilton as their player-manager.

Two days later and the draw was made for the League Cup. I couldn't believe it. Newcastle United in a two-legged affair with the first game to be played at St James' Park.

I was right. Pre-season was hard, especially the runs around Harlow Woods and the leg-sapping sessions on the sand dunes, which George kindly arranged, much to our displeasure.

The first game at home to Plymouth was a bit of an anticlimax as the fans turned out in force to see the newly promoted Stags, but all we could offer was a 0–0 and a Phil Stant disallowed goal given for offside after rounding Peter Shilton and sliding the ball home. At least we had Tuesday night to look forward to, with our visit to Kevin Keegan's Newcastle. He had been appointed the season before and big things were expected of him and his players.

This was the first time that I had been to this fantastic ground. The previous year, Newcastle had nearly been relegated to the Second Division, which would have been criminal. I just couldn't wait to get out there.

It was a fantastic atmosphere as I searched and found the small contingent of Stags fans in the top corner of the stand.

It was the type of game where you knew that you would play out of your skin.

There was no pressure, as everybody expected us to lose. If we won, however, we would have been heroes.

The first thing that I noticed as we kicked off was the roar from the crowd, especially from the Gallowgate end, which we would be attacking.

One minute had gone when Gavin Peacock scrambled the ball home for Newcastle. The crowd went berserk. 'Fuck me, here we go,' I thought. 1–0 down in the first minute. Fucking hell this is going to be a cricket score.

For the first twenty minutes we had to endure an onslaught with wave after wave of attacks. I hadn't had a kick, nor would Brian Kilcline let me win a header. I still couldn't get over the crowd. Every time Newcastle attacked, the crowd would roar and it seemed as though everything on the pitch was being sucked towards the goal that they were attacking. I had never experienced anything like it and never have since.

Once we had got through the first twenty minutes, we started to play and gain more confidence. It was a relief to go in at half-time only 1–0 down.

George gave us a pep talk at half-time. I remember him saying something about how well we were going. To be honest I wasn't listening. I was too busy admiring the size of the changing rooms. I was envious of the Newcastle players. What I would give to play at this level and at this club: 'How lucky they are,' I kept on thinking to myself.

The half-time break was quickly over and I couldn't wait for the second half.

I kept on thinking, just give me once chance. I would love to score here.

Newcastle had slowed down for some reason. Keegan was barking orders to his players to step it up. Back on the pitch, it was us who stepped up a gear. Steve Parkin crossed from the right, I got in front of Kilcline and scored with a diving header past Mike Hooper in the Newcastle goal.

Now it was my turn to go berserk. The place went silent, apart from the noise from our travelling faithful high up in the stand. I was screaming my head off as I ran past the Geordie fans all along the byline.

As they kicked off for the restart, the crowd came alive again. Newcastle threw everything they had at us, but we defended superbly. Then, in the last minute, Peacock got his second and it killed the game. We were gutted to have conceded in both the first and last minute of the game. We had deserved a draw.

I couldn't wait to get changed and get into the players' bar just to see what it was like. It was a great experience and as we pulled away on the coach I had one look back and wondered if I would ever play there again. The answer would turn out to be no.

Two weeks later, we put up another great performance in the second leg, which we drew 0–0, but we still went out.

We were finding it hard to pick up points in the league and from the early stages of the season I knew that it was going to be difficult.

The goals were still going in for me, but the difference in quality of most sides was turning out to be too much. George bought in one or two new faces, which helped.

We were also knocked out of the FA Cup in the first round at Shrewsbury.

In December, rumours were circulating that the club was short of money and, after a training session one day, George called me into the office to inform me that Cardiff City had offered £100,000 for me and that the board had accepted it.

I suppose it was good business. A £50,000 profit and a promotion with twenty-eight goals from myself. If the rumours about the club struggling for money were true, then I had to accept that it was very good business.

Cardiff were in the Third Division and were mid-table in the league. Their chairman, Rick Wright, was ploughing money in to get them promoted. I travelled down and met their manager, Eddie May, for talks.

Eddie was a giant, an ex-Charlton defender and a Cockney linguist. Terms were quickly agreed, but my main concern was moving house and uprooting my family yet again. The kids were settled in school and Carole now had a part-time job.

After speaking again to Eddie, it was agreed that on Tuesdays I could train at home, which meant that I would travel down on Monday and return after training.

Wednesday was always a day off, so I would stay down there Thursday and Friday nights, play the game on Saturday and then come home.

A lot of times it would work out even better when we played away. I could come home on Friday and get picked up by the coach for the game on Saturday. After the talks, I went home to have a couple of days to talk it over with Carole.

I thought about the football side. Mansfield were struggling, both in the league and for money, whereas Cardiff had the money and wanted to push on and get promoted.

I went to see George. He had a solemn look on his face.

'Phil the deal's off,' he said, as I sat down in his office. 'They were haggling over the payment of the fee and the deal is now dead.'

It was funny. I wasn't bothered. I was really happy at Mansfield. Mind you, I had been really happy at Fulham.

George was also quite happy that he wasn't losing his top goalscorer. They say that a week is a long time in politics but, equally, an awful lot can happen to a professional footballer during that time as well. It was what kept me motivated. Today, young kids can be on £4,000 a week right from the start of their career: that means that they only need to work for a few years before they're rich enough to retire. The uncertainty was good for me, though, as I stayed focused and knew that I had a family relying on me to do well.

Two days later, the deal was on again. I signed for Cardiff just a couple of days before Christmas.

Chapter Seventeen

I hadn't realised just what a big club Cardiff City was. Of course, I knew about their history and tradition with them winning the FA Cup in 1927, the only time that the Cup had been taken out of England, as well as great-name players, like John Toshack, who had worn the blue jersey.

I also knew that there would be a chance of playing in Europe by winning the Welsh Cup, which meant an entrance into the European Cup-Winners' Cup in which Cardiff had featured in some fantastic nights.

At the press conference, I was sat with Eddie May and surrounded by cameras. It was another thing that I hadn't really experienced before.

The club was run by a wealthy businessman, Rick Wright, who owned a holiday camp on Barry Island, twenty minutes down the road from Cardiff. However, he was on holiday when I signed. Rick had poured a lot of money into the club and had initially saved it from going out of business. Now he wanted to take the club out of the lower reaches and take them into the Second Division.

He had allowed Eddie to bring in players like ex-Leicester star Paul Ramsey and Welsh international Robbie James. Only a few days after my signing, he brought in the former Wales and Everton captain, Kevin Ratcliffe.

The club was in tenth position in the league and through to the second round of the Welsh Cup. My debut was to be at home to Hereford in the Freight Rover Trophy on the Tuesday night.

I still hadn't taken in the size of this famous club until I went into the treatment room for a rub down and a leg massage before the game and was informed by the physio, Jimmy Goodfellow, that the treatment table I was lying on was the same one that the Scottish legend Jock Stein had died on after the World Cup qualifier between Scotland and Wales some years earlier.

I had also heard about the passion of the Cardiff fans and I was determined to put on a good performance, not just for them, but also for Eddie, who had ploughed out £100,000 on me.

The lads made we feel welcome right from the start. I was brought in to play alongside Carl Dale, with Nathan Blake supplying the crosses on one side and Nick Richardson from the other. The match went like a dream.

I scored our first goal when I chipped Alan Judge, the Hereford keeper and another one of my former team-mates from my days at Reading, from the edge of the box.

We went on to win 2–1 and we were due to play them in the league the following Saturday. We won again, this time 3–2, with me scoring an identical goal. This time I couldn't resist the shout:

'Fancy some fish with that chip?' I shouted towards Alan Judge.

The fans were fantastic and were already chanting my name in the massive Bob Bank stand.

On Boxing Day we were 3–0 up against York. I had scored two of them, but we ended up drawing 3–3. It was the first time that I saw Eddie lose his temper, he went ballistic. It could have been even worse if York hadn't missed a penalty.

I just hoped that I wouldn't be on the end of an Eddie blast in the future. He would go purple, with the veins sticking out of his neck, and when he shouted at you he would spit.

We were moving up the league steadily and I couldn't stop scoring. We all felt that there was a real possibility of us gaining an automatic promotion spot and not just reaching the play-offs. We had also got through to the next round of the Welsh Cup, thanks to my hat-trick against Maesteg.

The spirit in the camp was excellent and, before a game, you knew we were going to get a result. We also had the magnificent backing of the supporters.

Carlisle United away. The score is 1–1 at half-time. Gavin Ward was our goalkeeper with Mark Crew as second choice. Blakey had put us in the lead before Carlisle had equalised with a header, which Wardy should have come for.

I grabbed my cup of tea, which I had always preferred to water or an orange at half-time, and sat down looking at the floor. I looked round at the lads and they were doing the same. We were all wondering and hoping that it wasn't one of us who was going to feel Eddie's wrath. My money was on Wardy.

Eddie walked in and took off his long coat and hung it up as he usually did. He was surprisingly restrained.

'Fuck me, Wardy, couldn't you have come for that?' he said shaking his head.

I looked up quickly, anxious not to have any eye contact with Eddie, which might have given him an excuse to have a go at me.

I looked at Wardy, who I could see was going to plead his innocence.

'Don't do it Wardy,' I thought to myself, but it was too late: the touch paper had been lit.

'But Eddie...' Wardy said as he stood up.

'You should have come for that, Wardy,' said Eddie, raising his voice and starting to turn purple.

'Uh oh,' I thought again.

'But Eddie...' Wardy tried again. Once again Eddie cut him off with his even-more raised voice.

'You should have fucking come for that.'

'But Eddie...' said Wardy once again, rising from his seat with us players now convinced that he had a death wish.

Eddie went up to him, face to face with hands on hips and said: 'Wardy, if you don't sit down I am going to fucking knock you out.'

With that Wardy quickly sat down.

I could hear the giggles from the lads. I had to hide under my shirt otherwise I would have burst out laughing. The lads couldn't wait to get back onto the pitch just so that they could release their laughter.

Once we were back on the pitch, we watched Wardy trudge back to his goal with his head bowed and laughed even louder when he gave a half-hearted handclap to the Cardiff fans.

We went on to win the game 2–1 with a rare Kevin Ratcliffe goal, a header from a corner. League-leaders Barnet were faltering and we were closing in. We couldn't stop winning games.

We had made it through to the semi-finals of the Welsh Cup and were rewarded with a draw against Wrexham. However, we had been knocked out of the Freight Rover Trophy during a live Sky televised game against Swansea.

Swansea and Cardiff were fierce rivals and I have never experienced such pure hatred between the two sets of supporters.

After scoring the winning goal away at Northampton, the

Cardiff fans swamped the pitch as usual and I noticed the Northampton goalkeeper, Barry Richardson, being slapped by a Cardiff fan. I just burst out laughing. I loved being part of this. When they went back behind the goal, they started chanting.

'Who needs Cantona when we've got Stantona. Who needs Cantona when we've got Stantona.'

I looked at Blakey and we just pissed ourselves laughing. The name stuck. I was called Stantona by the Cardiff faithful from that moment on. I found it quite embarrassing at first, but who was I to argue with these loyal fans who loved their club and its players.

I had to laugh when we were playing away. The opposition fans used to call us Welsh bastards or sheep shaggers. I used to shout back: 'I'm from fucking Bolton, and sheep shagging, don't knock it till you've tried it.'

By April we were in the top three and winning the championship had become a real possibility. We booked our place at the National Stadium for the Welsh Cup final after Blakey scored to knock out Wrexham in the semi-final.

Everything was going well. I had never played in a Cup final at pro level, but the thought of playing in Europe if we won was a fantastic feeling. We had secured promotion two weeks before the end of the season without kicking a ball. Barnet slipped up, meaning that we had been promoted with two games to go.

Our last home game of the season was against Shrewsbury. If we could win our last two games, the championship would be ours.

Unfortunately, once again the bookings had tallied up and I had to sit out the game due to a one-match ban. It was awful as it was a fantastic atmosphere. Almost 20,000 fans packed into Ninian Park to watch the lads win 1–0 in a carnival atmosphere. I just sat and watched in the press box as I was a guest summariser for the BBC. It just wasn't the same as being out there, though.

The following week we were away at Scunthorpe. As we drove along the M18, all we could see out of the coach window was blue and white. I was convinced that the whole of Cardiff was on its way to Lincolnshire.

The ground was packed with blue and white. Scunthorpe had kindly given up most of the ground to the away supporters with the home fans occupying just one side of the ground. Cohen Griffiths put us 1–0 up and I added another just before half-time. Cohen bagged his second and the game finished 3–0. We had won the league. What a feeling: my second promotion in consecutive seasons and a championship medal to boot.

The fans invaded the pitch. I couldn't get off, so I ran into the main stand where I could climb the wall and jump down into the tunnel. As I was climbing the wall, the Cardiff fans grabbed me and started to rip off my shirt. Once that had gone, they wanted my shorts. I quickly took them off and threw them into the air as they fought for them, which gave me enough time to scale the wall wearing just my underpants, socks and boots and jump down to the safety of the tunnel.

Carole, Hayley and Craig were at the game and I sensed that there would be a crowd invasion, win, lose or draw. I asked the ref how long to go.

'I'll blow the whistle as soon as I am near the tunnel,' he said.

'Good one,' I thought.

On that point, I saw Carole and the kids sat near the fence and I tried to motion to her just to stay there, because I was worried that they might get trodden on.

Jason Perry knocked a long ball forward and, forgetting what the ref had said, I chased it. As I got near the ball I suddenly realised that I was miles away from the tunnel and I could see the crowd ready to run onto the pitch. I looked around.

'Oh fuck,' I said, as I saw the ref standing near the tunnel and putting the whistle to his mouth. At that moment, the crowd started to run onto the pitch. I was relieved when I actually made it back to the dressing room.

Harry Parsons, our kit man, said: 'Stanty, where's your shirt and shorts?'

'Sorry H, don't know,' I replied.

'Well go and fucking get them back,' he said.

'You fucking go and get them,' I retorted.

'Fuck that,' he said and we both burst out laughing.

We had won the championship and it was a fantastic feeling. Now we had to clinch the Welsh Cup the following Sunday against part-timers Rhyl at the National Stadium in Cardiff, which would give us a league and cup double and ensure our passage into the European Cup-Winners' Cup.

However, there was discontent in the dressing room. The chairman had promised the lads a big bonus if they won the double. I was excluded because I had only arrived at the club halfway through the season and was only entitled to a £2,000 win bonus.

The week prior to the Cup final should have been a week of celebration, but the lads were determined to pursuef the case with chairman Rick Wright, who'd announced that he was selling the club. Rick was having none of it and the PFA were called in.

Brendon Batson came to the club to try and sort the argument out, but to no avail.

Some of the lads had reached agreement, but Nathan Blake, Nick Richardson and myself decided to take it further. After all, £2,000 was a lot of money to me. Blakey and Nick were entitled to more.

The situation at the club had obviously put Eddie in a strange position and I felt sorry for him.

We were going to be presented with the league trophy just

before the Cup final on Sunday, so at least we had something to look forward to.

As we had a pre-match meal in the hotel before the game, Eddie came over to have a private word with me. He pulled me to one side and said:

'Phil, the chairman has said to me that I can't play you in the final unless you drop your claim for your bonus.'

'You're fucking kidding, gaffer,' I replied, astonished. 'How fucking low can this get?' I thought.

'But I want to play Eddie,' I argued back. After all, I came to the club when they were tenth in the league and my goals, nearly twenty of them, had helped them to win the league as well as to reach the Cup final.

Once again I felt sorry for Eddie. It must have been an awful situation for him to tell his top scorer that he couldn't play in the Cup final.

Eddie went on: 'The chairman says that if you do play today, you will have accepted his ultimatum.'

'This is fucking bollocks,' I said. I was being blackmailed. Perhaps life in the Army and professional football weren't that different after all. As we made our way to the stadium, I still hadn't given Eddie an answer.

As we climbed off the coach there was once again a party atmosphere with all the fans cheering us in their fancy dress and scarves.

As I made my way down the tunnel to walk onto the pitch the fans had already started to filter in. As I stood in the centre circle, Eddie came up to me and said:

'Stanty, have you made your decision yet?'

I looked at Eddie and said: 'What do you want me to do?'

'I want to play you,' he replied.

'The only reason I won't be playing today Eddie, is if you don't pick me,' I said and walked off back to the dressing room.

Eddie came back in and named the side: No. 9 ... Stanty. This problem was not going to go away, but it would have to wait.

Perhaps I could speak to Rick Wright at the dinner later that night. Anyway, why should I miss the presentation of the league trophy?

The stadium was half full with 25,000 Cardiff fans taking up one side of the ground and a small contingent of Rhyl fans taking up the other.

We were presented with the league trophy before the game; it was a fantastic feeling.

The score of the final was never going to be in doubt after Cohen Griffiths had scored a brace and I'd done the same before half-time. In the second half, I completed my hat-trick to join Ian Rush as the only player to score a hat-trick at the National Stadium.

That evening there was a subdued atmosphere at the dinner. It should have been a happy occasion for everybody. Rick Wright stood up to give a speech, but was heckled by the lads who by now had a few beers inside them.

The next day I decided to go and have it out with Rick.

I was met with: 'Phil, by playing in the game you accepted my proposal.'

'Fuck off,' I shouted back. 'I didn't accept anything,' I carried on.

Then Rick and I had a bit of a slanging match, with him adamant that I would not be receiving any bonus.

Rick then went on to say: 'If you don't go now, I will call the police.'

With that I walked out.

'Wanker,' I shouted as I slammed the door.

I couldn't believe it. Why wouldn't he pay me what he owed me? The press was soon onto the story and it turned into a bit of a saga.

A month later, a tribunal ruled in my favour, which pissed Rick off big time. He was still trying to sell the club, but gave a press release saying that I would never play for the club again.

Chapter Eighteen

I still had a year left on my contract. Once again during the summer I worked hard on my fitness as I waited for the phone to ring. Eddie and I were in touch with each other most days.

When I returned to pre-season training, I just got on with the fitness work and kept my head down. Rick was still saying in the media that I had no future at the club.

Cardiff were due to go on tour to Northern Ireland, but with my Army background it was something I didn't want to do as plenty of people there would want to pick on my being an ex-soldier. Eddie made it easy for me by leaving me out anyway.

The draw for the first round of the European Cup-Winners' Cup was made and we were paired with the outstanding Belgian side, Standard Liège, but I knew I wouldn't be involved, even though it was a while off.

As the lads were on tour, I was left to train at home by myself. Then I got a call from George Foster saying they had agreed to take me on loan back at Mansfield. The Stags had been relegated after I had left and now had a new owner and chairman, Keith Haslem.

I agreed to go back to Mansfield for a month's loan, which would start at the beginning of the season. It was disappointing for me, as I really enjoyed playing for Cardiff.

We had had a fantastic season and all my dreams of playing in Europe had now died. How I hated Rick Wright at the time. He had gone to Australia on holiday for a month, but would regularly send press releases to the local media. The fans had also started a campaign to get me back, but at the moment my thoughts were with Mansfield Town.

Rob Phillips of the *South Wales Echo* would ring me every day with any news.

I hadn't really had a vigorous pre-season and as I helped Mansfield to an opening-day 1–0 victory over Shrewsbury, I felt my hamstring tighten, which would mean that I would miss the Tuesday night Cup game against Stoke City.

I knew that George was under pressure from the fans and the new chairman, who was obviously looking to make changes, so a good start was going to be vital.

Cardiff had also won, 2–0, on the opening day and the fans had been chanting my name. Rick loved the publicity and came up with a good stunt after being put under pressure by the Cardiff fans' campaign. He challenged them to buy £100,000 worth of season tickets and he would bring me back. It was laughable.

Cardiff had also signed another striker, the ex-WBA, Coventry, Villa and QPR striker, Garry Thompson.

A couple of weeks into the season things weren't going well for either Mansfield or Cardiff. Cardiff were due to play in Liège the following Tuesday night. It just so happened that George had been sacked and I got a welcome call from Eddie to tell me that chairman Rick Wright would allow me back.

He was going to throw me straight back into the side against

Hull at Ninian on Saturday and again against Liège on Tuesday night. It was great to get back to Ninian for training and to see the lads again. I was just glad that the whole episode was over.

We drew 2–2 against Hull and I was given a standing ovation as I came out to warm up. Yes, it was good to be back.

On Monday, we flew out of Cardiff heading for Belgium. I couldn't believe that I was actually going to play in a European tie against a crack European side managed by ex-Dutch international Arie Haan, who I still remembered for his goals in the 1978 World Cup finals in Argentina.

The morning of the game, we were given a tour of Liège in a coach, but what was more fascinating was watching the police chasing hordes of rampaging Cardiff fans. As we ran out onto the pitch, I could see all the Cardiff fans herded into an enclosure, surrounded by riot police.

The atmosphere was electric, but once the game had started I forgot about everything. I couldn't get near the ball; I was being marked by the Brazilian André Cruz and he had me in his pocket. Once or twice I tried to kick him, but I still couldn't get near to him.

Marc Willmots quickly opened the scoring for Liège, but Tony Bird levelled before we went 2–1 in front.

Our joy didn't last, though, as they stepped up a couple of gears and ran out 5–2 winners but, all said and done, it had been a fantastic experience.

Haan said in the papers the next day that I couldn't play, but I could kick.

'Cheeky fucker,' I thought, but at least we had the home leg to look forward to.

Things weren't going so well in the league and we were struggling. It was another Mansfield situation, where all we needed was a few more quality additions and we could have gone from strength to strength, but Rick was adamant that he was selling the club and that he wasn't going to be putting any more investment into it.

We'd been drawn away at Enfield in the FA Cup. We went through after a replay before beating Brentford 3–2 in the second round, which meant that we had reached the third round of the FA Cup, something I had never done before.

I had built up a good understanding with striker Garry Thompson. We became good friends and I was learning a lot from him. He was like a battering ram and I would just pick up the pieces. The goals would go in, but we always seemed to concede more.

I would time my runs off his headers, as he rarely got beaten in the air, but we rarely escaped Eddie's half-time bollockings. Sometimes they were funny, but we would have to wait until he had turned his back before giggling.

If you were ever getting the treatment off Eddie, you had to look him in the eye, but the other lads would try to make you laugh by waving or giving you the wanker sign behind his back and it was a real test not to laugh in his face as he was bollocking you.

One game away from home we were losing 1–0. As we trudged into the dressing room, I knew that Thommo and I hadn't played particularly well and that we were due some of Eddie's treatment.

To my surprise, Eddie tore a strip off the rest of the lads. Thommo and I just kept our heads down, with the occasional eyeball contact with each other.

Eddie paused and must have remembered that us strikers hadn't been performing.

'And you fuckers up front,' he ranted as he quickly got back into his stride... Thommo and I just looked back with that 'not-me-boss' look.

'I've seen more fucking movement in Subbuteo.'

I could hear a big groan inside me saying don't laugh, please don't laugh.

I couldn't wait to get back on the pitch. I noticed blood coming out of my lip, as I must have been biting it so hard in an attempt not to laugh in Eddie's face. He was really old school and an autocratic guy, but his technique appealed to the Army lad in me, as I always prefer to know where I stand with people and there was no mistaking the fact that you certainly knew what Eddie thought of you!

The FA Cup draw was made: Middlesbrough, who were now managed by Lennie Lawrence, at home. Another milestone would be achieved by playing in the third round of the FA Cup. No one gave us a chance, but after Paul Wilkinson had opened the scoring for Boro, I ran through on a one on one and beat Boro keeper Stephen Pears and scored. Allan Moore then put them 2–1 in front before Thommo grabbed an equaliser and forced a replay.

Once again no one gave us a chance in the replay up at Ayrsome Park.

It was a cold night, but we were definitely up for the game. We were 1–0 down at half-time, but we were playing well and had created a few chances.

I chased a long ball, but Pears got to the ball before me. At that moment, my studs got caught in the turf and my knee twisted. I thought that I had been shot in the knee, because the pain was unbearable. I had been quite fortunate in my career; with injuries and any knocks that I had had before I just carried on, even when I'd broken my toe. However, I had never felt anything like this before.

Still, I was convinced that I would be able to run it off. I was on the turf for about five minutes before physio Jimmy Goodfellow helped me onto my feet.

'Are you okay, Stanty?' he said, as I put my weight on it.

'Yeah, I'll be okay,' I said. 'But just keep an eye on me for five minutes,' I shouted, as he walked off behind the goal with his medical bag in hand.

As soon as I started to jog I knew that something was wrong.

The initial pain had subsided, but my knee felt like jelly and was wobbling. There was only one thing for it – I would have to come off.

All I could do was hobble, so I let Eddie know, who by now was giving me that is-it-or-isn't-it look.

The ref had restarted the game and I just wanted the ball to go out of play so that I could get off. Derek Brazil had the ball on the right-hand side and was surging forward. I hobbled into the area, in hope more than anything else. Derek crossed the ball, Steve Vickers, the Boro defender, missed it and I jumped on my good leg, headed the ball and it flew into the net, before I landed back on my good leg again.

The lads came running over to me to celebrate, but all I could scream was: 'Fuck off, keep off me, keep off me.'

With that Jimmy ran back on and helped me off. Later in the game, Nathan Blake scored our winner, but all I could think about was what my injury might be and how long I would be out with it.

The next day it was confirmed by the club doctor that I had a partial tear in my medial ligament and that it wasn't as bad as I had first feared. However, it still looked as though I would be out of action for about six weeks.

This was the first instance that I was going to be spending a lot of time in the treatment room. It didn't mean that I could spend more time with Carole, as attending physio was as much of a commitment as normal training. Injuries are the most frustrating aspect of professional sport and I was Jimmy's worst-ever patient. The most difficult times came when I was watching the lads playing from my seat in the stands.

Still, I got on with my rehabilitation, still working hard long after the lads had gone home.

We were drawn against Manchester City at home in the FA Cup fourth round, but there was no way that I would be fit for that.

Once again Blakey pulled off some magic and scored a cracker. Mark Grew, known as Barney by the lads, saved Keith Curle's penalty and we were in the fifth round of the Cup and drawn to play Luton.

That was my target: to be fit for that game, even though it would mean that I would have to come back earlier than expected. I made the bench. I hadn't played any games during my rehab, but I was confident that if I was needed I would be okay. I was just glad to be back involved in this live televised game.

Scott Oakes had put Luton in front in the first half. We knew how dangerous they were, especially Hartson up front, whose goal had knocked out Newcastle in the previous round.

We were huffing and puffing, but couldn't get an equaliser. I kept warming up, hoping that Eddie would give me the nod.

As I was warming up, I heard a shout from the dugout. I quickly turned around, but it was Luton manager David Pleat shouting to the linesman that he wanted to make a change. He replaced Hartson with my ex-Reading team-mate Kerry Dixon. Then I heard the unmistakable voice of Eddie.

'Oi Stanty!'

Within a few seconds, the sub suit was off and I was ready.

Five weeks of torture and I was back. The crowd cheered as I ran on. For the first few minutes I ran round like a headless chicken and was soon breathing out of my arse, but then a long ball was pumped forward. I could see Thommo jumping for it; he won the header and nodded it towards me on the edge of the box. I hit it first time with a left-foot volley and it flew into the net past Luton keeper, Juergen Summer.

Suddenly all those weeks of frustration – and the arguments with Jimmy the physio – had disappeared from my mind as I ran to the fans in the Bob Bank Stand screaming my head off.

Some of them ran onto the pitch as they sometimes did. We were back in it, but Luton regained the lead straightaway, with a disputed offside goal by David Preece.

Once again the crowd were on the pitch. It was total confusion for a few minutes. Eddie was having a fit on the touchline, but the goal was allowed to stand and we were out of the Cup in a cruel way.

Because of our FA Cup run, we had accrued a backlog of fixtures. We had reached the semi-final of the Welsh Cup, where we were due to play Swansea in a two-legged affair but, before then, we had to catch up with the league fixtures. We ended up playing Tuesday, Thursday, Saturday for two weeks, which was physically and mentally exhausting.

One of those games came on a Tuesday night down at Brighton. We desperately needed the points as we were being sucked into the relegation battle.

We were 1–0 up at the Goldstone Ground when I followed in a Blakey shot. The keeper spilled it, I reacted first, the Brighton fans packed behind the goal held their breath as I pulled my right foot back to slide it unopposed into the empty net. I was four yards out with an open goal, but managed to put it wide of the post.

I could hear the sigh of relief from the fans. I couldn't believe it and held my head in my hands knowing that I would have to face Eddie at half-time.

I walked forlornly out of the box as the Brighton fans took delight in chanting:

'Who's that No. 9? Who's that No. 9? You shit bastard, you shit bastard, who's that No. 9?'

I wanted the ground to open up and swallow me.

It was the first time that any opposing fans had gotten to me and I couldn't wait to get off at half-time so that I could receive Eddie's bollocking.

Eddie had been ranting and raving at me for ages for trying to smash the net either in training or in games.

'Stanty,' he would say. 'Why do you have to burst the net, just place the ball in.'

But I always loved smashing the ball in the net, that had always been me, so I was a little bemused at half-time during the bollocking after I had apologised for trying to pass it into the net and missing a sitter, when Eddie barked:

'Just smash the fucking thing home.'

Eddie's bollockings usually had the desired effect and I did just that, by smashing the ball home in the second half and took great delight in pointing out the number on my shirt to the Brighton fans.

It was a long ride back to Cardiff, even though we had won 5–3. It wasn't helped by the fact that we had another game on Thursday.

When I got home on Saturday night I was absolutely shattered. Carole and the kids were asleep on the settee as I got a beer out of the fridge and started to watch *Match of the Day*.

Then 'Goal of the Month' came on:

Goal A: Eric Cantona

Goal B: Ryan Giggs

Goal C: Phil Stant

Fucking hell. I spat my beer out. I couldn't believe I was on 'Goal of the Month'. It's one of those things that you dream about being on when you are growing up. I shook Carole to wake her up.

'Look I'm on "Goal of the Month",' I said excited.

But by the time she came round the goal had gone and they were showing Goal F: Matt Le Tissier.

'Make sure you lock the doors before you come up,' she said, as she grabbed the kids, one under each arm, and went upstairs.

I felt like shouting: I've been on fucking 'Goal of the Month.' Then I tried to work out, while opening another tin of beer, if my goal was the best.

By the time I went to bed I was exhausted, pissed and convinced that I was going to be a 'Goal of the Month' winner.

We managed to scrape through to the end of the season and avoid relegation.

Rick Wright still hadn't managed to sell the club and I was out of contract in the summer, but at least we had made it to the Welsh Cup final.

Once again the lads were in sombre moods as no negotiations had taken place and nobody knew what was happening. Rumours of a takeover had started, but we were all in complete limbo. We had one more game before the summer and, personally, I couldn't wait for the rest.

One the day of the Cup final we all met at the hotel for a pre-match meal unaware that our opponents Barry Town, who were flying in the Welsh League, had also booked in for a pre-match meal at the same venue. I think it was a little embarrassing for both parties, but the tension was eased when the team coach pulled up outside.

Both teams got up to make their way onto the coach when it was announced that it was Barry Town's transport. We watched their players get on the bus as we waited for ours, which was obviously running a few minutes late. We all stood outside kicking our heels. Time was pushing on and it was a ten-minute drive to the National Stadium.

Eddie started to make phone calls and he finally got through to the coach company when I heard him say:

'What do you fucking mean, no bus has been booked?'

The lads all looked at each other.

'Fucking typical,' said one of the lads.

Thommo and I just looked at each other, biting our lips again.

Eddie went rushing to the reception and ordered a fleet of taxis to get us to the stadium.

It was a three o'clock kick-off and it was now nearly two, which meant that we would have little time to prepare. We jumped into the taxis and Thommo said:

'Wait a minute, who's paying for the fucking taxis?'

'Don't look at me, I've no money,' I said.

A collection quickly followed to pay the driver as he pulled up at the National Stadium. The other taxis soon arrived.

The place was buzzing with Cardiff fans and they couldn't believe their eyes as we all jumped out of the cars and made a run for the players' entrance.

We were sat in the same dressing room in which we were celebrating last year. This time it was a totally different atmosphere, however, and I could sense defeat even before the game started. The whole preparation had been a shambles from start to finish.

It was no surprise that we went 1–0 down in the first half before I equalised after following in on a strike at goal from Thommo.

Late on, Barry Town clinched the winner from a corner and ran out 2–1 winners, securing themselves a place in the following season's European Cup-Winners' Cup.

I couldn't wait to get out of there. It was all a complete contrast to the previous visit twelve months before.

As I collected my losers' medal, I gave it to a young Cardiff fan who was still clapping us. What an end to a season.

During the summer I kept in contact with Eddie from Lilleshall, where I was completing my FA Advanced Coaching Licence. There was still nothing on the table and a few other clubs were sniffing around, including Swansea.

As we returned for pre-season nothing was happening, so we just got on with the training.

Just before the beginning of the season, a consortium based in Birmingham came in to take over the club. It was a relief; finally I could get a contract signed and get on with it.

They brought in ex-Wales manager Terry Yorath to oversee the football side of things and to help Eddie out.

After the first game of the season, Terry called me into the office to talk terms on my contract. It took five seconds to agree.

'Great, finally that's out of the way,' I thought. 'Now, I can concentrate on football.'

'There's only one snag,' said Terry.

'What's that?' I asked.

'You can't have the contract until January when the consortium officially takes over the club,' he said.

This was a blow. It meant that I would have to stay on the same money, even though it was costing me a fortune to commute to and from Cardiff.

I was a little unsure and took advice from the PFA. Their main concern was that I would be playing without a contract and what would happen if, for example, I broke my leg.

It was food for thought. Besides, I had been tapped up by a few clubs and these were pre-Bosman days. I decided to stick it out, even though it was risky.

The consortium were introduced to the fans at a forum and I was selected to represent the players as the fans asked questions. I sat next to Eddie as the new guys spoke about their intentions.

All the talking had proved worthless and, by December, the rumours had been circulating that the consortium couldn't raise the cash to pay off Rick Wright before the January deadline.

Now I was worried, especially as, by then, I was one of the top goalscorers in the league and Bury had been calling me every other day. I spoke to Terry Yorath and he confirmed my thoughts.

After speaking to Bury, I put in my seven days' notice and signed for them for a tribunal-set fee of £60,000.

Chapter Nineteen

I didn't know it at the time, but signing for Bury would provide another highlight of my career. It was also close to Bolton, where all my family still lived.

Bury – who were managed by Mike Walsh, with Stan Ternent as his assistant – had been in the top three for most of the season, but had dropped back down the table. However, they still had a great chance of making the play-offs.

At least my immediate future had been secured, as I had signed a two-and-a-half-year deal. It also didn't take me long to fit in with the culture, especially as I had been brought up just six miles down the road.

My first game was as a sub against Fulham away and the following week I made my full debut at Gigg Lane, scoring in a 4–1 victory over Colchester.

The dressing room was completely different to the one at Cardiff. It always seemed happy instead of the uncertainty and the doom and gloom. The place was full of characters, all of whom enjoyed their football, including the chairman, Terry Robinson.

Terry was a big, balding lad who was always on a diet.

'Get me pie, chips, peas and gravy,' he said to one of the office girls one lunchtime. 'And a diet coke.'

The secretary was Jill Neville, wife of commercial manager Neville Neville, mother and father of the Neville brothers, who would often come down to watch along with David Beckham and Ryan Giggs.

Once again I found myself going from a struggling side to a team that was a division below but who were going for promotion. It was another new challenge and this time with a forward-thinking club instead of one that was in turmoil with the owners trying to sell out.

Back at Cardiff, it didn't surprise me to find out that the consortium had pulled out, which meant that more players would either be sold or released.

Up at Bury things were going well. Once again the goals were going in and we were winning games. We had made it into the play-off places, but had a chance of gaining automatic promotion. We had also beaten champions-elect Carlisle 2–0 at home but, in the penultimate game of the season, we could only manage a draw against Walsall, which saw them claim the last automatic spot and condemned us to the play-offs.

I wasn't too bothered about this because I had every schoolboy's dream in my sights: a chance to play at Wembley.

I had been close to the twin towers once before with Notts County, but had had that snatched away from me on two occasions.

This time it could be different as I was a regular in the side. I hadn't realised it, but my goals at Cardiff and Bury had totted up to twenty-six, enough to win me another Golden Boot, which was going to be presented to me at Planet Hollywood in London by TV presenter Dani Behr.

Unfortunately, Walshy refused me permission to go, as we had a game the night after. We were due to play Preston North End, now managed by Gary Peters, as a two-legged play-off match with the first match to be played at Deepdale.

A few weeks before, they had trounced us 5–0 with a David Beckham-inspired performance, but at least he had now gone back to Manchester United.

There was a really good feeling at Bury and I was really pleased that I had signed for them. I would often pop off to see my mum, who was still living in Bolton, or my sister Shirley, who had since left the Army and was now raising a family.

Another mate, Ned Kelly, had left the Army a few years earlier and I would go down to Old Trafford, where we would have lunch together to discuss the good old days and, after one particular game, I arrived in the players' bar to find Ned with a few of the other Army Hereford lads.

We tried to relax for the play-off game with a day at Chester races, only to find that the Preston squad were doing the same thing. At least we drank more beer than them. '1–0,' I thought. 'That will give us a psychological boost.' The 5–0 defeat preyed on a lot on people's minds, but we had worked hard since then and we were more compact and organised now.

I was hoping for a draw, which could give us an advantage when we played them a few days later at our place. Preston had been to Wembley in the play-offs the previous year and had lost, so I knew that they would be as determined as us to win.

Deepdale was packed and, against the run of play, Dave Pugh, our skipper, put us 1–0 up. That's how it stayed at half-time. It was a really fierce local derby. Preston were piling on the pressure, but they couldn't score: our goalkeeper led a charmed life.

Pughy made a run down the left, he slid it to me six yards out with just the keeper to beat, but I lost my footing just as I was just about to make contact. I could hear the groans from the Bury fans behind the goal as I picked myself up.

Preston were piling forward and I just hoped that my miss wouldn't cost us. Fortunately for us it didn't: we held out with a 1–0 lead to take back with us to Gigg Lane for Wednesday's second leg.

I couldn't help thinking about my miss. Would it cost us in the long run? I had had a great opportunity to book our place in the final, but had fucked it up. It was even worse watching the replay, especially on TV in slow motion.

Gigg Lane was packed to the rafters for the second leg. All I could think about was the chance to play at Wembley. Preston battered us, but they couldn't get past our keeper, Gary Kelly. Just before half-time, I headed over from close range.

The game was reaching boiling point in the second half with us on the defensive most of the time but, with three minutes left, Tony Rigby hit a volley from twenty-five yards and it flew over the keeper and into the net.

The place erupted. We all ran over, jumping on Rigby, or 'Tigger' as he was known. I couldn't believe it, surely that's it, game over.

From the re-start, the ball was over near the dugout when our Tony Kelly and Preston's Paul Raynor had a scuffle, which ended up with Kelly being sent off.

I felt for him; I knew that he would automatically be banned from the final. Raynor only received a yellow card, but he had been the guilty party and he had been the one who had provoked Kelly. It was cruel. I called him a shithouse.

Shortly after, the whistle went for full time. The crowd invaded the pitch. We had done it. Bury were going to Wembley for the first time in their history. We celebrated well into the night.

It was decided that we would travel down to London the day before and have a walk round the famous old stadium. I climbed onto the coach, but couldn't get past the chairman, who was standing in the aisle scoffing a huge slice of pizza.

'Thought you were on a diet, chairman?' I said.

'I've lost two pounds, what more do you want?' he replied.

'About another ten stone,' I said, as I climbed over the seats to make my way to the back of the coach.

We set off in great spirits. Walshy and Stan were sat at the front of the bus watching the chairman stuffing his face with more food.

The lads all liked the chairman. Terry was a real character. Normally if your pay was short at any other club, you would kick up a fuss, but at Bury if you were short in the pay packet, you would approach Terry, tell him you were short and he would say:

'Fuck off, I haven't got it, but I will make it up to you next month.'

Because it was Terry, you knew that he would and you would just have to walk away laughing. At least he was up front about it.

Before we checked into the hotel, we made our way to Wembley for our walkabout. I took a video camera with me intent on capturing every moment.

It was funny as we had to bang on the big doors where the coach drives through.

'Fucking let us in,' shouted Stan.

Then all the lads started banging on the doors. Suddenly, a little door opened and a head popped out.

'Who are you?' said the man.

'I'll fucking show you who we are if you don't let us in,' said Stan.

The lads cheered as we were allowed in.

First we went into our dressing room, which was on the left. It was the home dressing room, the one that England always used.

OOH AH STANTONA

Even after all these years of professional play, I was in awe as I imagined some of the names that had sat in this dressing room over the years.

We then walked up the tunnel towards the pitch. I was tingling all over. I wondered what I would be like the following day at the actual game. The ground staff let us walk on the pitch, but insisted that it was players only.

The pitch was like a carpet and one of the lads mentioned that it was cut four times a day. Gary Kelly lit up a cigar and I lit up a fag. We walked to the top goal.

Gaz stood on the line, cigar in mouth, while I pretended to put a penalty past him with a fag in my mouth and then decided which corner I would run to if I scored. I looked around and had a mental picture of where Bobby Charlton hit that screamer against Mexico in 1966. I was sure that these were the original stanchions. How many goals had I witnessed being scored in this net on the telly, including all the Cup final goals.

All the lads then congregated in the centre circle pondering the game. I never asked, but I wondered if they were all feeling the same as me.

We made our way out and back onto the coach and I filmed the twin towers as we drove off.

My room-mate was John Paskin, a South African lad who was possibly one of the funniest characters I have met in the game. I filmed him as he had a shave and made it into an interview in which he mimicked Eric Cantona's seagulls statement in Afrikaans.

We tried to get an early night, but we were both just laughing all night. Perhaps it was nervous tension.

All the lads were up bright and early and were already eating breakfast as John and I made our way into the dining room. I couldn't eat much. I just wanted to get there.

Finally, we made our way to the coach outside. Walshy was standing by the door. I shoved my bag into the hold.

Kevin Hulme, or 'Reggie Kray' as we called him, asked Walshy if he needed his bag, to which Walshy replied no.

It obviously meant that Reggie wouldn't be involved. I was gutted for him, but at least it meant that I was playing.

Once again the twin towers came into sight, but this time there were thousands of supporters milling around outside. The Bury fans were cheering us, while those from Chesterfield, our opponents, gave us the V-sign.

The massive doors opened and the coach pulled into the tunnel. I couldn't wait to get off.

I dropped my bag next to the No. 9 shirt that had already been hung up and took a programme off the table and, along with the other lads, made my way up the tunnel to sample the atmosphere. When we reached the top of the tunnel we could see that a lot of spectators had already made their way in and were watching some charity game. Our supporters were down at the far end of the ground and we made our way towards them.

The first time I took it all in was when I looked at the match programme and read 'The Venue of Legends'.

It was time to get changed. That's all I wanted to do now, get the game started. I had taken in as much as I could and now it was time to get down to business. We were here for a reason, not for a day out. After all, that last promotion spot was up for grabs.

Back in the dressing rooms, the lads got changed and Reggie kindly took the video camera to record the proceedings for me. I was really touched to find a telegram from Cardiff Chairman Rick Wright waiting for me, wishing me all the best.

I felt quite good in the warm-up. The nerves had gone. Then we went back to the dressing room for final preparations as we waited for the bell.

It seemed like ages before it went. Everybody was shaking hands and wishing each other good luck. We were in the tunnel waiting when the Chesterfield players came out and lined up on the right-hand side. We all stood there for the signal to walk forward. The nerves started again as I heard the crowd. I looked up the tunnel, which was on a small incline: all you could see was the roof of the far end of the stadium. I stood there bouncing the ball.

I was second in the line behind Pughy our skipper. Suddenly I thought about my old headmaster, Mr Kenyon, who had insisted that I was more interested dreaming about playing at Wembley than schoolwork.

'How right you were, but I wish you were standing right next to me now. I wonder what your thoughts would be if you saw me now, sir,' I said to myself.

The signal came and away we went up the tunnel. The crowd suddenly came into view, as did the rest of the stadium.

When you actually walk through that tunnel and into 'The Venue of Legends' it is a feeling that you can't describe. Only those fortunate few who have done it can.

We kicked off attacking the goal where Geoff Hurst had scored his controversial goal off the bar, but within ten minutes we were 1–0 down. A long throw from the right-hand side saw Chesterfield striker, Andy Morris, control the ball with his arm, but the referee, Paul Adcock, didn't see it and the ball broke loose to Tony Lormor who scored.

As we placed the ball on the centre circle for the restart, I said to Adcock:

'Didn't you see the handball?'

With that he immediately pulled out a yellow card and displayed it, with great ceremony, to the crowd. I couldn't believe it. I just couldn't believe he was doing this. How I laughed a few years later when Paolo Di Canio pushed him, only for him to fall in a ridiculous manner.

'Oh, showing off to your fucking family?' I said, as we kicked off.

It got worse. Not too long after we were 2–0 down. We just couldn't get going and it was fair to say that it must have been a poor game to watch.

Before half-time I was already feeling fucked. We had all heard about the Wembley pitch and how it had tired some of the best players in the world. My legs had gone. I could only describe it as like playing on a sponge.

Tigger hit the post in the second half, but that was our only chance. Adcock blew his whistle and Chesterfield celebrated.

I sat on the turf absolutely drained and exhausted. We went up for our losers' medals first and made our way to our loyal supporters on a lap of honour before disappearing down the tunnel for the last time. Once the game was over, I just wanted to get away, as did everyone else.

On the way back to Gigg Lane, where we were going to have a drink, I reflected on the day. We hadn't played well and some of us had frozen, including me. But I was left with the consolation that a lot better players than me had never played at Wembley and, besides, I would rather have played there and lost than not to have played at all.

The fans were waiting for us when we arrived back at Gigg Lane that night and they gave us a great reception. We all went into the supporters' club to drown our sorrows.

The next day we had to attend a civic reception at Bury Town Hall before we could get off for the summer. Once again, I was really looking forward to the break.

Chapter Twenty

B ig things were expected for the 1995–96 season and we were favourites with the bookies for promotion, but the season started disastrously with a 4–1 defeat away to Northampton, a team who we had twice beaten 5–0 the term before.

As luck would have it, we were drawn against Chesterfield, our play-off final opponents, in the Coca-Cola Cup.

I scored in the first leg at Saltergate as we won 1–0, which gave us a little bit of revenge. We had had a steady start to the season, but a 5–0 home defeat to Plymouth was to be the end of Walshy. The job was given to Stan Ternent, his assistant.

Stan was respected by everyone, especially with his coaching ability, and I got on particularly well with him.

His first game in charge was the second leg against Chesterfield. We won 2–1 and went through to the next round, where we were drawn against Sheffield United.

OOH AH STANTONA

Stan had brought in Sam Ellis, the ex-manager of Bury who had left a few years earlier to assist Peter Reid at Manchester City. He had also brought in Bob Stokoe, the Sunderland legend who had taken the Black Cats to that historic FA Cup win against Leeds United in 1973. Bob was a real character and someone who I could talk with for hours.

We would often sit in the corridor after training with a cup of tea and he would enthrall me with his stories.

I found Bob to be an honest and well-respected guy. The pleasure that he must have had when Ian Porterfield scored the goal in that historic final was etched all over his face as he ran onto the Wembley pitch holding his trilby hat on his head.

The first leg of the Coca-Cola Cup-tie was at Bramhall Lane, the home of Sheffield United, who were managed by Dave Bassett. I scored in a 2–1 defeat for Sheffield, which at least gave us some hope in the second leg.

A regular occurrence would be a shout from Stan after training.

'Stanty, see me before you go,' would be the call, which would piss off Dean Keily and Dean West – nicknamed Fred by Shaun Reid – who were my travelling partners.

'Come in,' would be the shout as I knocked on the door.

I was hoping that Stan would be in a good mood. I got to know when to ask for a day off and when to keep my mouth shut.

On a good day he would give you anything, but on a bad day, keep out of the way.

I walked in and saw that he was relaxed. I sat down.

'Come on then, get the fucking fags out,' he said.

'Fucking hell gaffer, you never have any fags,' I said.

'Why should I buy any when you give 'em me,' he replied.

'Fair point,' I thought.

In all my time, I never saw him smoke his own fags, but he always knew where to find one. It was either off me or Pat, the laundry lady.

'What's up gaffer?' I asked.

I looked at him, waiting for his reply as he put his feet up onto the desk and leaned back in his chair blowing out smoke.

'Tell me some war stories,' he said.

And that was it. Now and again he would call me in to talk about my game, but more often than not he wanted me to entertain him with stories from my Army days.

Half of the time I would make them up, but Stan was fascinated with our little chats.

I couldn't wait for the Sheffield United second leg. We had nothing to lose, but with my goal in the first leg it gave us hope.

It was a great, entertaining game and we pulled off the major shock of the round by winning 4–2 on the night and 5–4 on aggregate. I scored two, with Mark Carter and David Johnson also getting on the score sheet.

I was also voted Man of the Match, which meant that I was to be presented with a mountain bike, courtesy of the sponsors, Coca-Cola.

After having a shower and doing the usual press interviews, I saw an irate Neville Neville coming down the corridor.

'Stanty, I've got the sponsors waiting up there ready to present you with the mountain bike,' he said looking flustered.

'Okay, I'm on my way,' I said.

'No not yet,' he said.

'Why?' I asked.

He looked round at me and said: 'Because someone's nicked the fucking bike.'

I pissed myself laughing. I just thought that it would be one of the lads having a laugh. I walked through one of the doors adjoining the corridor when I saw him again, shouting:

'Where's that fucking Craig?'

'Shit. Does he mean our Craig?' I thought. Then I heard him shout 'fucking hell' as he ran outside after being informed that our Craig was last seen riding a bike around the car park.

Panic over as the sponsors presented me with a muddy mountain bike and at least Nev saw the funny side later.

In October, we were due to play at Mansfield away. It was a fixture that I was looking forward to. We had recovered from a shaky league start and we were still in the Coca-Cola Cup. It would be my first time back at Field Mill since I had left for Cardiff a few years earlier. We were a goal down early on but, after a long kick by Gary Kelly, I scored after a one-on-one with the keeper.

Pughy put us 2–1 up just after half-time and I made it 3–1 not long after. David Johnson then put me through as I completed my hat-trick and, a few moments later, I scored my fourth.

I had scored a few hat-tricks in my career but never four and to do it against one of my former clubs was fantastic. After I had scored the fourth, the whole of the ground applauded, even the Mansfield fans were cheering.

Just before the final whistle, Johnno put me through again on the left-hand side just near to where some Bury fans were situated, but I was given offside. I heard a woman shout:

'Oh, not offside again, Stant.'

I couldn't believe it. I had scored four goals, we were winning 5–1 with less than a minute to go and a supporter was whinging because I was offside. I looked into the crowd and just said in the general direction of the voice:

'Are you fucking sure?'

It just goes to show that you can't keep everybody happy.

The win would set us up nicely for the next round of the

Coca-Cola Cup the following Tuesday night against another one of my former clubs, Reading, at Elm Park, with the competition now being decided on a one-leg basis.

We travelled down in torrential rain and wondered if the game was in doubt. By the time the game started the rain had stopped, but the pitch was heavy.

Tigger crossed from the right and I headed in off the bar, shortly after it started raining again and, after Tigger had put us 2–0 up, the Reading players, who were managed by player-managers Jimmy Quinn and Mick Gooding, started moaning to the referee, John Kirby, to abandon the game.

'Don't listen to them, John. I'll get a bonus tonight for scoring that goal,' I said, knowing that I was due a grand for scoring my tenth goal of the season.

But they kept on moaning. The rain was still coming down and little puddles were starting to appear in the goal areas. At half-time, the managers were called into the referee's room to discuss the situation. Stan was livid when he found out that, after Kirby's request to have the pitch forked, they could only find one pitchfork.

We thought that it was an obvious ploy to get the game abandoned. Kirby called the game off at half-time. We were 2–0 up and playing well, but it meant that we would have to come back and do it all again in a couple of weeks time.

Stan walked back into the dressing room and kicked the bin, spewing out its contents as he informed us of the decision.

In the return game, which had now turned into a grudge game because of the Reading players' actions – even though in hindsight Kirby had probably made the right decision – we had found some pitchforks and, as we ran out for the warm-up, me, Pughy, Gary Kelly and Tigger ran out waving them, much to the delight and humour of the travelling Bury fans.

Once again Tigger put us in front before Reading equalised. The tackles were flying in and we were desperate to get something out of the game, even a replay if we could hold on. But player-manager Jimmy Quinn came on and scored in the 93rd minute to kick us in the bollocks. It was a bitter pill to swallow after our efforts over both games.

As we all walked down the tunnel after the game, emotions were running high and, after some funny comment from a Reading player, it went off outside the changing rooms: twenty-two players in a small area trying to throw punches at each other, it was comical.

Stan tried to calm everybody down and ushered us back into the changing room. As we filed back in another comment was made and Stan was soon in the thick of it as we all piled out again to give our manager our backing. At least over two games we had put up a good fight, one way or another. It was our turn to calm Stan down now. He was fuming.

'Let's get on the bus away from this shit hole,' he said.

'Stanty, go and get some beer in for the coach,' he carried on as he gave me £20.

'I'll drink to that gaffer,' I said.

By the beginning of November I had scored twelve goals, but come the turn of the year, I had gone ten games without a goal. It was the worst run without scoring I had been through since I had become a pro.

I couldn't score whatever I did. I had had little spells before and I knew that all strikers had lean times during the season, but it was starting to play on my mind and my game suffered as a result.

Stan would often say: 'Don't worry, one will bounce off your arse and go in.'

But every time it bounced off my arse it was either saved or it missed the target.

I loved the sound of the swish when the ball hits the net, there is no other feeling like it and then the cheer of the crowd, it's a real buzz and it puts you on a high that takes ages to come down from. It was the same in the schoolyard or at the end of the street on Mrs Skilling's wall after rounding 'Jackie Charlton.' The longer it went on, though, the more it became inevitable that I would lose my place in the side.

Stan called me in after training on Friday, the day before the away game at Chester. I was hoping that it wouldn't be a football-related chat, but I knew that it would be when I walked in and saw Stan relaxed.

'Have a seat, Stanty,' he said.

I sat down and couldn't believe my eyes as he pulled out a packet of fags from his desk drawer and threw me one.

'Fuck me, that's a first,' I said as he lit his and chucked over his lighter.

I knew that he was buttering me up for the incoming bad news.

'I'm resting you tomorrow,' he said.

'You mean you're dropping me,' I replied.

'No. I mean I'm fucking resting you,' he said.

I wasn't going to argue, there would only be one winner, but I knew I was being dropped. Deep down I also knew that he was right. At least I had the consolation of being on the bench at the very least.

'Okay gaffer, I'll see you tomorrow. At least I'll be on the bench, won't I?' I asked.

'No,' he replied as he blew out his smoke. 'I'm giving you a rest,' he said.

Fucking hell. I'd been bombed completely.

As we drove away from the ground, I was fuming again. I thought I would be worth a place on the bench.

'Fred, stop the car and turn back to the ground,' I said to Westy.

I went back into the ground, burst open Stan's door, who had by now been joined by Terry Robinson the chairman, and walked up to Stan who was still sat behind his desk.

'Don't ever ask me for another fucking fag,' I shouted at him. I then turned round and made my way to the door. Before I had the chance to shut it, Terry put his hand up and said: 'Alreet Stanty lad.'

I turned round and said: 'And you can shut the fuck up.'

I felt a bit better that I had let off some steam.

A couple of weeks later I was back on the bench, but with Mark Carter and David Johnson playing well and scoring goals my chances were limited.

Gary Kelly found himself in the same position as me, with Dean Kiely playing out of his skin.

We were both left out altogether for the away trip to Leyton Orient on Grand National day, so we just stayed in the players' bar all game and watched the race getting slowly pissed, which cost us a bollocking and a fine on Monday morning, courtesy of Stan.

We got promoted on the last day of the season, beating Cardiff and clinching the last promotion spot. At least I was involved, coming on for the last twenty minutes.

It had been a case of two halves that season for me. The first part of the season I was among the top scorers in the league, but I had played only a small part in the second half and was wondering if it was time for a move again.

I knew the writing was on the wall the following season. Stan had signed yet another striker, Ronnie Jepson from Huddersfield.

Ronnie and I got on well, probably because he was also a smoker and we would often hide in the stands having a fag before training as Sam Ellis searched for us.

We would duck down behind the seats in the main stands trying to hide the smoke floating above us and breathing a sigh of relief when Sam turned around and made his way back up the tunnel. We would then quickly extinguish the fags, run into the gym and start pumping weights. When Sam came in to see us, we would be breathing heavily.

'Oh there you fuckers are,' Sam would say.

With Ronnie's signing, you didn't need to be Einstein to work out that we had a surplus of strikers and that one of us would have to go. I went to see Stan, who I still got on well with, and he promised that he would try to get me a move nearer home.

He still involved me and I was on the bench now and again and even scored on my only appearance, in a win against Bristol Rovers.

In November, Stan arranged for me to go to on loan to Northampton, who were managed by Ian Atkins and assisted by my former Cardiff team-mate, Gary Thompson.

Bury, by this time, were still looking to recoup some money for me and although I enjoyed it at Northampton, scoring a couple of goals, I knew that they had no money to pay for a fee.

My last game for the Cobblers was a 0–0 draw away at Lincoln City and Atkins pulled me over after the game and asked me to stay for another month.

It appealed to me, simply because I was playing regularly again, so I agreed.

On the Monday after training, I came home and Carole said:

'Stan's been on the phone.'

'What did he want?' I asked.

She carried on: 'John Beck wants you at Lincoln for talks.'

'And what did you say?'

'Is that the same John Beck who throws buckets of cold water over his players before games.'

'And what did Stan say?'

'Stan said he will only do it to Stanty once.'

The next minute the phone went. It was Stan, telling me of Lincoln's interest.

Over the past few years, John Beck had been heavily criticised for his teams' style of play at Cambridge, where he had been very successful, at Preston and now at Lincoln.

He had taken over the previous season and had rescued them when they had been virtually down and out by taking them to comfortable safety. However, this year they were having a better season and could, with a push, make the play-offs.

I rang a few of Beck's ex-players, all of whom informed me that it wouldn't work out and that it would be better to stay away from him.

I arranged to meet Beck and the chairman John Reames for talks, but I had already decided that, because of their style of play and also because of my past experience of the loan spell at Sincil Bank, I would only talk to them out of courtesy.

The ground had been upgraded since my days at Notts County and looked great with its new stands.

It was funny meeting John Beck, but I got on well with him straightaway as he showed me round before our meeting with the chairman.

The clubs had agreed a fee of £30,000 for me, which for a thirty-four-year-old was a lot of money. The talks went well and I was slowly coming round to the idea of signing for Lincoln. The deal was wrapped up after John Reames offered me a two-and-a-half-year contract. At my age, there was no way that I could turn down that sort of security.

Chapter Twenty-One

As I walked in the next day for training and to meet my new team-mates, I was surprised at how much the club had changed. The place was buzzing and the dressing room was full of guys who all made me feel welcome straightaway.

It was the first time that I had been at a club so full of characters. We had had a good team spirit at Bury, but this was by far and away the best dressing room for personalities and that was all down to John Beck.

John was assisted by John Still and Shane Westley. I was immediately introduced to John's strict training regime, which included Eddie Baronowski, a fitness consultant.

Fitness consultant: what the fuck's that? And for the first time at any club I'd been to, there was a meal provided after training.

I couldn't believe it, as I thought back to the return journeys with travelling partners when we had all stopped off for a sandwich or a McDonalds.

OOH AH STANTONA

My first game was away at Hull just after Christmas. As we sat on the coach stuck in traffic, Beck called me down to the front and tried to introduce me to his style of play with the aid of a pen and a notepad.

He described certain areas of the pitch, such as Heartbreak Hotel, which meant a place on the pitch that we didn't play in. It was certainly interesting listening to his 'method' as he called it.

People had called it long ball and it was certainly that, but the way he described how we would get the ball into Quality Street – the channels – had really got me interested, especially as I had just qualified for my UEFA A coaching licence and was now into coaching big time. I managed to score on my debut yet again, but we lost 2–1.

From Monday till Thursday we would not see a ball and were continually on the running track with Eddie or in the weights room with the music blaring out, another favourite tactic of John's.

In our dressing room, we had a speaker blasting out music to drown out the opposition manager's team talks. It must have driven them mad.

As well as this, we were required to train both in the morning and in the afternoon every day, which was also new to me. Being one of the old school, I was used to being away from training by 12.30pm tops, so it came as a real culture shock.

The atmosphere in the dressing room, however, was a pleasure to be part of and it certainly made up for the long days. In fact everybody used to get to training early, just for the crack of it, and nobody was in a hurry to leave afterwards.

John was a strange character. If you saw him in the morning and said hello, sometimes he would just blank you or sometimes he would reply and start talking. I think it was a psychological exercise to keep you on your toes. It certainly did that.

Another thing about John was that he would be the first to help you out if you had a problem. I only saw him lose his temper in the dressing room on one occasion.

The lads also had a secret competition: they were having bets on who could stay on the pitch for the least amount of time before getting hauled off. John wasn't frightened to make substitutions, if you had fucked up in the first minute or the last: the record was held by Dutch striker Gijsbert Bos, another one of John's signings, who had lasted just four minutes in the away game at Blackpool before being dragged off because he had lost a header.

It was after that game that John embarrassed me in the dressing room in front of the rest of the lads by saying, in his Cockney accent: 'Phil, you're a fucking credit to your profession my son,' simply because I had raced back and dispossessed Blackpool midfielder and my former Bury team-mate Gary Brabin.

Our skipper Terry Fleming loved this, as he could impersonate Becky and his accent down to a tee, which he did all the way home.

However, the following week, after the game at Darlington, which had been a real battle, the type of game I loved, he said: 'Phil, you're a fucking pub player son. Fucking tattoos and all that, you just want to fight everyone.'

I looked at Terry and I just fucking knew that I wouldn't hear the last of that one. But sorry for being a winner. Yes, I may be passionate, but it always hurt me to lose. I even hated it when we had won and I hadn't scored. I have always been a bad loser and I would never accept people taking the piss out of me.

We were racing up the table and a play-off spot had become a real possibility and instead of easing off in training John stepped it up even more. Personally, though, I could feel the benefit of this training programme.

I may have been thirty-four, but I felt fitter than I had ever done and I was also more mentally prepared and focused.

It was going well on the pitch, too. Gareth Ainsworth supplied the ammunition and I scored the goals. I even managed to score my 200th league and cup goal at home in a game against local rivals Scunthorpe in a 2–0 win.

On the last day of the season, we needed to beat Rochdale at home to clinch a play-off spot, but we didn't play well and lost 2–0. However, we had a good squad and, maybe with a few more quality additions in the summer, we could go further the following season.

After not being involved in the first part of the season at Bury I had moved to Lincoln and ended up with eighteen goals in twenty-one games, which I didn't think was bad.

I had heard all about Becky's pre-season training, so I made a real effort throughout the summer to keep my fitness levels up. However, the pre-season programme was the hardest I have ever done.

At Bury, Stan would get the balls out and finish off with a bit of running in the July heat encouraging us in just his Y-fronts as he topped up his tan, but this was something else. I quickly grew to hate the word Fartlek, which means something like endurance in Swedish.

A Fartlek was a run, a jog, a walk and a sprint and, after forty-five minutes of that – which incidentally is supposed to simulate a game situation – we were fucked. That was before the day had begun. Becky would be riding a bike at the side of us giving lots of encouragement.

On one occasion, in the heat, we were doing a Fartlek, supposedly for forty-five minutes, when John hadn't realised that his watch had stopped. An hour and a half later, the lads were dropping like flies and, after a flood of abuse, he had to concede. It was so bad that he had to give us the next day off to recover.

On the first day of the season we lost to Chester away and we were also knocked out of the Coca-Cola Cup in the first round by Chris Waddle's Burnley. But the spirit in the camp was still good. John Still had left to take over at Barnet, which was a big blow to all of us.

The next game I was looking forward to was Notts County away. I still hadn't been back there for a competitive match since I'd left for Fulham, but I couldn't wait for it.

Notts had been relegated the year before and Devon White put them in front before we equalised.

In the second half, big Devon got involved in a tussle with our John Witney and the referee, Phil Richards, showed him a red card. We all pissed ourselves laughing as the six-foot-four-inch gentle giant Devon pleaded with the ref like a scolded schoolboy, insisting with arms outstretched that 'it wasn't my fault ref, he started it'.

We smelled victory and it was even sweeter when Steve Holmes crossed from the right and I buried a header from ten yards out and clearly a yard or two offside, but the linesman never flagged.

Off I went to celebrate and remembered the rule that the lads had made after our end-of-season do in Ayai Napa. That was that every goal we scored would have to relate to our holiday in Cyprus: I picked the 'oops upside your head' song, where everybody sat down and did the actions of a rowboat. All the lads had quickly sat down behind me in a line and we reenacted our night in the Car Wash Disco in May.

Suddenly a blur went past me.

'What the fuck's that?' I thought.

As we got up, I looked across and saw that a supporter had

run across the pitch and attacked the linesman for not giving me offside.

The match finished 2–1 and not long after the fan was sentenced to three months in prison.

Not long after that, I pulled a hamstring and was out for a few weeks.

The results were not going as planned. I couldn't get back into the side and Becky was under pressure.

I had once again been restricted to the subs' bench and once again it was very frustrating. For some reason I couldn't reach the form of the previous season. One of the reasons was the record sale of Gareth Ainsworth to Port Vale, whose service from the right I missed.

From the team's point of view things improved, though. We started to pick up results and, at one stage, even topped the table, but we soon slid down to tenth place.

The worst thing for me, though, was the training regime. I was running all week and had no game to play in at the end of it. Even if you were on the bench on Saturday, Shane Westley would run the bollocks off you after the game. It pissed me off big time.

If I had put my coach's head on, I would have realised that fitness levels had to be maintained, just in case I got back into the side, but I had misinterpreted the situation and thought that Becky had ordered Shane to run me just to piss me off.

After one game, in which I had been on the bench and didn't get on, Shane had ordered us to go for a run.

'Fuck this. I've had enough of this,' I thought, as I set myself up for the running.

'What's up with you?' said Shane.

'I ain't fucking running,' I replied.

'Oh you ain't aren't you?' said Shane.

'No I fucking ain't. What are you going to do about it?' I

278

said, as the other lads looked on as pissed off as I was and, just like me, didn't realise that everything was done for a reason. The red mist was descending again. I kicked the advertising hoardings as Shane called me a wanker.

'What did you say?' I said.

'You're a wanker,' he replied.

'You're all talk,' I said.

'Okay. Meet me outside after, I'll be there, but you fucking won't be,' he said.

It was like a red rag to a bull. I'd never backed down from a fight and I wasn't going to start now, especially given the mood I was in.

Paul Smith, who we had signed from Nottingham Forest and who was my travelling partner, was waiting in the car for the drive home.

'Come on, Stanty,' he shouted at me as he saw me come out of the players' entrance, only to be interrupted by a few autograph hunters. 'I want to get off.'

'Okay Smudge,' I replied, as I signed my last autograph.

Suddenly Shane came out of the manager's entrance. We looked at each other and made our way to the gate that led to the training pitch.

'Come on, Stanty. He's not worth it,' said Smudge, leaning out of the car window.

But it was too late. Before we nearly came to blows, a thought suddenly came to my mind.

'If I hit a member of staff I will be sacked. I still have eighteen months left on my contract and, at thirty-five years of age, there's no way I'm going to get another.'

There was a bit of pushing and shoving as well as name-calling before I decided to get into the car with Smudge.

On the Monday, Becky called me into the office to inform me that he was suspending me from the club and that if I didn't leave now he would call the police. He was also going to fine me two weeks' wages.

It pissed me off because, as a senior pro, I felt as though I had more to offer, but what I didn't know was that John was on dodgy ground, not just because of our results, but because he had taken a break skiing in the middle of the season while the chairman was in Australia. The chairman had come back and John was relieved of his duties pending an investigation.

The chairman, John Reames, returned from Australia and put Shane in temporary charge. I was still on suspension after the previous week's events.

I spoke to Terry Robinson, the Bury chairman, and told him my point of view. That Sunday night, John Reames rang me at home and told me to be at the club at nine o'clock the following morning.

It sounded ominous. John Reames called me into the manager's office with Shane and Keith Oakes, the physio, and announced that we would be the new management team until the end of the season. It surprised me as much as it surprised Shane.

The previous week we had been ready to fight each other, now we were part of a team. It was hardly inspiring for a new management team and the players were well aware of the tensions between us. We got on surprisingly well, though, and the team worked. We clinched promotion on the last day of the season – sound familiar? – with a home win against Brighton with Lee Thorpe scoring two.

Chapter Twenty-Two

Shane was named manager for the new season and I was made assistant manager. We started the season with two new signings – Leo Fortune West from Gillingham and Tony Battersby from Bury.

Wally Downes, the ex-Wimbledon player, had also joined us as first-team coach; he had been the youth-team coach at Bury under Stan.

I was a very inexperienced coach, but I learned a lot from Wally in those first few months. We had also signed left-winger Lee Philpott, who we hoped would provide the ammunition for the front lads.

During the summer the only money we had paid out was £80,000 for Battersby, which was a lot of money for Lincoln, but it was soon put into perspective when we were beaten by Gillingham, who had forked out £1.5 million for their strike force Carl Asaba and Robert Taylor. I knew then that it would be a struggle.

It soon turned out that there were divisions within divisions and that you needed money to survive.

By November we were struggling. We had suffered unlucky defeats at Millwall and Bristol Rovers, but following a defeat at Walsall on a Tuesday night the chairman had lost patience. The goal had suddenly become to stay in the division.

The next day I turned up for work. Shane and Wally were clearing the desks.

'What's up?' I said.

'We've had the bullet,' Wally replied.

'Oh no,' I thought. 'What am I going to do now. I've lost my job, shit.' I panicked.

A call came through. I had to go and see Reames in the boardroom.

I made my way to the boardroom and looked out of the window as I waited for John Reames. I saw Wally leaving in a taxi with all his belongings in a black bin liner. Reames walked in.

'Hi Phil,' he said.

'Here we go,' I thought.

'Right. As you know, there have been some changes,' he said.

'Yes chairman,' I replied.

He went on: 'I will now be manager, assisted by you.'

'Fucking hell. The chairman is going to be the manager assisted by me,' I thought.

My first reaction was one of relief. At least I wasn't going to be sacked, but I felt for Shane and Wally, especially Shane, as I had become good friends with him since our little spat.

We were struggling in the league and, on Saturday, we were due to play the Conference leaders Cheltenham in the FA Cup in a televised game.

The chairman left all of the preparations to me and we beat them 1–0 with Lee Thorpe scoring. I was suddenly in at the deep end with all of the coaching duties on my shoulders.

I was very apprehensive because as a player it's easy. You think you know all the problems and have all the answers and that your coach doesn't have a clue. I know because that's what I was like as a player if things were going wrong. But here I was, a fully qualified coach, worried in case I fucked it up.

As a coach you have to have all of the answers, because it doesn't matter if you're right or wrong, the players will always respond to mob rule. I had recently gained my UEFA A qualification, but when they present you with that certificate they don't say to you: 'And by the way, you are now a good coach.' You learn your trade by experience. All the certificate meant was that you were competent to coach at that level.

It was certainly a great learning curve for me, especially after all the managers and coaches I had worked with, which enabled me to draw down on my own experiences of how to do it and how not to do it.

We beat Stevenage, another top Conference club, in the FA Cup second round, 4–0 at Sincil Bank. The third-round draw handed us a plum home tie against Peter Reid's Sunderland.

In that game, a first-half Gavin McCann goal condemned us to a 1–0 defeat, but at least we had reached the third round, an achievement that had secured us, after a promise from the manager-chairman, a holiday in Ayai Napa at the end of the season. After having been well adrift at the bottom of the league table, a run of a few victories handed us a real chance of survival. The chairman even won the Manager of the Month award.

One morning John called me in.

'I am going to sign Bruce Grobbelaar,' he pronounced.

'You're joking chairman,' I responded.

'Phil, please call me John,' he said.

'Okay chairman,' I said.

'No. I am not joking,' he replied.

Bruce joined us for a few games, which pissed off our regular keeper, Barry Richardson, big time, but following a 4–0 defeat at Wycombe, he was soon released.

After John's holiday to Australia, he brought back a Crocodile Dundee-style hat, which he wore with pride in the dugout.

After one game, we went to do the usual press conference, but John had left his hat in the changing room. Afterwards in the boardroom he said to me:

'Phil, have you seen my hat?'

'No chairman,' I said and thought nothing more of it.

On the Monday morning I was going through the scouting report when John walked in looking pissed off.

'What's up chairman?' I said.

'Phil, please call me John in here,' he replied again.

'Sorry chairman,' I said.

He had received a letter in the post. It was a ransom demand for the return of his hat and enclosed in it was a Polaroid of the hat with a message saying:

'If you don't put £100 into the players' pool, the hat gets it.'

I found it hysterical, but the chairman was annoyed, after all, he wasn't used to the dressing-room sense of humour.

He called a players' meeting and demanded the return of the hat, but everybody pleaded ignorance. He wouldn't pay the ransom and he never saw the hat again.

We lost the last game of the season at home to Wycombe again and were relegated.

At least we had made it to the last game of the season, but for me it was heartbreak, as I experienced relegation for the first and only time of my career.

John announced that he would carry on as manager for another season and that he would then hand over the reins to me as his successor.

At the time, I thought that John's presence was a hindrance and felt that I could do the job myself, but after working closely with him I soon found out how a football club was run. After seeing the budget sheet for the first time and going through it with John, the figures were frightening.

The job itself was a far cry from simply looking after the playing side. My title may have been assistant manager, but I was also a player. I ran the reserves and coached the first team; I was also scouting most nights. The job was exhausting but I loved it, it was a real challenge and that season we finished just below halfway in the league and in safety as Chester were relegated away at Macclesfield, who had been relegated with us the previous season.

During the game with them the previous year, both sides had been involved in a twenty-two-man brawl when we lost 1–0. Playing against them this time round, we were losing 1–0 and were being hassled from the fans behind the dugout. After Lee Thorpe equalised from a long Jason Barnett throw, Reamsey jumped up and banged his head on the roof of the dugout and slumped to the floor. Of course, we were all celebrating and it was a while before physio Keith Oakes noticed the chairman, who was a little dazed but okay.

John then stood up outside for the rest of the game; in the dugout we could not stop laughing and I for one couldn't concentrate on the game.

Near to the end of the season, John had also spoken to me about who I wanted as my assistant for the following year. I told him that I wanted George Foster, my ex-Mansfield Town manager who was now working on the coaching staff at Birmingham City. George was an excellent coach and had been coming in to help me with the coaching on his day off.

The summer came and John handed the reins over to me. It was then that I really found out what it was like to be the manager of a league club. However, John had also decided that he was going to sell the club.

The problems started soon after the season had begun. I had managed to bring in one or two players, including Dave Cameron from Brighton and Justin Walker from Scunthorpe.

A wage cap had been introduced by the club and I soon found out that even with all of my contacts within the game, I couldn't compete with other clubs when trying to sign the players I thought we would need to give us a chance.

All the bigger earners at the club had gone, as we couldn't afford to keep them, which knocked the wage bill down drastically. The club was in real financial trouble, so the chairman and chief executive, Jerry Lonsdale, had a meeting with the bank and had agreed a three-year business plan: the result was the wage cap and the cutting of the wage bill as a whole.

It would have been a tough season for an experienced manager, let alone a young rookie who was still learning his trade.

I also needed a second keeper to give young Alan Marriott some competition, but was told that I would have to use loan signings or a trialist. The great team spirit that had been there when I had first arrived at the club had now gone, as had most of the players. My mission at the start of the season was simply not to finish bottom.

I asked Jerry if we could go public on that and let the supporters know the state of play: the answer was no. So there I was saying how we were going for the play-offs this year knowing full well that survival, not only in the league but for the club, was the aim. I didn't know it at the time, but I had made a rod for my own back.

John Reames had now left the club and Jerry was virtually running it on his own, constantly fighting off the creditors. A transfer embargo had also been served on the club by the PFA, which tied my hands even more.

Gavin Gordon was our top scorer and when Bobby Gould from Cardiff enquired about him, I told him that we would sell him for half a million. I knew that any reasonable offer would have taken him away anyway.

Two days later, the deal was done. That meant that with the saved wages and Gavin's transfer fee, I had brought in £800,000 in six months. I went into the boardroom for the monthly board meeting with the few remaining directors, as well as newly appointed interim chairman, Rob Bradley, a representative from the Supporters' Club who, after years of supporting the club, had now found himself in the top job. The directors were full of smiles, but I knew that the money I had brought in merely scratched the surface of the financial difficulties that beset the club.

'Well done Phil. That's great business, half a million for Gordon,' said Rob. He carried on. 'We have decided now that the transfer embargo is off and that you can go and replace him.'

I couldn't believe my ears. After working so hard with my hands tied so tightly behind my back, they were now giving me permission to sign more players.

'That's great chairman, how much can I have?' I said.

Rob coughed and lowered his head as he looked at the other directors before looking at me and saying: 'Sorry Phil, there is no money available, but you can sign another player if you want to.'

I stood up with my hands in my dirty tracksuit bottoms.

'I have just sold our top scorer and the league's top scorer for half a million and you want me to go and replace him with nothing,' I said.

It went quiet, and then Rob said: 'Yes Phil.'

I pulled my right hand out of my pocket and put it in the air before shouting.

'Here's a fucking rabbit.'

Did they think that I was some kind of magician? I just walked out of the meeting, but I also knew that if they had had money available they would help me out.

Anyway I went down to see George who was waiting in my office and told him of the outcome of the board meeting. He leaned back in his chair, took a deep breath and ripped up our hit list of targeted players.

We were in the bottom half of the table and scraping a draw here or a win there, but we were losing points through silly individual errors.

A week before our FA Cup-tie at home to Dagenham and with the winner getting an away tie at West Ham, our young keeper Alan Marriott was injured.

The only keeper I had other than him was a young trialist called Matthew Ghent from Villa. Fortunately for us I had signed him on a non-contract basis and he would have to play in the Cup-tie, as the rules stated that you couldn't sign anybody a week before an FA Cup-tie.

We just couldn't score and I could see Dagenham scoring. We were holding out to a lot of pressure in the final stages until, in the last minute of stoppage time, Matt let a weak shot through his legs, which trickled over the line and didn't even touch the back of the net.

I was more gutted for him than for me, but that was it, we were out of the FA Cup, even though I had warned the board at the start of the season that we needed another keeper, and an experienced one at that.

There was no point crying over spilt milk: it was just another kick in the bollocks, but at least we were on target with the first year of the bank's business plan. The following season I wouldn't have to operate under the same severe restrictions.

However, the local radio station had started a talk show and I listened to it on my way home as the broadcaster fed the supporters ammunition to call for my head.

The situation was still the same. I wasn't allowed to go public about the club's situation and, as the weeks went on, the noose tightened.

Fortunately, though, a group of local community business-men had agreed to take over the club. The restrictions couldn't be lifted yet, but at least it gave me hope.

We beat Chesterfield to reach the Northern Final of the LDV Vans Trophy with an emphatic 4–0 win. Was the tide turning?

No. We lost 2–0 at home to Macclesfield after Steve Holmes was sent off ten minutes into the game for kicking out. And, on the following Saturday, we lost 3–2 at home to Orient after losing four players at 12.50pm with a flu virus, which had swept through the club. That meant that I had to send out a patched-up team with one or two reserve players, all of whom had been given little preparation time.

The following day I had arranged to take the players away to Blackpool for a few days' rest and a few beers. I thought that the change of scenery would do them good.

After the game, I walked into the boardroom and, as usual, if you had won people would pat you on the back, but if you had lost then they would turn away and engage themselves in conversation elsewhere.

One of the new directors, who I didn't know from Adam, came up to me and said, as he took a swig of his drink: 'Think you got your tactics wrong today.'

He walked away. I didn't even bother replying. After all, what did he know about what goes on in the dressing room and the problems that I'd had before the game?

I chuckled inside: 'Prick,' I thought as I walked out.

I rang George on the way home, who had already left. We were all going to meet on the Sunday in Blackpool and George had planned to join us after scouting at Kidderminster.

'George, don't go to Kidderminster tomorrow,' I said.

'Why?' said George.

'Because we are going to get the bullet,' I said.

'Yeah, okay. I'll come up with you tomorrow then,' George replied.

I knew that it was coming simply by observing people's body language in the boardroom. Alan Buckley had been linked with my job for the previous few weeks as had other people, including John Beck who, before the Orient game, I found sitting in my office. I had just patched up the side and had gone off to my office for a bit of sanctuary.

'Hi Phil. Alright?' said Becky.

'What the fuck are you doing in my office?' I screamed at him.

John was pleading that he was just coming in to say hello as I was pushing him out of the door. But I thought he was after my job, unaware that it was Buckley who had already been lined up.

Come Monday morning I was nursing a hangover when the phone rang at the hotel. It was our secretary Fran Martin.

'Phil, can you and George get back for a board meeting at two this afternoon?'

'Yes, I'll be there, Fran,' I replied.

With that I woke George and the other lads and called a team meeting as captain John Finnegan had also taken a call from Fran requesting that all players be at the club for three o'clock. All the lads sat down and I told them what was going to happen. Even though it wasn't official yet, I knew. I thanked them for their efforts: after all, the players on the pitch don't make errors on purpose.

George and I made our way back to Lincoln from the hotel in Blackpool, but we got held up in a snowstorm. As we drove back, I reflected on my season in charge.

We had had a wage cap imposed on us, we had been forced to release players over a certain wage, there had been a transfer embargo and we had to sell our top scorer. The money that transfer had brought in had kept the club going. We had also reached the Northern Final of the LDV Trophy. Fucking hell, if this didn't stand me in good stead nothing would. We were stuck in traffic when George's mobile rang. It was Fran.

'Can you get here as quickly as you can,' she said.

George explained our predicament with the weather, but told her that we would get there when we could. After all, why rush to get the sack? Perhaps it would fuck up their plans.

We finally made it to the boardroom where all of the directors were waiting.

I walked in, patted Rob Bradley on the shoulder and said: 'Fuck me, Rob, don't look so worried, I know this is all new to you.'

Rob told us that the board had agreed to terminate my contract and that the same applied to George. That was it. Out we went to clear the office of our personal belongings.

I was putting some stuff in the boot of my car when a photographer snapped me.

There was a great picture the following night with the headline: 'The Boot'.

I sat down in the office with George for the last time with a cup of tea. The phones started to ring. Word was out. We looked at Teletext to find my name up there with the words 'sacked' next to it.

Roy Macfarland of Cambridge had also been sacked – at least I was in good company – to be replaced by John Beck. How ironic that was. Only a few days earlier I had booted him out of my office thinking that he was after my job.

The phone didn't stop ringing from other managers wanting to wish me well. The first call came from Peter Reid at Sunderland. The phone went again. It was Orient's assistant manager Paul Clarke. He hadn't heard the news and was enquiring about Lee Thorpe. Another call came; this time it was Micky Adams at Brighton.

'Fuck them. Come and play for me,' he said.

'Are you kidding Mick? I've just got the fucking bullet,' I replied.

'Well ring me tomorrow,' he said.

With that George and I left the ground, went to a pub and got pissed.

Chapter Twenty-Three

The next day I rang Micky back. He wanted me to come down and help him out by being on the bench and coming on for the last fifteen to twenty minutes. I agreed to help him out for a couple of weeks. Meanwhile, Alan Buckley was appointed as the new manager of Lincoln on twice my salary and was allowed to break the wage cap.

'What had happened to the three-year plan?' I thought.

Ironically, Brighton, who were tenth in the league, were due to play at Orient, the last team Lincoln had played when I was manager.

I travelled down on the Thursday and met my new team-mates on Friday for training. On the Saturday I sat on the coach with the players instead of in my usual seat at the front. It seemed a little weird reverting back to a player's mentality. After all, I was now thirty-eight years old.

Micky's assistant was Bob Booker and he shouted down:
'Sleep alright, Stanty?'

'For the first time since fucking August,' I replied.

It was now the beginning of March. Micky shouted down: 'That's right Stanty. These fucking players have no idea.'

I got on well with Mick and Bob. Before the final leg to any ground, Micky would make the coach driver blast out 'Heroes' by David Bowie on the stereo.

I came on for the last twenty minutes to replace Bobby Zamora, who had put us 2–0 up. I just used my experience and held the ball up in the corners.

I still had my bleached blond hair, which was dyed to raise money for a young Lincoln supporter, Nathan Bradley, who needed an operation. The Brighton fans fortunately took to me after questions had been raised about Micky's sanity for signing a bleached-blond thirty-eight-year-old who had been nicknamed 'Eminem'.

I had initially said that I would help him out for a couple of weeks, but ended up staying until the end of the season, in which we won fourteen games out of fifteen, including a 2–0 win over Lincoln. I scored my last league goal for Brighton in a 3–0 home win over Hull. We clinched the championship with a 2–0 win at Plymouth.

I had even qualified for a championship medal, which was presented along with the trophy at our last home game of the season and I felt great joy as I pointed to my medal on the Sky TV cameras, hoping that Lincoln's people would see it. At least as a player I would be finishing as a winner.

After leaving Lincoln I began to doubt my own ability. I was left wondering what I did wrong. What would I do differently next time; after all, the saying was: 'You're not a good manager until you've been sacked three times.'

I took some consolation by watching Micky prepare his side for each match: it was only the same as I had done at Lincoln, in fact I would go as far as saying that we were more prepared than his side were and I told him so.

'Better players, Stanty. Better fucking players,' he replied.

He was spot on, which led to me regaining both my confidence and my appetite to have another crack at the job, but with who?

Shortly after the season had finished, another mate, Keith Alexander, rang me to tell me that he was joining Alan Buckley at Lincoln as his No. 2. He had said that he had recommended me for the manager's job to the Northwich Victoria board before he left.

Keith had nearly joined us at Lincoln as youth-team manager, but had decided to stay at non-league Ilkeston Town, because we couldn't match his wages.

I had two interviews for the job, but lost out to Jimmy Quinn, my old adversary from the Bury-Reading game.

John Still rang me from Barnet and suggested that I come down to do a bit of coaching for him, he also gave me a bollocking for treating Becky the way I did.

I was applying for jobs all over the place, but nothing came up over that summer. All the managers' jobs or coaching jobs seemed to go to the experienced, but failed, manager or to personnel who were already there, which saved a club's money.

Nobody seemed to want to employ a coach who had been a manager as you were seen as a threat to their jobs. I even applied for positions with the PFA's Football in the Community Programme, but didn't get a sniff. It was a really frustrating time, especially when I surveyed the situation.

A lot of people were in jobs who had no qualifications but who were simply there because the manager was their mate. After spending years getting my badges, I soon discovered that they didn't get me anywhere ... they didn't even get me an interview.

David Platt got the Forest job. He was unqualified, blew £12 million, nearly sent the club out of business and soon landed the England Under-21 job.

I knew that I had done a good job at Lincoln under restrictions that even Alex Ferguson would have found hard to cope with but, to be fair, I had taken the job knowing what the financial problems were.

A year later, Lincoln survived bankruptcy by the skin of their teeth. If only they had stuck to the three-year-plan. The Supporters' Trust, which had taken over the club, celebrated outside the High Court claiming victory for saving the club. The real truth was that they had placed the club in that position by giving Buckley the freedom to break the wage cap.

John Barton rang me from Worcester City, who were in the Dr Marten's Premier League, and I agreed to help him out for a couple of weeks in a playing role. I stayed until Christmas and then Neville Southall rang me from Dover with the same request. After that it was Hayes, also in the Conference, and then my last port of call was with Hinckley United, also in the Dr Marten's.

It was a season I had really enjoyed. I loved playing, even at the age of thirty-nine.

At the last count, I had applied for fifty jobs within football and had only had one interview with Northwich Victoria. I still believe I have what it takes to become a manager in this fantastic game.

I often look back and think how lucky I am to have been a professional footballer. It's every kid's dream and to be still playing in the league at thirty-eight when the average age of a pro is twenty-eight. It is an achievement that fills me with pride.

I was also proud that, even though I wasn't good enough to play at the highest level, I had reached my ceiling and had maintained it for a good number of years. I had scored plenty of goals ... and that had been the best feeling in the world ... ever.

The Falklands Return

It is nearly 25 years since I last looked out of the small window on the RAF Hercules transporter plane, watching as the Falkland Islands slowly disappeared out of sight and thinking I never want to go back to this place, I just want to get back to England as quick as possible. From the air, the Islands looked so peaceful and tranquil, the ocean below me with its splendid colours of aqua green and silver blue poured over golden beaches, beaches that I had never seen before. In fact you wouldn't have ever known that this had been hell for a lot of people for many months, the place where hundreds of men had been killed and seriously wounded who weren't lucky enough to be heading back home on a noisy aircraft.

Up in the sky, I had time to reflect. I had hated that place, vowing never to return. It had been hell and I never wanted to experience anything like it again. Of course I would miss Bill and Evelyn, especially after they had looked after me so well and treated me as one of their family. It wasn't long before I drifted off, the noise of the engines oblivious to me as the aircraft made its journey to Ascension Island and then on to RAF Brize Norton back home and hopefully a welcome pint.

The Falklands are 8,000 miles from Britain, 300 miles from South America and only 600 miles from Antarctica. They are very bleak with hardly any trees, and visitors will notice straight away the unrelentingly strong winds which even in summer produce a wind-chill factor below zero.

As a young lad back in 1982 I hadn't a clue about the Falklands and how Britain became involved in its first expeditionary war all those miles away. I say war – some people call it a conflict but to me it was a war because people died, some horrifically.

It was only as the years passed that I took some interest in the politics of this war and why it had started. Argentina had always laid claim to the islands – Las Malvinas as they call them – and even today bringing them back under Argentine rule is a stated intention of the government. The Argentine military government, the Junta, seized power in 1976 and immediately started what was called The Dirty War. This state-sponsored violence against normal citizens continued for seven years and was started as a campaign against any suspected dissidents and subversives. Anyone deemed a threat to the Junta was put under surveillance, some subjected to torture, thrown from planes at 13,000 feet into the South Atlantic after being stripped and drugged, or simply 'disappeared' – taken to secret detention centres and never seen again. It didn't matter who you were, you may have been just a friend or a friend of a friend. Secret police would raid homes at night and kidnap people just because they could, including students, trade unionists and even teachers and lawyers. Pregnant mothers were kidnapped, with their babies passed onto military officers, never to be seen again.

Nearly 30,000 people became known as 'los desaparecidos'

('the disappeared'). As the years passed some of the mothers of the disappeared formed an organisation called The Mothers of Plaza de Mayo, aimed at finding out the truth about what had happened to their sons and daughters. The Plaza de Mayo is a square in the middle of Buenos Aires where they would gather every Thursday afternoon, walking around wearing white headscarves to signify a nappy; some still do it today. Eventually, the organisation joined forces with trade unionists which signalled the Argentine middle class uniting against the Junta. With unemployment soaring, the Junta needed a cause to reunite the country and try to regain popularity.

In 1980 an Argentine businessman named Constantino Davidoff bought a disused whale slaughterhouse in the nearby islands of South Georgia, situated to the south-east of the Falklands, which were also under British rule. Davidoff decided to dismantle the slaughterhouse and sell it for scrap metal. Three years later he returned with an Argentinean Navy ship and started to work. During the course of the work, his labourers displayed the Argentinean flag which upset the South Georgia residents who then complained to the British Governor in the Falklands. The Governor sent HMS *Endurance*, the British navy ship who was on patrol in the area, to take it down.

The Argentine Junta under the leadership of General Leopoldo Galtieri had been planning an invasion of the Islands and this latest development in South Georgia was just the excuse he was looking for. He believed that after the invasion his government would gain a quick negotiation with Margaret Thatcher enabling Argentina to keep the Islands, thus solving his domestic problems. He was wrong.

I came to the conclusion that because the war was won by the British, the Junta was soon ousted for a democratic government and changed the culture forever. It should also be noted that in Britain at the time we were in recession and that our victory reunited Britain, enabling Margaret Thatcher to win the next general election by a landslide – an effect known as the Falklands factor.

I couldn't believe I was stuck in traffic yet again trying to get out of south-east London after completing a technical inspection of Crystal Palace FC Youth Academy in my role as Youth Development officer for The Football League. My role is to ensure that all Football League Academies and Centres of Excellence are being run as they should.

It was hot and sticky in the middle of June when I found myself in the jam approaching the Blackwall tunnel. As I sat there I switched on the radio for information but I started to listen to the news while pondering my day's work at Palace.

As my ears pricked up I found myself reaching for the volume button following an announcement on the air by the then junior defence minister Tom Watson that major celebrations were to take place the following year to commemorate the 25th anniversary of the Falklands War. He stated, 'There will be a major celebration to commemorate the war,' and his own view was that it should be both celebrated in the UK and The Falklands. He also added, 'Given the bold, courageous leadership of Margaret Thatcher and the bravery and dedication of our armed forces, it is welcomed that the events of 25 years ago will be commemorated so prominently.'

I had to be honest, I had never heard of Tom Watson, probably because I spend most of my time listening to sports channels. My first thoughts were of real sadness, words from some MP who wouldn't know what a war is if it bit him on the arse. If only MPs could be enlisted and thrown into a war zone I thought. No such luck. It also made me feel angry as my thoughts drifted back to 1982 and the air attack that caught us so unaware. I still remember that day, 8 June 1982, watching helplessly as *Sir Galahad* and *Sir*

Tristram were bombed 500 metres from our trenches in Port Pleasant, a quiet stretch of water near Fitzroy settlement.

I shouted at the radio, 'Major celebrations!' I couldn't believe what I was hearing. 'It was a war, people lost their lives, you fucking idiot.' Celebration no, remembrance certainly. I am sure if you ask people who have been involved in a war situation they would agree that war is not for celebration.

I began to get angrier. Was it because I was stuck in traffic and another motorist was looking at me as though I had come off another planet? I suppose it's not every day you see someone shouting at the radio in your car. It wasn't the traffic, it was because I had a mental picture of MPs getting pissed at some celebration on the back of a war, a war that had caused a huge amount of suffering and misery. Thank God I am now moving, I thought. I was nearly out of the tunnel; think I will listen to the sports news.

As the years had passed, I was more concerned with my career as a professional footballer than revisiting my experiences on the battlefield. I had always been popular with the fans of the teams that I played for; I suppose it was because I believed I always give a hundred per cent and also because I always appreciated how lucky I was in fulfilling every boy's dream by playing football professionally.

But I also understood more. I came to the conclusion that unless war involves you personally or somebody close to you, nobody gives a shit. As somebody who is very patriotic and prone to nostalgia, I feel that we seem to have lost sense of our heritage and community. It's the people who have fought and died in wars and conflicts who have given us today's society who are my heroes. In recent times the news has been dominated by the conflict in Iraq. The latest incidents are soon chip paper and people are more interested in watching talentless celebrity wannabees on some crap TV reality show. Perhaps we should start another reality show with these wasters and parachute them into Baghdad, let's see how many sign up for that!

Returning troops soon find out when they return from duty in theses regions the majority go about their business not bothering about what's happening to our forces around the world, especially in the Middle East, as long as they know who's been voted out of the jungle or the house.

A few months after hearing Tom Watson on the radio, I was late as usual for a meeting at The Football League Operations Centre in Preston where I was to do a presentation to the FA Premier League, The PFA (Professional Football Association) and colleagues from the Football League. I was going to talk about exit strategies for under-16 footballers who have not been offered a professional contract, which include the organisation of trials for potential young footballers.

The phone rang. 'Hi, is that Phil?'

'Yes, unfortunately it is,' I replied, expecting problems as normal.

'This is Phil Braund from ITV. Is it convenient to talk?'

'Not really, can I ring you back later?' I replied.

My presentation went well and during lunch I remembered the call. Better ring back, I thought.

I returned Phil's call and was interested to learn that he had read an earlier edition of my book and wondered whether I would be interested in returning to the Falklands as part of a documentary team to do a programme on my story.

I confirmed my interest and he said he would ring me back. I couldn't understand why they wanted to tell my story, as I only played a small part, perhaps he should speak to the Paras, Commandos or the other Infantry Battalions. After all, they were the real heroes of that war. I had never thought I would go back or even get the opportunity – nor did I know whether I wanted to – but after more thought I came to the conclusion that it didn't matter how big or small the part played, as every person has a story to tell. In fact, I had already told my story.

I met up with Phil and a couple of months later was introduced to my new colleagues who would accompany me, producer Frazer Sheppard and cameraman Paul Leuenberger. A week before departure we had a final briefing which included me obtaining some new walking boots and a fleece courtesy of ITV.

As the week passed, I started to get excited but also apprehensive, especially about my return to Fitzroy. But most of all I was looking forward to seeing Bill and Evelyn again after research had found them well and still living in the same house.

On 30 January 2007 I left RAF Brize Norton with Frazer and Paul on probably the oldest jumbo jet in circulation, which as a nervous flyer didn't fill me with confidence. I noticed that Brize had changed dramatically since I landed there back in 1982. The plane was mostly full with other media crews as well as squaddies travelling back after leave. I decided it was best to snatch a few hours sleep on the way down to Ascension Island where we would have to land and refuel, but the turbulence was unbelievable and I found myself staring at the stewardess in case she gave away any signs of an emergency.

I kept dropping off and was eventually woken by one of the girls who was serving some food, which consisted of a battered panini and some warm orange juice. That was just about it as no alcohol was allowed because of abuse from previous passengers, probably squaddies, I thought. On landing at Ascension I noticed that the place hadn't changed much, it was still the same red-brown volcanic island I saw a quarter of a century before. I couldn't wait to get off and stretch my legs with Frazer and Paul.

The aircraft parked near the arrivals lounge which was like a small shed with a fenced compound. Everybody was told to stay in the compound. I am sure everybody felt like sheep. It was so hot even so early in the morning. Frazer bought us a coffee as we had a chat about the flight and what else was in store for our journey. Two hours later we were herded back on the plane and were soon in the air for the final leg of the flight, only another eight hours to go and more fucking paninis and turbulence. This second leg seemed quicker. Soon the captain was giving us an update and informed us that we would be escorted by two RAF Tornadoes.

As we approached, the islands came into view. I tried to pick out certain familiar points but I couldn't recognise anything. I thought I recognised Fitzroy but the truth was it all looked the same to me. We landed at Mount Pleasant Airport which now comprises a large military complex and the home of the Army. After eventually disembarking we were herded to a small arrival lounge with one conveyor belt for luggage. It was chaos, with no room for manoeuvre, especially with a luggage trolley with a dodgy wheel. Waiting for us outside was a Falkland Island tour bus ready to take us to Port Stanley.

I had remembered that there were no roads on the Islands; however one had been built during the Mount Pleasant construction and linked the airport with Port Stanley and other places on the island. The road was horrendous as it was mostly all gravel with the occasional few hundred metres of tarmac. How these buses survive the wear and tear I will never know – the only vehicle suitable would be a 4x4 or equivalent. During the forthcoming week we would also notice that every vehicle on the Islands has big cracks in the windscreens which nobody replaces simply because as soon as you go back on that road, you're bound to get another one. The bus was only small but already I had concluded that the young driver had a death wish. It felt funny as years before I had left unscathed, but this time around felt there was a distinct possibility I wouldn't! Instead, I concentrated on the landscape during the 45 minute journey to the world's most southerly capital. Also on the bus were other members of the media and soon I was lost in my own thoughts. It really annoyed me that I was shaken from these thoughts by the sound of laughter from the other passengers, after all, these people weren't here in 1982. To me it was a sacred place and they should show respect, but that was me being selfish.

As we entered Stanley I was surprised to see how much it had changed, with new buildings and houses on practically every street. For a moment I thought we were in a different place as so much had changed. We had even arrived by a different road. I was expecting to arrive via the famous Falklands Road past Moody Brook, the scene of the original British surrender and into Stanley itself. It is funny how after a period of time the mind works; it took me a while to get my bearings. I was convinced before I arrived that I would know exactly were things were. Perhaps in 1982 this road wasn't here, I just couldn't remember. Even though you have clear pictures in your head, they sometimes just don't match up.

Eventually we arrived at the famous Upland Goose to drop off the other media passengers. We were going to be staying at a bed and breakfast five minutes away called Lafone House. It is run by Arlette Betts, who straight away made us feel welcome. We had the place to ourselves, which added to the comfort. I had a lovely view of the sea from my bedroom window. Arlette was to make us extremely welcome during our stay and even became a member of our team, driving us around in her 4x4 during the week.

We only had time to drop off our bags before making our way to the media centre for a briefing, then it was on to the Globe Tavern in Stanley for a welcome pint and the chance to plan the week. The bar was quite noisy with a few pissed up young squaddies who were probably only about 18 or 19 and trying to

Minutes after the attack on HMS Sir Galahad in Bluff Cove, known as the War's saddest day. It remains one of the biggest tragedies in military history.

© PA Photos

The memorial to the Welsh Guards at Fitzroy overlooking Port Pleasant. Though the trenches have long since been filled in, I managed to find my spot and soon found myself vividly re-living an aerial attack by the Argentine Air Force.

Above left: Taking time off from filming at San Carlos Bay, with the infamous 'Bomb Alley' in the background. It was hard for me to believe that this seemingly peaceful place had been such a scene of devastation.

Above right: The team at work: Frazer Shephard and Paul Leuenberge in Port Stanley.

The spot on Darwin Hill where Colonel 'H' Jones of the Parachute Regiment was shot dead. He was posthumously awarded the Victoria Cross for bravery. For an ex-serviceman, it was very moving to pay one's respects at the spot where he fell in action.

chat up the young locals, reminding me of myself at that age. Fortunately, Frazer had the foresight to book us into a restaurant before he came out, another thing that had surprised me – a brasserie in Port Stanley, never!

There we could talk in peace. I still couldn't believe where I was. I was desperate to get on with some exploring but after the flight and something to eat all I needed was some sleep. Before we left the restaurant it was decided that we would revisit Fitzroy in the morning and then have a reunion with Bill and Evelyn. I was looking forward to the second part of the day but I didn't know how I would cope with Fitzroy so early in the week, I had expected to visit it perhaps later on. I started to get nervous as we made our way back to Lafone House but I was also excited. Paul and Frazer were chatting away just like the professionals they were. I started to think back again to that day, a day I will never forget. It wasn't just the attack I remembered, it was also the constant battle with the elements, the freezing weather, howling winds, sleet and snow, lack of proper food, no shower or toilet facilities, feet like blocks of ice, living in a trench and also the psychological battle that you have with yourself wondering if an air raid will be coming straight for you and wondering how long it will last. I was just glad I was back there under totally different circumstances.

Frazer had decided to employ Arlette as our driver and guide. The next day I was up at 5 o'clock with the light morning. It was summer time, something I found strange after coming out of the great British winter and long, dark days. Frazer and Paul weren't far behind me and after a very welcome cooked breakfast off we went back down that horrible MPA (Mount Pleasant Airport) road towards Mount Pleasant and Fitzroy.

I had no idea how long the journey would be. All I could remember was that it was a 20-minute helicopter ride from Port Stanley. As soon as we got out of Stanley it all became so familiar as I looked at Mount Tumbledown to my right, scene of the historic battle involving the Scots Guards. I remembered the rock rivers which I had seen so clearly before.

As we went along, Arlette slowed down and I noticed a small sign which said Fitzroy, indicating a left turn. Back when I was last here there were no roads. This one had been built during the late eighties. It was more of a track and just as bad as the MPA road. As we approached the Fitzroy settlement one of us had to get out and open gates. This was my designated task during the week. Once through the settlement I got my first glimpse of Port Pleasant, the small stretch of water and scene of one of the biggest tragedies in British military history, a tragedy that I was a witness to.

We parked the car in a little parking area that had been set aside. For some reason this surprised me as I had never stopped to think that people would have wanted to visit this place. Already the mind was playing tricks.

I noticed a few memorials had been erected. Again, for a moment I had to concentrate. I was sure I would be able to walk straight to where our trenches were. It then came to me that after the war had finished, the Welsh Guards had erected a temporary memorial out of stones on the hill. I looked and found it was still there. I recalled that when I was in my trench the memorial was located over my left shoulder, so I stood with the memorial on my left which helped me to pinpoint our exact location. I waited impatiently, forgetting that I was part of the documentary team. I just wanted to move on, but I had to wait as Paul organised his equipment and made sure I was audible from the microphone he attached to my jacket. The idea was that they would follow me and just see what happened as I described everything I could remember of that day and about my time in this location. Understandably, they didn't want to miss anything.

I soon forgot that I was being shadowed, with my every word recorded as I walked down the hill towards the little cove where the survivors from *Sir Galahad* had rowed ashore. I still remembered faces as they came ashore, some laughing and smiling still in shock or just grateful that they had survived. As I moved on I started talking, oblivious to the team. I described that where we were standing right now, people had died. As I walked on I was desperate to find my trench, blurting out that I had to find it because I had left my wallet there, just trying to ease the moment.

The ground had changed and the trenches had been filled in. The environment had also changed but I was adamant that I had found it, or where it had been. I described that day as it happened and I found it really weird to sit in exactly the same spot as I was when the attacking aircraft came in. It was as though it was happening right now and I had never been away, the feelings were incredible. I had often talked about this day to people but nobody can understand unless you were there.

I described the landing of a chopper on the same spot as a marine came out with his leg blown off, an image which stays with me to this day. Twenty-five years ago the locals used to tip scrap metal over the cliffs. Back then there was only a handful of scrap. Today I noticed it came right to the top of the cliffs, seeing beer bottles scattered possibly from the tip by the wind which made me really sad. It was funny as the wind was howling just as it used to. The elements didn't bother me at all, and being out in them was a wonderful feeling.

We then walked down to the little cove where I had run down with the boys to help the survivors. The tide was out and it gave a bit of a false impression. I spoke with Frazer on camera about how I felt that day. As we talked I became annoyed again as I remembered how well led and guided we were by our officers, our Company Sergeant Major (CSM) Kevin Townsend and senior NCOs (Non Commissioned Officers). Their professionalism on that fateful day was second-to-none as we were only young lads. Imagine how we would have coped without them, they were so calm. I remembered the CSM who took total charge of the situation. I felt annoyed because looking back they never received any recognition. It was usually the top brass who was mentioned after the war. Our brigade leader was Tony Wilson, someone I don't think I'd ever seen. To my mind, praise for the higher ranking officers unfairly excluded men who made such a difference on the guard.

We walked back to the car. Frazer suggested I spend some time on my own which I was grateful for. I walked back to where our trenches were, expecting one of the lads to pop his head out of a trench saying 'Stanty, the brew's on.' I even replied 'Two sugars.'

I was now alone with my own thoughts without intrusion. I sat down again in what in my mind was my seat on my land. I kept staring at the water, it was so peaceful, I could have stayed there all night. I didn't want to leave as I was in my own little world. I don't know how long I stayed there but I realised it was time to move on. I looked in the distance where I saw Paul, Frazer and Arlette waiting for me. I walked back just to have one last look at the monuments; one is dedicated to the Royal Fleet Auxiliary (RFA) personnel who died on the ships. On it was the name of Yeung Shui Kam who was a sailor on *Sir Tristram* and probably the guy I was working with at the back of the ship before I disembarked.

It was funny but after having feelings of wanting to stay there I suddenly got the urge to leave immediately, it's something I couldn't explain to myself or Frazer but I did know I had to leave. It was as if I had done what I had to do. It had been a very emotional visit, I was glad that I had got it out of the way and now in the afternoon I was looking forward to a reunion with Bill and Evelyn. As we drove away I had a last look, I noticed that the track was still there in the distance that had ferried the injured to Fitzroy settlement. I hadn't really noticed it before.

I had really saturated my mind with pictures and that was all I needed to do. Frazer commented that they had been filming for two-and-a-half hours non stop. I couldn't believe it, I had been waffling on for a long time, I couldn't even remember what I had been saying, I just hoped I hadn't embarrassed myself.

It was decided that we would go back to Lafone for a cup of tea while Frazer arranged the visit to see Bill and Evelyn. A cup of tea was more than welcome. Frazer rang the Pooles and they would be expecting me. Apparently Bill had said 'Don't worry, I have had my nap and will be ready.'

This was something I was looking forward to. I wondered how they looked now after all this time, I hoped they would be as excited as I was. Frazer called a cab, another example of how the capital had developed.

I remembered the address in Fitzroy Road, we stopped at the end of the street so Paul could once again mike me up. They wanted to capture the reunion as it happened without anything planned. All Bill and Evelyn knew was that I would be knocking on the door sometime during the afternoon. The cab dropped us off at the top of the road. Frazer and Paul walked in front looking for the house, but they couldn't find it, I looked and yet again everything seemed to have changed even though I was sure I could walk right up to the door. My memory was playing tricks. I had to ask a young couple walking down the street who pointed it out.

Of course, how could I be so stupid! The entrance was round the back, so off we went. I knocked on the door, so nervous and hoping they would remember me. I knocked again and waited, the door opened and it was Evelyn with a big smile on her face. Then Bill appeared and gave me a hug. It was a wonderful feeling to walk back in to that house again. Straight away Bill got the beers out, the lads were still filming, Bill put his arm round me and wouldn't let go and I felt the same.

It suddenly dawned on me that the Islanders also suffered

during the occupation of the Argentines. Bill showed me round the house. I needed to see everything, including the bedroom I had slept in. I remembered how good clean sheets felt after spending so long in the field. The small table was still there where we used to eat mutton and potatoes every night, the Islands favourite meal. We all sat round the table and started talking, Evelyn reminded me of a story during the occupation when instead of coming home for his tea, Bill decided to have a pint in the Globe which was still open. Of course, after a few pints Bill decided it was time for home, when he came out he started abusing the Argentines and was promptly arrested. He was taken away to the cells. When Evelyn found out, she was furious, not with the Argentineans but with Bill for missing his tea. Eventually Bill was released and was upset as the Argies threatened to hang him. I bet he didn't know whether to stay in his cell or go home and face the wrath of Evelyn. One thing was for sure, he learnt his lesson!

After our beers, it was time to go with a promise I would come back to see them before I left. It had been a long day, an emotional day and I was absolutely knackered. We headed back to Arlette's who had promised to make a chicken curry which I was looking forward to. After the meal we sat in the lounge talking about the day.

I left the lads for my bed and it wasn't long before I was asleep. The day had taken so much out of me. I wanted some time to reflect on it, because everything seemed to have gone so fast.

Next morning I was awake again as the sunlight came through the bedroom window at about 5am. I looked out and saw the wind was howling again, the sea was so choppy. Just another normal day in the Falklands, I thought. Frazer was soon up and with Paul decided that as the previous day had been really heavy, we would take some wildlife shots, which was fine by me as I was still tired.

OOH AH STANTONA

As we waited for breakfast we looked out from the conservatory and noticed that a cruise liner was docked just around the opening to the bay, ferrying passengers in a small tender crashing up and downs in the waves. Rather them than me I thought, as we laughed at the misfortune of others. Since the conflict, up to 20,000 visitors a year visit the Islands, providing a major source of income for the gift shops that have opened. I felt pleased that there do seem to be a large number of people interested in the war and willing to visit the key sites.

We managed to get a lift with a rep from the Falkland Islands tourist board who took us up to Gypsy Cove about 20 minutes drive away, another place I had never heard of. We walked round the cliffs enabling Paul to get some great shots of the penguins on the beach. The area was gorgeous; places that we didn't know existed during my time here before. Unfortunately, we could not go down to the beach as it was still mined – another reason to thank the Argies I thought!

The views were stunning. You looked south in the direction of Antarctica, and once again I noticed how peaceful it was. The penguins were just waddling up and down as we watched from a cliff about 50 feet up; down below us dolphins played. I watched as they swam up and down in the cold waters of the South Atlantic.

Frazer decided to talk to me again on camera, so I positioned myself next to a nest of penguins. One came out and had a nosey while I talked away about the beauty of the place, and my thoughts at this time were well away from war. It was a real contrast from the day before. I hadn't realised how beautiful the place is, with its dramatic coastlines as well as the wildlife, and spectacular views.

The shoot also allowed me to recite a saying they have in the Falklands: 'Photographers build relationships with wildlife built upon trust and an unspoken promise never to abuse nature's hospitality.' I thought it was really fitting. You also realise that places like this at the end of the earth are a painter's or nature-lover's paradise.

Paul took his time taking shot after shot, ensuring he didn't miss a moment. Frazer had told me before we came away that a lot of the time would be boring for me as we waited for the filming to finish. I didn't care. I was taking everything in and was enthused by the commitment and passion of these guys. We had only been together for a few days and had quickly become good friends in such a short space of time. That evening we were invited to a social occasion along with other dignitaries and media personnel at Government House for drinks with the Governor of the Falkland Islands, Alan Huckle. It was the scene of the Argentine surrender by the commander of the Argentine forces General Menendez.

Menendez had surrendered, ignoring orders from General Galtieri back in Buenos Aires. Galtieri had actually ordered him to counterattack the British, but Menendez had the foresight to see that if the British came to attack Stanley it would have been a bloodbath and would certainly put the civilians at risk as well as his own troops. His actions probably saved hundreds of lives and he must be commended for that.

Prior to arriving in the Islands we were fortunate enough to organise a football match with the Port Stanley team against HMS *Edinburgh*, as Phil Braund thought it might be a good angle to the programme. It was something I was looking forward to as it would take my mind of why I was really here, even if some of the game was to be filmed. Thanks to The Football League I had also arranged to make a presentation of a glass football to the Governor and The Falkland Islanders and thought it would be appropriate to make it at this social occasion even though the game was in the morning at 9.00am. How I managed to take a glass ball 8000 miles without breaking it I will never know.

I made the presentation and a speech on how pleasing it was to see how much the Islands had developed and progressed during the postwar years, which in my mind had made it all worth while.

Once again the following morning I was up at 5am, I just couldn't get used to the time difference. Doug Clark, who was captain of the Port Stanley team, would be picking us up at 7.45am to take us to the MPA venue of the fixture. He arrived right on time. As we helped Paul with his equipment I noticed his windscreen had so many cracks in it I wondered how he could see through it. It turned out that Doug worked at the MPA and drove to work every day down the MPA road. What me and the guys hadn't planned for was that Doug obviously thought he was in a formula one racing car. It was a hair-raising journey, how I wished Arlette was driving. I could see us not making the game. Obviously Doug used this road twice a day but that was no consolation. I looked at Frazer and Paul and knew they were feeling the same way, especially when Doug had great pleasure in telling us about the time he hit a sheep, which forced him off the road. Great, I thought!

Eventually we arrived at the MPA needing a change of underwear and minus a few nerves. We got changed at the side of the pitch as I got ready to make my full international debut at 44 years of age. The game started and we were a goal down after just 20 seconds, but soon levelled a minute later thanks to yours truly. The game was a release for me. I enjoyed it so much as we ran out winners 5–4. The lads from the HMS *Edinburgh* were fantastic and afterwards we were talking for ages. Some were even Fulham fans. I felt really proud to present both teams with shirts from my playing days. The Port Stanley lads also presented me with Falkland Islands FC shirts which I will treasure.

When we got back after another hair-raising ride down the dreaded road courtesy of Doug it was time for a long soak in the bath. I still play football like I am a pro and never learn that old age creeps up on us. By the time I got out of the bath I couldn't move. Frazer and Paul had gone into Stanley to do some general view shots known in the trade as GVs.

When they got back I was ready and raring to go. That afternoon I was to interview a guy called John Phillips. John was another Falklands veteran who was defusing a bomb with his mate Jim Prescott on HMS *Antelope* in bomb alley when it exploded, sinking the ship. Miraculously, John survived despite losing his left arm but Jim was killed instantly.

It was a very moving interview as John recited that day minute by minute and even though he lost his arm, he still thanks God that he is still here to tell the tale. Quite a few of the bombs dropped by the skilled Argentine pilots did not explode simply because they were dropped at such a low altitude that the bombs didn't have time to arm themselves.

I knew the next day would be a long one as we had planned to go to San Carlos, the location of the beachhead and of the infamous Bomb Alley. After that it would be on to Goose Green and Darwin. We were up early because San Carlos was about three hours away. Not another three hours on that fucking road I thought! Oh well, at least Arlette would be driving.

Eventually we arrived in the area. We came over the hill and there in the distance was Bomb Alley. It appeared like a monster coming out the water. We arrived at Blue Beach in San Carlos and as we drove down I saw on the hill remnants of the trenches that the British forces had occupied. I could make out the jetty where everybody came ashore from different ships, remembering the hive of activity as the beachhead was established. Once again, it was so peaceful and quiet. We carried on to the San Carlos memorial which had been constructed shortly after the war. We parked up and I saw the memorial for the first time. I had never even seen a picture of it. It was eerily quiet. A circular wall guards headstones of some of the men who died in the war including Colonel 'H' Jones of the Parachute Regiment. The memorial was in immaculate condition and is proudly maintained by local residents. It also overlooks San Carlos water, which I much preferred as Bomb Alley suddenly sounded inappropriate.

I laid a wooden cross down with a tear in my eye and walked out and down to the waters edge for a few minutes on my own again. I looked into the water, wondering whereabouts my ship RFA *Stromness* had anchored before we had been ferried ashore on a landing craft. I also remembered John Phillips from the day before and wondered how he feels when he comes here knowing his mate went down with the ship. This was very moving and I had to keep reminding myself not to cry on camera. Not long after, we went back around the hill to what was the beachhead. I looked at Paul and said, 'I don't care if you film this but I just have to walk down this jetty again'.

For some reason I had the urge to complete this task, why? I don't know. The jetty is now very run down and at the end where the landing crafts pulled up and the troops disembarked is now dangerous and cut off, isolated except for some inquisitive geese. I walked back down it and expected to see the shed with the slogan 'last stop before Goose Green'. It wasn't there anymore. I had to keep reminding myself that it was 25 years on and that things couldn't stay the same.

Flashbacks came back to me. The last time I had walked down here I had been wondering how long we would be on these Islands as well as thankful for firm land after weeks at sea. Before we left I jumped in one of the trenches and had another look at the beachhead. As I surveyed it I imagined the noise, with men digging trenches, choppers flying about and senior NCOs shouting orders to the troops, but now it was eerily silent.

'Time to move,' said Frazer. Away we went and I didn't look back.

Goose Green and Darwin were places I had never been to before so I was looking forward to this visit very much as I could visit them more as a tourist than an ex-serviceman. After another long drive we could see the Goose Green and Darwin settlements as we passed the Argentine Cemetery, a place I was determined to have a look at on our way back to Stanley.

Darwin Hill was to my left and I could see in the distance the small memorial where Colonel 'H' Jones had died as he attacked an Argentine gun position. He was posthumously awarded the Victoria Cross. The memorial was located about half a mile from the road at the bottom of the hill. We parked up and made our way down to pay our respects. As we headed down I tried to imagine what it was like that night for the Paras. After a long march they then had to go into battle, I wondered what would have been going through their minds, perhaps they would have been chatting between themselves, maybe making a brew and wondering what was in store. The Hill was defended by the Argentinean 12th Regiment. I noticed the scorched landscape all the way up the hill. As I got closer, white pebbles had been laid next to the memorial which signified the exact location that Jones had died. The now famous radio transmission 'sunray is down' echoed down the airwaves in my mind.

Some said he was irresponsible, some said he was incredibly brave. For me, he was certainly the latter. With the Paras pinned down he attacked the nest and was hit from a trench behind. His attack forced the Argentines to open fire which identified other gun posts and trenches for the Paras which in turn were duly obliterated. I couldn't help thinking about him with sadness, especially as a mere 20 minutes after his death the Argies surrendered.

I looked up the hill in the direction he was attacking before looking round and identifying the trench (or what was left of it) that had delivered the fatal shot. I walked over to it, possibly 50 metres away and saw that a simple stick wrapped in black and white tape gave away its position. I couldn't help feeling how privileged I was to be standing on such an historic spot.

We moved on again, this time for a well-deserved cup of tea in Darwin before some GV shots of Goose Green and then on to the Argentine Cemetery. The cemetery is located about half a mile away from Darwin Hill on the road to Darwin and Goose Green. The weather had turned blustery again. There was a little car park where we pulled up and again got out Paul's equipment. The cemetery is enclosed by a white fence and I could see a lot of little white crosses. At the top was a big white cross looking over the whole of the cemetery. The entrance was a white wooden gate which was blowing in the wind. I noticed how desolate it was. As I got closer I made out a distinct lack of maintenance – the grass was long in places, not like the superbly maintained British memorials and San Carlos cemetery. There was a sign at the entrance which stated that the maintenance was the responsibility of the Argentine Government and not that of the British.

While having a cup of tea in Darwin we found out that there used to be pictures of the dead on the crosses but these had been taken down. We also learned that the Argentine government saw these people as an embarrassment to their country, a fact that astounded me. It was because of theses guys and because the British had won the war that Argentina was able to move towards being a more democratic society. Surely that can't be cause for embarrassment.

It annoyed me that these people had just been left up here by their own country. After all, they were soldiers who had fought for their country. The crosses were also in poor condition with flaking paint, plus sheep droppings on the headstones. There were some headstones with 'soldier known only to god' in Spanish. Some had names, one was Felix Ernesto Aguirre, and I made a point of saying, 'I don't know who you were son, but you have my respect.'

It's funny looking back and thinking how I hated these guys, but as you get older you see things in a different light. Maybe I will upset some British guys with my observations and thoughts – so be it, it was just how I felt.

I laid a wooden cross at the base of the big white cross before walking away with the promise that I would try to do something when I got back to try to get the cemetery in better condition which hopefully would allow theses guys to rest in peace, no matter what you thought of them.

It was a long drive back after a long day out. We arrived in Stanley about 9pm just in time to get a bite to eat. As we were eating, much to his delight, Frazer received a call saying there would be a helicopter available in the morning for us to do some aerial shots. As my head hit the pillow I couldn't help thinking of what I had seen and felt that day.

The next morning we made our way to the rugby field on the outskirts of the town. Frazer revealed to Arlette that he had been in discussion with the RAF and she would be allowed to join us in the Sea King helicopter. Her face was a picture as she had never been in a helicopter before. For me it was going to be exciting as the last one I went up in was a Chinook after the surrender, I was looking forward to seeing the Islands from the air again.

We took off heading for San Carlos with the intention of flying down bomb alley. I saw that the landscape hadn't changed at all; first we had to stop off at the MPC to refuel. As we refuelled we went inside the operations room and had a cup of tea, the weather closed in which worried me a little. Soon after we were in the air but right in the middle of a storm, the pilot quickly banked round and landed again as the weather was too bad to continue, much to my relief,

As we waited I started to talk to the winch man of the aircraft, a lad called Aidie. We talked about his job which usually entailed helping people in the Cairngorms in Scotland, we also talked about the war and my return. He hoped that my visit would enable me 'to put some things to bed.' As I drank my tea, I thought 'yeah, you're right.'

Not long after, the weather cleared and up we went, unfortunately not enough time for San Carlos but time for a flight over Fitzroy and Port Pleasant. I made sure I got a good last look, but alas no sign of my trench. As we disembarked we waited to give the crew a wave. The pilot flew right over our heads at about 30 feet with Aidie hanging out waving to us and give us a final salute. It was a fantastic exit.

Our last night and we took Arlette out to dinner to thank her for all the help she had given us during the week. We were planning to leave in the morning but had got word that the jumbo had not been able to leave Ascension due to strong winds, so the flight was delayed, giving us an extra day. That was great as it would enable me to visit Bill and Evelyn in the morning. There was only one thing for it, more wine please.

We got up early yet again and packed before we made our way to Bill and Evelyn's for a last cup of tea and goodbye. I noticed the winds had dropped which should ensure a plane arrives on time – I was still worried about turbulence but promised myself that I would do some writing and then get some sleep after the refuelling stop at Ascension.

When we were finally in the air, I wondered if I would ever return. I wondered how many other veterans would get the chance to return. I also wondered if some of them wouldn't want to. One thing was for sure, for me personally it had been a very emotional, exhausting but very rewarding trip, and as Aidie said, it allowed me to put some things to bed, which I was very grateful for.